The Rhetoric of White Slavery and

the Making of National Identity

The **Rhetoric** of **White Slavery** and the **Making** of **National Identity**

LESLIE J. HARRIS

Michigan State University Press | *East Lansing*

Copyright © 2023 by Leslie J. Harris

Michigan State University Press
East Lansing, Michigan 48823-5245

Library of Congress Cataloging-in-Publication Data
Names: Harris, Leslie J., 1978– author.
Title: The rhetoric of white slavery and the making of national identity / Leslie J. Harris.
Description: First. | East Lansing : Michigan State University Press, 2023. |
Series: Rhetoric of power and protest |
Includes bibliographical references and index.
Identifiers: LCCN 2022043344 | ISBN 9781611864595 (paperback) | ISBN 9781609177331 | ISBN 9781628954999 | ISBN 9781628964950
Subjects: LCSH: Human trafficking—United States—History—20th century. | Slavery—United States—History—20th century. | Prostitution—United States—History—20th century. | National characteristics, American. | Women, White—United States—History—20th century. | White people—Race identity—United States. | United States—Civilization—20th century. | Rhetoric—United States.
Classification: LCC HQ281 .H3525 2023 | DDC 306.3/08262—dc
LC record available at https://lccn.loc.gov/2022043344

Rhetoric of Power and Protest
Series Editors: Leroy Dorsey and Shawn Parry-Giles

Cover design by Shaun Allshouse, www.shaunallshouse.com
Cover art: "If Only I Could Get Out of Here." Illustration
from Ernest Bell, *Fighting the Traffic in Young Girls: Or War on the White Slave Trade* (Chicago, 1910). From Special Collections, University of Wisconsin–Milwaukee Libraries.

Visit Michigan State University Press at *www.msupress.org*

Contents

vii ACKNOWLEDGMENTS

ix INTRODUCTION

1 CHAPTER 1. Slavery Up North: White Women's Displacement in the Wisconsin Northwoods, 1887–1889

25 CHAPTER 2. Mobility and the Danger of the City: Moral Reform in Chicago, 1907–1914

49 CHAPTER 3. The Science of Social Mobility: John D. Rockefeller Jr. and the Science of Reform, 1910–1917

71 CHAPTER 4. A National Solution: Protecting Whiteness Through the 1910 Mann Act

97 CHAPTER 5. White Slavery and Yellow Peril: Immigration and Transnational Threat

125 CHAPTER 6. White Slavery and Transnational Flow: International Sex Trafficking Activism before World War I

149 CONCLUSION

161 NOTES

209 BIBLIOGRAPHY

229 INDEX

Acknowledgments

I find writing acknowledgments to be both overwhelming and humbling because this writing has benefited from the support of so many different people and organizations. First, I received research support from the University of Wisconsin–Milwaukee and the Rockefeller Archive Center. The National Communication Association's Mid-Career Scholars Writing Retreat was enormously valuable, giving me time and support to complete this book. Throughout the research process, I have been reminded of the importance of librarians and archivists who made material accessible during a global pandemic, helped contextualize a vast archive, suggested a source I would have never found on my own, or made an extra phone call to help track down a document. Librarians and archivists are amazing people, and I am so grateful for their work. In particular, librarians and archivists from the University of Wisconsin–Milwaukee, Rockefeller Archive Center, Johns Hopkins University, National Archives (Washington, DC), Chicago History Museum, Wisconsin Historical Society, University of Wisconsin–La Crosse, and Frances Willard Library and Archives were helpful, kind, and patient.

I am eternally grateful to the many friends and colleagues who have read all or parts of this book at different stages. In particular, Karrin Vasby Anderson, David Cisneros, Lisa Flores, Lydia Huerta, Alyssa Samek, Mary Stuckey, and Kirt Wilson generously offered ideas and suggestions at critical points. I had conversations with many more people, including Karma Chávez, Lisa Corrigan, Annie Hill, Matthew Houdek, Jo Hsu, Zornitsa Keremidchieva, Lucy Knight, Ersula Ore, Catherine Palczewski, Bonnie Shucha, and Sara VanderHaagen, who have influenced my thinking in meaningful ways. I also taught a graduate seminar on rhetoric, space, and mobility, and the University of Wisconsin–Milwaukee graduate students in that class, especially Alex Parr Balaram, Alisa Hardy, and Kristin Wagel, helped me (in ways that they may not realize) think through the concept of the mobile imagination that I offer in this book.

Finally, I am grateful to my family. John, Anna, and James have been tremendously supportive in my travel for archival research and time away for writing. Also, Lynne Harris, possibly the best mother-in-law ever, proofread the entire manuscript. Of course, any remaining errors are my own.

Parts of the introduction and chapter 2 are from Leslie J. Harris, "Rhetorical Mobilities and the City: The White Slavery Controversy and Racialized Protection of Women in the U.S.," *Quarterly Journal of Speech* 104, no. 1 (2018): 22–46, and are reprinted by permission of the publisher (Taylor & Francis Ltd., http://www.tandfonline.com).

Introduction

In 1911, the *National Prohibitionist* wrote, "Awful as the story is, we invite attention, not to its horror—the horror of herds of little girls sold at a per-head price below the value of pigs—but to the practical questions of responsibility and cure."[1] At the turn of the nineteenth into the twentieth century, the United States was in the midst of a crisis commonly known as white slavery. There was widespread fear that white women and girls were being "trapped, ensnared, deceived, and sold into dens of vice," and any white woman who dared to venture out of the safety of her home was thought to be at risk.[2] Yet, white slavery was not simply understood as a personal problem. For those who attempted to warn the country about white slavery, the risk to white womanhood represented a threat to the nation. As activists Clifford G. Roe and B. S. Steadwell explained:

> A hideous monster, known as white slavery, has crept in among us and is undermining our homes. Its poisonous venom has corrupted and diseased our boys. It has coiled its slimy tentacles around our girls and strangled

purity and innocence. It has thus demoralized the sanctity of our homes and destroyed peace and happiness. In time, if not killed[,] it will crush out decent government, for when our homes are destroyed our government is ruined, because the home is the foundation of all government.[3]

Given the perceived stakes, it is not surprising that the controversy had far-reaching consequences, prompting international treaties and sweeping national laws, expanding the federal police force (later known as the FBI), regulating immigration, and instituting a variety of state and local policies. Yet, the controversy was not simply about protecting women and children; it was also about harnessing white womanhood to constitute national identity and belonging.

In *The Rhetoric of White Slavery and the Making of National Identity*, I insist that white slavery functioned as a rhetoric that was used to shape national space. Advocates for reform represented white women as vulnerable, precious, and in need of protection. As a result, perceived dangers of white slavery justified extraordinary measures to attempt to keep white women within the home because they were supposed to be safe if they stayed in their culturally appropriate place. White women were not the people most at risk of sexual exploitation, yet they became weaponized in the controversy to target populations deemed undesirable. Similarly, there was no evidence that immigrants and people from non-white communities posed a threat to white women. Nonetheless, government officials and activists used the fear of white slavery to discipline people who failed to perform appropriate American whiteness, representing many immigrants and similarly undesirable people as dangerous white slavers. Consequently, the rhetoric of white slavery controlled the ways that people existed and belonged within national space.

The story, however, extends beyond the material consequences of white slavery rhetoric on specific American populations. Through analysis of the white slavery controversy, I conclude that white womanhood was a symbolic construct used to make sense of home and nation.[4] The risk to white womanhood was understood as a risk to the nation, and under the guise of protecting white women, white slavery rhetoric solidified ties between national identity and, to use the words of bell hooks, "imperialist white supremacist capitalist cisheteropatriarchy."[5] By moving through the different scales of the controversy, this book makes the case that the confinement of Chinese migrant women by immigration agents, the targeting of Black men by the federal police force, and the "helping" of Indian women by US missionaries traveling through *chaklas* (state sanctioned brothels in India), were part of the same spatial network that shaped fundamental understandings of national identity. White womanhood was mobilized to justify and sustain this construction of nation. In this sense, the white slavery controversy offers a window into the rhetoric that constituted the fundamental identity of the United States.

White Slavery

The story of white slavery is most often represented as an example of moral panic. Existing research on the white slavery controversy tends to focus on understanding the material realities of prostitution, attempting to uncover the truth of white slavery, and tracing the implications of the supposed mass hysteria that gripped the United States and Europe during the Progressive Era. This research has identified how the controversy was used to reify racial hierarchies in the United States, led to the expansion of the FBI, and participated in the Progressive Era development of newspaper and print culture.[6] A significant amount of scholarship argues that there were very few instances of white slavery, and some explicitly label white slavery as a moral panic that was used to justify a massive expansion in state power to regulate the lives of individuals.[7] However, as Ruth Rosen argues, we need to be mindful to avoid the obfuscation of real violence and exploitation in prostitution.[8] While there is some historical evidence to suggest that the most extreme forms of forced prostitution were rare (Rosen estimated less than 10 percent of all prostitution), sexual exploitation was more widespread.[9]

We know that someone who has consensually practiced prostitution can also be raped, entrapped, or exploited, and during this time period, women had limited economic and political rights. Reformers were attempting to address a wide variety of problems related to the entry of women into, the treatment of women within, and the removal of women from prostitution.[10] Further, agency is complex and multifaceted, suggesting that there may not be a clear dichotomy between consensual prostitution and white slavery. To be clear, I am not attempting to argue that there were many white slaves in the Progressive Era United States or Europe; rather, I am looking to shift the question from the factual claim of whether white slavery was a problem to the critical question of what the controversy was doing in public culture. In this book, I argue that the white slavery controversy was about constructions of white womanhood and the shaping of national identity.

This study differs from much of the existing literature on the white slavery controversy because it utilizes an explicitly rhetorical framework.[11] Thus, rather than attempting to uncover the material reality of lives lived behind closed doors, I turn to the primarily discursive representations of those lives. I am operating under the assumption that the rhetoric of the controversy was not a transparent reflection of the reality of prostitution, but such rhetoric matters because it both reflects and constitutes larger cultural understandings. In other words, I turn to the white slavery controversy not because I aim to understand the reality of Progressive Era prostitution, but because this controversy functions as a case study to understand larger questions of gender, race, and national space.

The language of "white slavery" was not new when it came to be evoked in controversies over sexual exploitation. In the early nineteenth-century United States and Europe, "white slavery" was often associated with class conflict and used to challenge working conditions of white workers by associating white slavery with enslaved people of African descent.[12] In the United States, the term was also used in captivity narratives to fuel fear and anger toward Indigenous American and Catholic populations.[13] This wide use speaks to the evocative nature of the phrase "white slavery." The metaphor of slavery has proven to be tremendously powerful in the United States, and it remains powerful because it evokes "moral repugnance."[14] Perhaps more significantly, slavery has remarkable rhetorical power when connected to whiteness. According to Nell Irvin Painter, freedom is at the heart of whiteness, and it gains cultural meaning in its opposition to blackness.[15] The cultural connections among Black, abject, and slave participated in constituting whiteness in terms of superiority and freedom. This freedom also entailed ownership of property. According to Mishuana Goeman, "The presumptuous *guarantee* of property through whiteness was common in nineteenth-century settler nations and led state legislation to codify settlers' heighted race consciousness around whiteness as property."[16] The connections between whiteness and property, then, worked in different directions. Whiteness opened space for ownership, an agency exercised through possession. Thus, being owned evacuated whiteness, creating an inherent contradiction in the term "white slavery." Furthermore, as whiteness functioned as property, only some people had access to that property. Black, Indigenous American, and many migrant people were effectively excluded from laying claim to whiteness. The term "white slavery" was not only a startling disjuncture, but it put whiteness itself at risk, collapsing borders between Black/white and abject/citizen.[17]

By the end of the nineteenth century, the term "white slavery" was firmly connected to prostitution and sexual exploitation, and it gained widespread traction in Europe prior to being appropriated by American activists. Increasing international communication networks, especially among purity and temperance activists, propelled concern over white slavery from Europe to the United States and beyond. As I will argue, white womanhood came to be appropriated in sex trafficking rhetoric in ways that traveled across the globe, but it appeared to emerge as a significant issue in the United States after William T. Stead published a multipart investigation in England's *Pall Mall Gazette* titled, "The Maiden Tribute of Modern Babylon."[18] Stead did not invent the language of white slavery, and he was not the first to warn of its dangers. However, many activists marked Stead's 1885 exposé as the moment when Americans began to see their white women and girls as in danger, prompting the beginning of a movement.[19]

Other than the association with sexual exploitation and prostitution, there was little consensus about the meanings of white slavery. For some reformers, the term was used to describe the perceived problem of "young white women ... being lured from their homes by traffickers and forced into prostitution."[20] Others, however, could not imagine white women's consensual prostitution and explicitly classified all prostitution as sex slavery. Still others defined white slavery as a middle ground between the two poles, placing a vast swath of sexual exploitation ranging from physical and financial coercion to verbal threats and manipulation within the category of white slavery. The dramatic discrepancy in the operational definitions of white slavery, led to vastly different quantifications of the problem by reformers.[21] Regardless of the specific definition, white women were not the people who were most frequently victimized or exploited. Nevertheless, white womanhood remained symbolically important to the development of the controversy in the United States and Europe.

The rhetoric of white slavery moved. Consequently, white slavery emerged as a significant issue at a variety of geographic scales, including in the wilds of northern Wisconsin, official diplomatic letters between nations, the halls of the US Congress, and the rough streets of Chicago. Following Peggy Levitt, I utilize a transnational optic to read across the different scales of the white slavery controversy, drawing attention to the complexity of space that may not align with formal geographical boundaries. In other words, while spaces on a map may appear stable and clearly defined, a transnational optic reveals the way that rhetoric reshapes space and calls for multifaceted readings of geography. As Raka Shome argues, "The global and the national are thus not neat separate objects or domains. They constantly inform each other through shifting transnational circuits of power."[22] Likewise, feminist geopolitics identifies geopolitical power as simultaneously situated in and reinforced by different scales such as the body, home, and nation-state.[23] Thus, by drawing attention to the complex movement among scales of the white slavery controversy, I establish how white womanhood works to structure national space.

Progress and White Womanhood

National identity is never static. I am conceptualizing nation as an "imagined community" that comes into existence in response to rhetorical technologies that include shared symbols, mythologies, and histories.[24] Yet, the turn of the nineteenth into the twentieth century was a period of significant change in the United States. Immigration, the Great Migration, the perceived loss of the Western frontier, industrialization, and urbanization all challenged conceptions of the American imaginary. Developments in global communication and transportation infrastructure dramatically changed possibilities for mobility, and historic shifts in gender roles changed the ways that women negotiated public space. The ways that people moved through and existed within the nation felt irrevocably altered.

Change appeared most acute in American cities. In his 1914 study of the urban United States, sociologist Edward A. Ross explained that the great peoples who had supposedly conquered the West were being supplanted by a shockingly diverse population, many of whom were "sub-common."[25] American cities demonstrated evidence of excessive wealth and abject poverty. For instance, John D. Rockefeller Jr., one of the wealthiest men in the world, had a home in New York City, as did migrants from all over the world who lived in crowded tenements.[26] The first wave of what has come to be known as the Great Migration also brought large numbers of Black Americans north, changing the racial composition of many American cities.[27] At the same time, racial segregation, upheld by the US Supreme Court's 1896 *Plessy* decision, institutionalized racial discrimination and perceptions of racial hierarchy.

About twenty-three million immigrants came to the United States between the 1890s and the 1920s, and this surge in immigration prompted questions about "what should be done with the immigrant or for the immigrant."[28] Increasingly Americans were distinguishing between "old" immigrants, primarily from northern and western Europe, and "new" immigrants, from southern and eastern Europe, Asia, and elsewhere. While the old immigrants tended to be represented as desirable and easily able to assimilate, new immigrants were less likely to speak English, and many were poor and uneducated.[29] Some activists responded to changes in immigration patterns by increasing efforts toward Americanization, essentially teaching immigrants how to become good Americans, but others advocated for immigration restrictions.

Just as the composition of the nation was changing, a confluence of factors contributed to changes in women's roles at the new millennium, spurring what came to be called the "new woman." The new woman tended to be more educated and independent than previous generations of white American women. While women have always worked, industrialization and urbanization shifted much working-class paid employment out of the home, and opportunities for women's employment also expanded.[30] Middle-class women in the United States tended to have more leisure time, and significant numbers of women pursued educational opportunities, leading to a first generation of college educated women.[31] Although many educational opportunities were only available to white, middle-class women, by the turn of the century, many Black women also had access to unprecedented educational opportunities, and public education was becoming more prevalent.[32] There was increasing evidence of widespread change in American women's lives.

In the wake of massive social change, white Americans tended to embrace a version of American exceptionalism. A central component of this American public imaginary was the linear progress of civilization. The popularization of Darwinism encouraged a view of humanity as progressing from savagery to civilization, and perceptions of this progress were intimately connected to race.[33] In the Progressive Era, people tended to approach perceived challenges to progress by embracing possibilities for change through the state and other institutions. Drawing on earlier Darwinian ideas, it was common for progressives to accept racial hierarchy, and these hierarchies were frequently naturalized through scientific classification. For example, Ross based his conclusion about "sub-common" immigrants on his observation of the physiognomy (such as eye shape and the slope of the forehead) of immigrants.[34] Similarly, the 1911 *Dictionary of Races or Peoples*, published by the Immigration Commission (also known as the Dillingham Commission), created a racial hierarchy based in seemingly objective anthropological and ethnographic data.[35] However, progressives tended to deviate from earlier Darwinism by embracing eugenics. While Darwinism was often understood as individualistic and even laissez-faire, eugenics demanded intervention because it posited that racial progress could happen with institutional support. The alternative to intervention was regression or even "race suicide."[36] In other words, theories of Darwinism positioned evolution as natural and, in many cases, inevitable, but eugenics, on the other hand, embraced artificial selection to ensure progress. Eugenics permeated Progressive Era understandings of the world, shaping scientific, social, and economic reform.[37] It was a spatiotemporal understanding of society that seemed to necessitate reform to ensure the forward march of civilization.

White womanhood was central to this imagining of progress. For instance, Charlotte Perkins Gilman represented women as "enlightened society's eugenic agents" through their ability to select partners and procreate.[38] Theodore Roosevelt, along with other progressives, warned of "race suicide" because good white women were thought to be having fewer children, while less desirable women tended to have large numbers of children.[39] Additionally, many women harnessed their supposedly natural morality to influence social reform and ensure moral progress.[40] Through their reproduction and moralizing influence, white women were critical to perceptions of national progress.

White womanhood as a symbolic construct also retained a powerful hold on the American public imaginary. Anne McClintock has established that women are often represented as "symbolic bearers of the nation."[41] In the United States, white womanhood was often tied to the home. Working from Barbra Welter's conception of the cult of true womanhood, extensive research has confirmed that, throughout the nineteenth and into the twentieth century, good womanhood was judged based on expectations of "piety," sexual and moral "purity," "domesticity" and proper performance of motherhood, and "submissiveness."[42] Not only did these cultural norms create impossible standards for good womanhood, but they also became used to justify white women's limited civic identities, as well as to sustain women's roles in the private sphere of the home.[43] Beyond physical procreation, the home was represented as training ground for citizens and a microcosm of the nation. Progressive Era rhetoric often connected home and national identity, and by situating home as critical to the American public imaginary, there was a public interest in maintaining women's place within the home.[44] White womanhood was emblematic of national virtue, and women were represented as housekeepers of the nation and molders of the next generation of Americans. These perceptions sustained a contradictory mix of fixation on individual bodies for the purpose of protecting womanhood, disregarding the needs and desires of many actual women, and failing to address systemic and structural violence against women, especially women of color.[45]

Reading the Mobile Imagination

The white slavery controversy was animated by supposed violations in mobility. Some white Americans perceived that undesirable people were moving through American spaces, white women were being moved into sites of danger, and even the nation's movement toward civilization seemed to be threatened. These movements were cultural threats because they challenged what I am referring to as the "mobile imagination," the ways that people were thought to exist within space and time. Imagined mobility can constitute and reflect spatiotemporal belonging within national space, making a consideration of the mobile imagination valuable to understanding the imagined community of the United States. My conception of the mobile imagination guides my reading of the white slavery controversy, drawing attention to white womanhood in shaping national identity.

My reading of the mobile imaginary is grounded in an assumption that space is constructed and dynamic. Henri Lefebvre argues, "(Social) space is a (social) product," suggesting that space does not have intrinsic meaning outside of its cultural context.[46] Further, Doreen Massey has been influential in conceptualizing "social relations stretched over space," rather than space or place as a static concept.[47] As a result, any consideration of space should also include a consideration of the ways in which people use space and exist within space that is necessarily marked by power relations within culture.[48] Even in everyday spaces, there is a constant flow between human performance of identity and the space of that performance, and this flow shapes agential possibilities.[49] To conceptualize these relationships, Massey's research established that "space is a product of interrelations; it is the sphere of the possibility for the existence of multiplicity; it is always in the process of becoming, is always being made."[50] Moving from a topological understanding of space to a conception of space as relationally constituted makes space ripe for rhetorical engagement.[51]

While rhetorical studies of space/place often implicitly engage issues of mobility, it is increasingly becoming a focus of rhetorical research. Mobility involves a confluence of time and space. As Tim Cresswell argues, "It is the spatialization of time and temporalization of space."[52] It is the movement of people or things from one point to another, and it is the central act in a variety of phenomena of concern to rhetorical scholars (such as migration, transportation, and tourism). For example, Daniel C. Brouwer describes mobility "as both a key topic for analysis and a conceptual resource" in his analysis of the AIDS quilt and its move to Atlanta from San Francisco.[53] From running and walking to driving and other forms of transportation, rhetorical scholars have explicitly analyzed corporal mobility as a way to engage issues of space and power.[54] Additionally, rhetorical scholarship has established that corporeal mobility is structured by race. For example, police traffic stops of those who are Black function as a regulation of Black people's mobility and, as Armond R. Towns argues, is one part of "a long-held White mastery over mobility maintained by controlling the movement of people of color of all genders, sexualities, and classes."[55] This control is significant, in part, because free mobility is often used as a marker of full citizenship and humanity.[56] This research has been important in highlighting mobility as a significant area of concern for rhetorical scholars, bringing attention to the rhetoricity of the moving body, and identifying connections between mobility and space/place. Furthermore, attention to the material elements of mobility has helped advance complex understandings of agency that move beyond the human power of the rhetor toward explicitly considering how agency not only is constrained by context but also resides in places and bodies.

Although material mobility remains significant, discourses of mobility help shape understandings of the material.[57] The co-constitutive relationship of discursive and material mobility calls for deeper rhetorical engagement. Some scholarship has engaged the figurative dimensions of mobility such as Carly S. Woods's consideration of mobility metaphors in intersectional rhetorical history.[58] Lisa A. Flores uncovers the intermingling of corporeal and figurative mobility in her analysis of the racialized control over mobility through "stoppage," which "is both a phenomenon related to the forced immobility of bodies—literal and figurative—as it is also a rhetorical mode of racialization."[59] Flores argues that stoppage creates a set of spatiotemporal relations that shape identity, especially in relation to place and belonging.[60] I find Flores's argument to be especially significant because it gets at some of the rhetorical mechanisms of what Cresswell has called the "geographic imagination" and what Massey has called "spatial imagination." Rhetoricity provides the link between the geographic imagination and the material. That is, the rhetorical both reflects and constitutes imaginations of racialized place and belonging in ways that shape material, embodied experiences.

By turning to the mobile imagination, I foreground concerns of representation and cultural entanglements in the ways that people exist within and move through space. Rather than focus on the space itself, the mobile imagination draws attention to the intersection of space, people, and time.

The analysis of the mobile imagination accordingly demands reflection on who or what can move, how the mobility occurs, the material and social constraints to mobility, and the cultural meanings of mobility within particular contexts. Rather than only focus on the material, rhetorical understandings of mobility call for an imagining of possibilities and reflecting on the meanings of representation within mobility. These questions can help lead us to a better understanding of how the rhetoricity of mobility can shape space and belonging—even in cases where mobility does not appear to be the focus of controversy.

I identify three central components of mobile imagination. First, it calls for an analysis of the meanings of mobility and immobility. Mobility is not neutral. Because mobility involves a person moving through time and space, meaning is bound up with embodied identity and spatiotemporality. Stasis, an absence of mobility, can connote safety and security, but forced stoppage, on the other hand, can be a way of regulating mobility and belonging. Cresswell identifies a sedentary and nomadic metaphysics to describe the moments when mobility or stasis becomes culturally valued. He argues that mobility is valued when it is a citizenship practice, and within this framework, mobility connotes possibility, freedom, flow, and advancement.[61] On the other hand, stasis can be valued when it creates a sense of rootedness, belonging, stability, and security. The privileging of home, for example, is a privileging of stasis. While there is a strong cultural connection between stasis and womanhood, mobile citizens ("autonomous individualized agents") are often considered to be ideal, and mobility is commonly understood as a basic right of citizenship.[62] Yet, not everyone has the same access to mobility because of material constraints, socially perpetuated fear, or cultural expectations.[63] When the possibility for mobility or stasis is stripped away, people are marked as incomplete. Free mobility is often associated with citizenship and belonging, but there can also be associations with escape, adventure, tedious obligation, or exploration. An analysis of the meanings of mobility and immobility helps uncover relationships between embodied identity and spatiotemporally.

Meanings of mobility can also emerge through the interactions between time and space. A spatiotemporal alignment is part of what creates a cultural identity. Massey explains that we can imagine cultures and societies "as constellations of social relations configured as forming a time-space."[64] To create a sense of a people at a particular moment is to also create the possibility that people can be perceived as dislocated either spatially or temporally. For example, labeling a culture as "developing" or "backward" rhetorically positions it as temporally dislocated,[65] and nostalgia can be imagined as a spatiotemporal yearning. Rhetoric can also create a sense that different spaces move at different rates. Joan Faber McAlister insists that communication scholars need to challenge the time compression thesis—the idea that that global communication technologies shrink the world.[66] It is true that there is not only unequal access to technologies that create a sense of compression but also different emotional valences associated with compression in relation to particular spaces.[67] If the city, for example, is imagined as fast-paced, that space-time compression may be deemed inappropriate for women if women's space is that of the home, a site of stasis and preservation of tradition.

A second component of the mobile imagination is the representation of the ways of movement. The ways of movement can be analyzed through both paths and modes. At its most basic, a path is how one gets from point A to point B, but considering the rhetoricity of paths helps explain how people move through space and time. For example, one space can be represented as a natural or inevitable path to another space. Likewise, some paths may be represented as safe and others as dangerous or off limits. Topography can be rhetorically folded, expanded, nested, stretched, collapsed, or networked to facilitate or limit pathways and, thereby, change the meaning and interaction with space. Jan Nespor describes topology as "the ways places are connected, rather than their relative locations in map-space," and this understanding of connection can help us identity the "folds and stretches" of space.[68] Other research has identified theories of assemblage as a way of understanding social space through connection. As people move through and between space, they develop networks of connections that, in turn, create a complicated and layered understanding of social space.[69] When space is conceptualized as a complicated and rhetorically constructed network, rather than a stable container, mobility becomes critical to understandings of space and the ways that people exist in space.

The mode is the tool or technology that someone uses for their movement. Communication research has analyzed the technologies that enable, sustain, and shape these networks of mobility.[70] A bicycle, for example, may have been a technology of freedom and independence for some nineteenth-century women, and it may currently work as an environmental statement for those who use it to commute to work instead of a car.[71] Similarly, buses can be understood as markers of class and race, leading some communities to eliminate or reduce bus lines in order to control who can move through their community.

Finally, the mobile imagination considers the potential for mobility, which involves an interplay of power and constraints, necessitating an understanding of agency. Karlyn Kohrs Campbell's conception of rhetorical agency has been deeply influential. She explained "that agency (1) is communal and participatory, hence, both constituted and constrained by externals that are material and symbolic; (2) is 'invented' by authors who are points of articulation; (3) emerges in artistry or craft; (4) is effected through form; and (5) is perverse, that is, inherently, protean, ambiguous, open to reversal."[72] In this sense, agency is always constrained by context and constituted in the enactment of rhetorical performance. Other scholarship has found that agency has a complex relationship with identity, both shaping and reflecting the discursive production of identity at individual and communal levels.[73]

Even as constraints limit some agential possibilities, resistance can happen because of constraints.[74] Josue David Cisneros positions this duality in reference to the border, arguing "the border cuts and divides but also provides the possibility for contact and crossing."[75] Similarly, in her analysis of Black women's geographies, Katherine McKittrick argues that Black women exist within geographies of domination that include displacement and containment.⁷⁶ However, Black women also inhabit what Jenny Sharpe calls "the cervices of power . . . [where they can] manipulate and recast the geographic terrain."⁷⁷ Thus, agency and identity function as important components of the mobile imagination.

Mapping the Study

The white slavery controversy was complicated and multifaceted, and the inconsistent boundaries of the controversy make a historical account difficult to map. This study considers the white slavery controversy within concentric scales, ranging from the local to the transnational. This organizational structure can elucidate the rhetorical intermingling of these scales. Often rhetorical studies of space are isolated to a single scale, such as a specific region, border, or monument, but human controversy always exists simultaneously on different scales. An issue may manifest in different ways on a local or national scale, but we cannot understand one without the other. Spatial scales are inextricably linked, and the structure of this book can help tease out some of the complexities of those connections.

The following chapter begins with a local controversy that gained national attention. When innocent white women were thought to be trapped in prostitution in the Northwoods of Wisconsin in 1887, the Woman's Christian Temperance Union and Wisconsin lawmakers entered into a conflict over place and belonging. I argue that place writes meaning onto bodies, and the apparent displacement of white women in the Northwoods forced these women into a perceived dichotomy between irredeemable whore and innocent victim. There is a stability that can become imagined onto local places, and as a result of that seemingly stable meaning, some people are thought to not belong. When Americans were forced to confront the reality of pretty, young white women moving into the Northwoods, they changed the meanings of the bodies, rather than challenge the meanings of place.⁷⁸ Perceived possibilities for women's mobility differed depending on the character of the woman and the sites of mobility. It was inconceivable that good women could have traveled to the Northwoods by choice, so the public debate was about classifying the women as innocent and trapped or whore and mobile.

The analysis then moves from the local scale to the scale of the city. While the geographical space of the Wisconsin Northwoods is larger than Chicago or New York, it was constructed as local, isolated, and particular. In contrast, the image of the city was increasingly represented as a vast site of danger. In chapter 2, I consider white slavery at the scale of the city through an analysis of moral reform literature primarily centered in Chicago. I argue that the danger of the city was tied into the mobile imagination. The inability of activists to contain vice necessitated the containment of women. In contrast, in chapter 3, I analyze the scientific reform rhetoric that gained prominence when John D. Rockefeller Jr. developed an interest in white slavery and spearheaded New York reform efforts. This rhetoric situated white women as redeemable. Women's safety was thought to depend on a carefully controlled environment, specifically the environment of the white American home. At the same time, women who did not properly perform whiteness were erased as reformers treated many women of color and immigrant women as symptoms of the diseased city from which white women needed to be rescued.

In chapter 4, I analyze the debate over and enforcement of the 1910 federal White Slave Traffic Act, also known as the Mann Act. I argue that through restricting movement by evoking the commerce clause, this legislation constituted whiteness as integral to national identity. Although the Mann Act was ostensibly color-blind, the rhetoric reveals connections between race, the mobile imagination, and citizenship. The mobility of people of color, particularly Black men, was represented as dangerous and threatening, especially when that mobility challenged the color line through interracial sex. Thus, the Mann Act became an enforcement mechanism to limit the potential mobility for people of color, and the prosecution of heavyweight boxing champion Jack Johnson functioned as a warning about the consequences of both movement across geographical space, as well as mobility in crossing the color line.

I then shift from mobility within the United States to a consideration of the international border. In chapter 5, I analyze the rhetoric about white slavery, yellow slavery, and yellow peril, and I argue that concern over immigration and Asian prostitution functioned as a way to protect white women and enforce whiteness. The immigration rhetoric figured Chinatowns and migrants from Asia as an invasion of American cities, threatening white womanhood and, thus, the nation.

I finally turn to the transnational scale in chapter 6. I argue that globalization and colonialism transformed the mobile imagination of white womanhood. Increasingly countries perceived women of their nation as endangered, and international coalitions were used to shore up both national boundaries and expressions of empire. However, as the controversy slipped across borders, in much the same way as women were feared to slip into transnational danger, reformers rhetorically appropriated white slavery to meet their different rhetorical needs.

I conclude with connections between current human trafficking rhetoric and the Progressive Era white slavery controversy. While the white slavery controversy was certainly about prostitution and sexual exploitation, in this book, I identify the protection of white womanhood as a rhetoric that is deeply imbued with racialized belonging and the whiteness of nation. In what follows, I examine how white womanhood intersects with the mobile imagination, shaping perceptions of space, time, and public identity. In moving through the different scales of the controversy, I aim to uncover how overlapping rhetorics about white womanhood reinforce white national belonging while expelling or erasing those who do not conform to norms of whiteness. Rhetorics of sexual precarity are about much more than sex; they are also about belonging, identity, and race.

CHAPTER 1

Slavery Up North

WHITE WOMEN'S DISPLACEMENT IN THE WISCONSIN
NORTHWOODS, 1887–1889

In 1886, the northern woods of Wisconsin remained a fairly isolated location. Dense pine woods and fast-moving rivers made it an ideal site for logging, and small towns scattered the area. Marinette was one such town, tucked into the northern woods but still accessible by rail. Despite rapid growth, Marinette retained the ethos of a lumber town and had few amenities that may have been expected in the eleventh largest city in the state.[1] Those northern woods may seem like an unlikely location for sordid tales of abduction and sex trafficking, but by 1887, reports of "slavery up north" made northern Wisconsin the focus of both national outrage and reform efforts.

Julia Howden was certainly not the first to share her experience in the Northwoods, but when Howden, a "hansom" twenty-five-year-old white woman, walked into a Chicago police station one October afternoon in 1887, she started a wave that would reverberate to the Wisconsin governor's office and ultimately across the rest of the country.[2] She described a harrowing ordeal of being tricked into traveling to northern Wisconsin with the promise of a job only to become trapped in a saloon and brothel. She said that she was raped and starved, but she ultimately escaped, making her way home to Chicago.

When Howden's story reached the newspapers, there had already been small ripples—occasional stories of missing girls, accusations, and reporter investigations. Howden's story, however, seemed to join with and amplify the previous murmurings of suspicion. Julia Howden's story became part of a larger narrative about white slavery that ultimately led to legislative action in Wisconsin and national attention. Stories such as Julia Howden's created gaps in the perceived borders that separated good and evil. Accounts of white women and girls being tricked, imprisoned, and manipulated into prostitution made Wisconsin the focus of national outrage, eventually leading the state to adopt pioneering (although largely ineffective) legislation in response to sex trafficking. Wisconsin became the locus of national controversy, and the question of white women's place was at the root of the controversy.

The case study of the Wisconsin white slavery controversy illustrates the ways in which space maps onto women, and the specific contours of the map make the difference between a woman who is a victim in need of saving and an irredeemable whore. In the Wisconsin Northwoods, these white women were moved out of place, and the meanings of that displacement were "inflected by the governing metaphors of flesh: race, gender, and sexuality."[3] The white slavery controversy provides an opportunity to understand how people make sense of moments of displacement. This chapter explores an early moment in the white slavery controversy. Wisconsin was not only the first major flare in what came to be a significant national issue, but it resulted in one of the first attempts to legislate a solution to white slavery in the United States. The Wisconsin white slavery controversy uncovers how the mobile imagination of a place shapes meanings of white women's displacement and, thus, possibilities for redemption.

Place and the New North

Although northern Wisconsin may seem like a stable place, meanings of places are always infected with "geographical layers" that, while place is contingent and mutable, can create a sense of stability and permanence.[4] As Ronald Walter Greene and Kevin Douglas Kuswa explain, "Regions are rhetorically drawn into maps of power as actors, objects, and techniques of governance."[5] Defining and making sense of place is inseparable from the complex power dynamic within, across, and around the space. Thus, northern Wisconsin is not simply the northern part of a northwestern state, but it was a liminal site that marked the boundary between the tamed and the untamed. It was a place of possibility and danger.

The place of northern Wisconsin, commonly known as the "New North," "Northwoods," or the "pinelands," covered about three-fifths of the state, and the 1860 census indicated that only one-twenty-fifth of the state lived in the primarily unsettled North.[6] The Homestead Act of 1862, federal legislation that encouraged western settlement, was used by many who eventually settled in the area, and the last federal land office in Wisconsin did not close until 1928.[7] Northern Wisconsin settlement was largely driven by farming and the lumber industry, and, by some accounts, there was a mutually advantageous relationship between these two groups of settlers.[8]

The massive northern forests of pine were integral to expansion of the lumber industry in Wisconsin in the four decades preceding the turn of the century.[9] It is difficult to underestimate the influence of the lumber industry on northern Wisconsin. One historian of the state notes, "The seeming epitome of malign monopoly, large mill owners dominated whole communities and even counties, controlling practically all employment, wage rates, retailing, law enforcement, and services."[10] The 1880s were a peak time in the growth of the lumber industry through much of northern Wisconsin.[11] The burgeoning lumber and mining industries worked to tame the land and supply the West with resources for continued expansion. Yet, despite its population growth, the Northwoods retained an ethos of wild and untamed territory.

Place writes meaning onto those within it. Places and spaces, as Isaac West argues, are "integrally linked to the rhetorical production of identity and agency."[12] Thus, the creation and maintenance of place is rhetorical and infected with power, and place operates rhetorically not only as a site of rhetorical action but also as a mechanism of identity creation. In the Northwoods, as with much western expansion, white Americans attempted to evacuate racialized Others, namely Indigenous populations, to tame the land. The prevailing assumption was that interacting with Indigenous Americans would corrupt white people—degrading their civilizing influence.[13] As such, it is perhaps unsurprising that the narrative of Wisconsin expansion explicitly erased the native populations from the land after 1848.[14] Nevertheless, there is a plethora of evidence that Indigenous populations

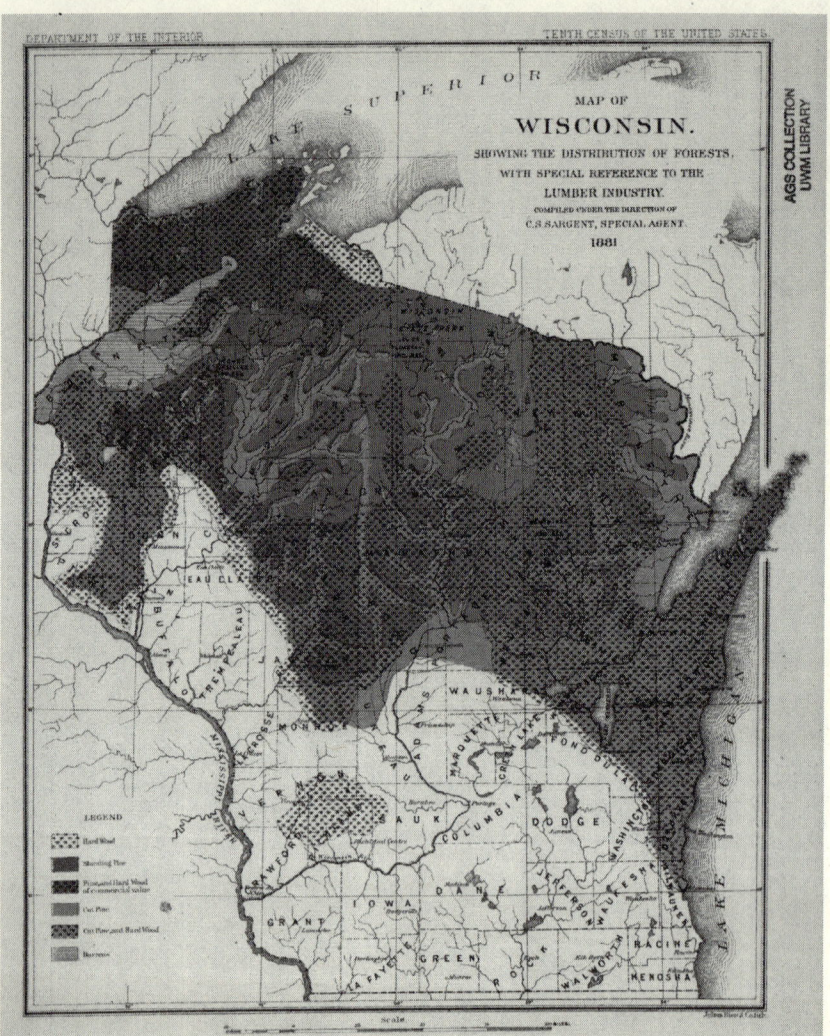

FIGURE 1. Map of Wisconsin showing the distribution of forests with special reference to the lumber industry, 1881. Compiled under the direction of C. S. Sargent, special agent; Department of the Interior; Tenth Census of the United States. From the American Geographical Society Library, University of Wisconsin–Milwaukee Libraries.

remained (and continue to remain) in Wisconsin, but their rhetorical erasure was an important part of the white, masculine conquest narrative.

Historian and Wisconsin native Frederick J. Turner argued in 1893 that the frontier, "the meeting point between savagery and civilization," was the site of the "most rapid and effective Americanization" because as people moved toward the frontier, they were forced to strip themselves of European markers of civility, ultimately developing a distinctly American civilization.[15] Turner's argument, which has come to be known as the frontier thesis, has been both celebrated and critiqued, but it is perhaps most useful in understanding late nineteenth century conceptions of the frontier within the US public imaginary.[16] Rather than being consistently defined as the trans-Mississippi west, the frontier was understood as a moving site of liminality between the civilized and the savage, although Turner lamented that the frontier was quickly disappearing.[17] Implicit within this understanding was the assumption that white men became called upon to tame the wilderness and write meaning on the virgin landscape.[18] Thus, both whiteness and masculinity became indelibly written on the imaginary of the American West.

Women's Place

By the 1880s, white woman's place remained firmly rooted in the home. Even into the turn of the century, the cult of domesticity retained a powerful hold on the American public imaginary of the good woman, and women in public often had the taint of "fallen women."[19] Western women were not exempt from these expectations, rather they were supposed to extend womanliness to the frontier in service of white male conquest mythology.[20] Despite the clear constraints of domesticity, women have long utilized domestic ideologies in the service of public action, and the Woman's Christian Temperance Union is one of the most successful examples of such a strategy.[21]

When Frances E. Willard assumed the presidency of the Woman's Christian Temperance Union (WCTU), the organization became the largest and most influential women's organization in the United States, growing from about twenty-seven thousand members to nearly two hundred thousand members in the course of the 1880s.[22] The WCTU Department for the Promotion of Social Purity began in 1886 in an effort to promote an equal standard of morality for men and women and protect the purity of women, aligning social purity with temperance.[23] In their announcement to the press, the WCTU explicitly referenced the "recent terrible disclosures in England [that] have caused an 'arrest of thought' to Europe and America alike," invoking William T. Stead's 1885 white slavery exposé in London's *Pall Mall Gazette*.[24]

Not everyone praised the new department of the WCTU. For example, a New York newspaper commented, "The author of it [the circular announcing the new department] is skating upon such mighty thin ice that we would not dare to follow her. We shall only say that it comes evidently from earnest women, aiming at a good end."[25] The critics typically expressed a concern that public discussion of sex would reduce innocence and purity in white youth and women. Nevertheless, by the summer of 1886, Willard reported:

> Organized in ten thousand towns and cities, with State and Territorial auxiliaries embracing the entire Republic, and now stretching out in the World's W.C.T.U to every corner of the globe, we are, in the providence of God, the strongest single power yet raised up among women to do battle for this sacred cause.[26]

The strong associations between temperance and purity, along with the WCTU emphasis on mothers' meetings and home protection, quickly raised the profile of the new Social Purity Department.

The growth of the WCTU involvement in social purity was rooted in the language of home protection, which implicitly justified white women's public involvement while reifying the home as women's proper place. Yet, Willard developed a framework of home protection that centered the home as critical to humanity for both men and women—a framework that was consistently emerging within the WCTU since the founding of the Social Purity Department but most full articulated in Willard's 1890 pamphlet, *A White Life for Two*.

In *A White Life for Two*, Willard framed her argument as a progress narrative, where social purity was necessary for human progress. That progress, according to Willard, corresponded to a godly ideal of home. Calling that ideal into existence, Willard argued, "The American home, with its Christian method of a two-fold headship, based on laws natural and divine, is steadily rooting out all of that remains of the mediaeval continental and harem philosophies concerning this greatest problem of all time."[27] Willard's association of American with Christian created space for a clear contrast with the supposedly barbaric past. By deftly naming the American and Christian home as a site of equality with "two-fold headship," Willard constituted an ideal that was not consistently in practice at the time. The chain of reasoning posited progress as Christian, a link reinforced when Willard named "modern womanhood" as working on "a high plane Christianity."[28] By Willard's logic, the more modern and advanced a society, the closer that society was to God, and the home functioned as evidence of that advancement. Within this framework, white women's mobility was social and spiritual; while remining within the physical space of the home, white women could move toward greater social status and closer to God. Indeed, this social mobility could only occur through white women's physical stasis within the home.

While Willard's assertion that protecting the home was the route to progress may have been uncontroversial, her means of protecting the home was fairly radical for the time because it was rooted in women's rights both inside and outside of the domestic sphere. Through a series of six rhetorical questions, Willard planted a sense of injustice that clustered rights, social progress, and purity. For example, she asked, "Why are laws so shamelessly unequal now? ... Why [in one state] is the age of protection or consent ... only seven years? ... The answer is not far to seek. Women become, in barbarous ages, the subjects of the stronger."[29] Establishing the significance of purity, Willard forwarded an argument that men and women needed to both be held to equal standards for purity. Behind this argument were two assumptions. First, Willard privileged self-control. Men were faced with "sins that do most easily beset them, and from the mad temptations that clutch at them on every side."[30] Without cultural expectations for men to exercise self-control, they were more likely to succumb to temptation. In appropriating the trope of self-control, Willard was building off prevailing cultural expectations of white masculinity, while extending those expectations to purity, a condition previously imposed almost entirely on women.

A second assumption was that virtue could be learned. Willard stated, "Innocence may be founded on ignorance, but virtue is ever more based upon knowledge."[31] This assumption was critical for the development of the WCTU White Cross Army because when virtue is understood as malleable, people are not inherently sinful and, thus, capable of being saved by the WCTU. As a result, the White Cross Army had a persistent threat that needed to be fought. While they maintained a need to teach men virtue, they also assumed that previously impure men and women could be rescued by learning virtue, hence WCTU concern over rumors of white slavery. The virtue of men and women harmed by the white slave trade were not irrevocably lost; they only needed a White Cross Army to save them.

Locating White Slavery

By 1887 white slavery had come to Wisconsin. The public controversy developed through the interrelationships between newspaper reporting, public speeches and advocacy, and nearly one hundred letters to the Wisconsin governor. In developing the case against white slavery, each rhetoric existed in conversation with others, reflecting an intermingling of official and vernacular discourses that functioned as part of a complex web constituting a reality of white slavery in Wisconsin. Wisconsin and the nation not only debated the existence of and appropriate response to white slavery but also participated in an ongoing negotiation of white woman's place and sites of belonging.

The role of newspaper reporting in the controversy is understandable given the dramatic rise in literacy rates during the 1880s that also supported a rise in newspaper, magazine, and dime novel circulation.[32] Often considered to be a heyday of sensationalist journalism, this time period also saw a rise in activist journalism where an organization like the WCTU both recognized and utilized the power of the press to shape perceptions of reality.[33]

Following the white slavery controversy in England, there had been occasional newspaper reporting of white slavery in the United States, and by the end of 1886, the lumber camps of northern Wisconsin and Michigan provided the most frequent fodder.[34] However, Julia Howden's dramatic entry into a Chicago police station, along with her sensational story, captured the attention of the American public. Howden was apparently married with no previous record of misconduct, and she gave the names of two other entrapped girls to the police, one of whom was taken from a reform institution under suspicious circumstances and the other, a fifteen-year-old orphan, was eventually recovered from a brothel.[35] While some remained skeptical of the veracity of Howden's account, there was enough evidence that newspaper readers expressed their outrage by writing Governor Jeremiah Rusk of Wisconsin demanding that he act.

Newspapers across the country reported on white slavery in northern Wisconsin. In Iowa, readers learned, "Hidden away in the gloom of Wisconsin forests, there are houses of prostitution, presided over by human devils, who beat the miserable women inmates without mercy, and when they escape hunt them with dogs, and bring them back to a slavery worse than death."[36] Such dramatic imagery was not unusual. The Northwoods were commonly represented as isolated, impenetrable, or wild, and the dives were thought to cater to rough men in the lumber camps who descended on the brothels at the beginning and end of the logging season.[37] *The Great Wisconsin Pineries Scandal* vividly described two dens as "built into the forests stretching along a lonely road leading to Pestago" from Marinette. "The country between the two towns," the dime novel continued, "is wild and dismal." In that dense wood, there were reportedly few signs of civilization, and some of the few homes were "owned and occupied by the remnant of the once powerful bands of the Winnebagos and Chippewas [sic]."[38] Descriptions such as these reinforced a sense of frontier isolation, as well as the risk to white women.

With few exceptions, writers represented the white women trapped in the brothels as young and innocent.[39] Not long after Julia Howden's story, papers began reporting on the story of Blanche Boneville, a "pretty" fifteen-year-old girl who was rescued from a "horrible dive." According to one report, she was found with her "hair cut close to head; she has to give up every vestige of clothes she wears, and is compelled to appear before the drunken frequentees of the place with a very scant calico Mother Hubbard reaching to the knees, with underwear and hosier to match [sic]."[40] Newspapers repeated Boneville's story as an example of how innocent white girls were lured and trapped. She responded to a seemingly reputable job offer, only to discover the truth too late. She was reportedly transported to the Wisconsin wilderness, isolated, plied with alcohol, threatened to be chased by dogs if she attempted escape, fined and kept in debt, and told that she would never be accepted back into her family.

Letters to the Wisconsin Governor

In the years 1887–1889, the governor of Wisconsin, Jeremiah Rusk, and starting in 1889, William Hoard, consistently received letters from across the country on the topic of white slavery, most of which exhorted the governor to act. Groups and organizations such as WCTU chapters or philanthropic organizations sent some of the letters, many of which appealed to a universalized sense of morality in protecting womanhood and the home.[41] Many more people, however, wrote as individuals, often assuming a deeply personal tone in corresponding with the governor. Letter writers frequently included newspaper clippings, suggesting a strong relationship between media representations and the letters.

Letters to public officials can be a valuable source of vernacular rhetoric. While public opinion is often understood through survey results, such as numerical representations of what a "public" thinks or believes, we know that this understanding of public opinion is limited at best, failing to account for depth of opinion, moral authority behind the opinion, or the reasoning and narrative supporting the opinion.[42] Furthermore, public opinion polling as we now know it did not exist in the 1880s, making the numerous letters that the Wisconsin governor received on the topic of white slavery some of the best evidence available of the depth and breadth of public sentiment. These letters reflected the concerns of ordinary citizens, often connecting personal experience with newspaper or secondhand accounts. Following Gerard A. Hauser, they exposed attempts to "understand and respond to the *vernacular* exchanges that exist outside of power and are normative of it."[43] Furthermore, the letters reflected an implied relationship between official sources of power and citizens. Through using what Mary E. Stuckey calls "political vocabularies," letters implicitly built on and participated in establishing norms of authority.[44]

In the case of the Wisconsin letters, writers drew on authority from a variety of identity locations. While some authors posited themselves as "a humble citizen," a common identity was that of woman.[45] Large numbers of letters arrived from women who explicitly drew on their identities as women, some signing their letter "a mother" or "a woman."[46] Letters such as these drew on women's limited citizenship status. Rather than writing as voters, these women wrote as keepers of national morality and seamlessly moved between familial and governmental scales. These letters framed women's civic identities in terms of home, motherhood, and morality.

Other authors derived their authority from personal experience. Writers commonly shared their experiences or personal investigations with the governor, positioning themselves as authorities on the issue.[47] For example, one author insisted that he had "personal knowledge and observation" that newspaper reports were accurate, and another writer said that he investigated and listed specific sites with "disreputable women" and "intoxicating drinks."[48] A corresponding secretary of the Methodist Episcopal Church Mission Rooms in New York wrote, "I am receiving letters from our preachers of Wisconsin assuring me that the statements made by Dr. Bushnell [a prominent speaker on the topic], concerning the outrages upon defenseless girls committed in Northern Wisconsin, are true."[49] Word of mouth and personal experience functioned as sufficient truth for white slavery accusations because writers were able to place themselves within a larger cultural narrative.

Just as the letters constructed authority for authors, they also established a framework for understanding the identity of the governor. Most letters began with honorifics (such as "Esteemed Sir," "Honored Sir," or "Your Excellency") that positioned the governor within a position demanding respect. Some letters were explicit in their praise. For example, "I know you are a brave soldier, and, of all Governors, in this country, you know how to handle riots; but I hope you will not lightly pass over the statements of Dr. Kate Bushnell [an advocate investigating Wisconsin white slavery]."[50] Others, such as the following writer, praised the state of Wisconsin stating, "I appeal to you as chief executive of a grand state."[51] Statements such as these positioned the governor as already good, caring, and noble, thus naturalizing a prompt response to the perceived reality of white slavery. Other writers implied that the governor had not already responded because of ignorance or misinformation. Many of these writers included newspaper clippings, suggesting that if the governor understood the problem, he would immediately act to rectify the situation. Letter writers commonly expressed an assumption that the existence of the problem was an established fact, and given the correct information and opportunity, the governor would act accordingly.

Other writers, however, appeared to frame the civic role of the governor through the seemingly private and domestic scale of manhood and protection of white women. One writer, for example, asked, "Are you a man?" She continued, "In the name of manhood and decency, put a stop to them, or give up your title of manhood."[52] In this example, the writer, who signed the letter "a woman," did not challenge the performance of the governor as a political leader; she challenged the governor's performance of masculinity and, in doing so, explicitly drew on protection of white women as integral to masculinity. Another author wrote, "Shame—Shame. Have you no love for a daughter? Do your duty."[53] Much like the others, these letters assumed the fact of white slavery into existence. Instead of positing the governor in a distant position of authority, these writers implied an intimate connection seeped in gendered and familial norms.

Dr. Katherine Bushnell

The final strand of the web that created white slavery as a significant public controversy was public speakers and national advocates, and none were more influential than Dr. Katherine Bushnell. By the end of 1888, Kate Bushnell had become a prominent national advocate, especially among the growing social purity reformers. A significant number of letters to the Wisconsin governor specifically referenced Bushnell and implored the governor to listen and act on her report.[54]

Dr. Katharine Bushnell was born in 1855 and moved with her family to Evanston, Illinois, in the 1870s.[55] Bushnell attended Northwestern University where she worked closely with Frances Willard, who was then dean of women, and she graduated from Chicago Woman's Medical College in 1879.[56] Bushnell grew up as a devout Methodist, a disposition that was only nurtured after moving to Evanston (which was known as a "Methodist mecca"), and after her graduation, Bushnell accepted a missionary position in China where she remained for three years. After returning to the United States, Bushnell quickly joined the WCTU serving as head of the Colorado chapter before assuming the position of National Evangelist for the WCTU's new Social Purity Department.[57]

Bushnell was active in addressing the issue of prostitution prior to her appointment as National Evangelist. While in Denver, she was superintendent of "work among fallen women," in addition to her state-wide work with the WCTU.[58] Her early approach to the issue can be seen through a letter to the Colorado WCTU newspaper, *The Challenge*. She began by asking, "And the practical question for the W.C.T.U. of Colorado to consider is, Do we wish simply to take care of a small fraction of those who are being daily led to ruin, or do we wish to become a power for purity that will be felt in every city and village in the State?"[59] The answer for Bushnell was, of course, to become a power for purity. However, the real significance of this letter rests in how the WCTU was to become this power for purity. For Bushnell, the key to real change resided in addressing the reformers—not simply the women to be reformed. Bushnell was direct in her admonishment of reformers saying,

"The 'I am holier than thou' method cannot be made to work." Bushnell called on the readers to treat so-called fallen women with respect and not "invite people into the Kingdom until you are ready to welcome them."[60] In addressing potential WCTU reformers, Bushnell worked to constitute women practicing prostitution as deserving of respect and unfairly trapped in conditions that pushed them into prostitution. Nonetheless, Bushnell's work in Colorado did very little to address national perceptions of prostitution. Indeed, there is little evidence to suggests that she was even successful within her state in addressing methods of reform and intervention.

In her role as National Evangelist for the WCTU (after leaving her Colorado position), Bushnell investigated reports of sex trafficking in northern Wisconsin and shortly thereafter went on a prolific national speaking tour to bring attention to the situation and advocate for reform. Described by the *Chicago Tribune* as having "somewhat masculine features" but a "particularly feminine and mellifluous voice," Bushnell gained national attention.[61] She delivered the speech "Slavery up North" to an audience of ladies at First Methodist Church in Chicago on January 5, 1889, and based on reports of her other speaking engagements, "Slavery up North" appears to be representative of the type of speech that Bushnell delivered during this time. The letters to the Wisconsin governor, as well as newspaper reporting, suggest that these speaking engagements were influential in developing awareness of the issue, but, just as significantly, Bushnell participated in defining the problem as a type of slavery where prostitutes were victims, rather than immoral seductresses.

In the 1880s, sex remained an unacceptable topic of public conversation, especially for women. Bushnell attempted to address this social stigma by framing herself as a Christian woman, directed by God, in much the same way as women who were writing to the governor. Bushnell recounted a reluctant journey that brought her from the safety and comfort of home to the dangers "up North." She explained, "I would wake in the quiet hours of the night wondering what was the matter, and then the thought of those girls up in Northern Wisconsin would fill my eyes with tears and my heart with sorrow. In May I went North."[62] Bushnell depicted her story as a parallel to the women she was attempting to save—a story of dislocation and uncertainty. She experienced a type of dislocation, wandering "through those towns, wondering where the next few dollars will come from to pay [her] way," but she framed this dislocation as a sacrifice to save the white women who were in even more perilous conditions. Furthermore, Bushnell depicted herself as unable to experience the comfort of home while other women were trapped. The short, direct sentence, "In May I went North," appears to resolve the tension that Bushnell experienced. In turn, Bushnell implicitly directed the white women in the audience to feel that same conflict and discomfort until they too acted to resolve the problem. The speech was punctuated by two central (and overlapping) antitheses that centered on the location of slavery—slavery/whiteness and slavery/North. Indeed, it is these antitheses that characterized and located Wisconsin white slavery throughout the duration of the controversy.

Whiteness and slavery were thought to be antithetical. Bushnell described the condition of white women in northern Wisconsin as "a slavery of soul and body." Women were kept in what she described as "stockade dens," evoking both the confinement of livestock and chattel slavery. In her speech, Bushnell told a detailed story of a chained white woman attempting to escape and another story of a brothel owner claiming, "I paid $25 apiece for them." The explicit labeling of slavery, as well as the accompanying language of slavery—chains, purchase of humans, entrapment—created a clear connection in the public imaginary with the enslavement of people of African descent. Yet, the slavery in Wisconsin was a slavery of *white* women. In Bushnell's speech, whiteness was implicit. The victims were, according to Bushnell, "innocent and good" and "as pure hearted as any of your [the white audience's] daughters."[63] Innocence and purity were cultural markers of whiteness.

The slavery/whiteness dichotomy was not a characteristic unique to Bushnell's rhetoric. Many who wrote letters to the Wisconsin governor clearly evoked the memory of the Civil War, and slavery emerged as both an analogy and a moral threshold for action, especially when associated with whiteness. A letter from Eva A. Wolfe encompassed both of these appeals. She wrote, "Hundreds of thousands of lives and billions of dollars worth of property were sacrificed on the altar of our country that negro slavery might be wiped out but how infinitely worse is this white slavery of innocent, unsuspecting, respectable girls?"[64] Letter writers labeled the situation in Wisconsin as a form of slavery, and some made claims such as "negro slavery was happiness in comparison."[65] While rape, sexual exploitation, and violence were common and often accepted in the enslavement of people of African descent, the letter writers marked whiteness as a key moral differentiator. Governor Rusk was known as a hero of the Civil War and a potential future candidate for president of the United States, and writers appealed to his reputation as a "brave solder" in calling for the governor to save white girls trapped in slavery in Wisconsin.[66]

Writers further amplified the risk to whiteness in their framing of those assumed to be doing the enslaving, while the whiteness of the victims reinforced perceptions of purity and innocence.[67] For example, one author explained, "These den keepers are almost wholly foreigners, while the inmates are almost wholly American girls."[68] The lumbermen who were thought to frequent the prostitutes were also depicted as violent foreigners. One publication explained, "The first floor is used almost exclusively for orgies. It is here that the coarse and untutored woodsman hangs his mackinac on a peg and dances with his cork boots."[69] Woodsmen were often reported as beating the innocent girls either with hands or large work boots. Thus, advocates represented the problem as a threat to whiteness by uncivilized foreign men.

A second site of dialectical tension emerged in spatial location. From the title and throughout the speech, Bushnell located the slavery as "up North." This was a powerful rhetorical choice because it generated a contrast to the Southern legacy of enslavement. Bushnell further described "stockades" and bulldogs used to chase escapees, drawing on images of Southern enslavers. This contrast not only evoked racial difference but located enslavement in what seemed to be the wrong place (North as opposed to South). Just as whiteness is inscribed on bodies, it is also inscribed onto space. With the Civil War vivid in the national memory, the North had a strong association with freedom and whiteness.

The Northwoods, however, were not simply the North, but they were the "new north."[70] As immigrants and Black Americans moved to cities like New York and Chicago, the Northwoods seemed to hold a possibility that evacuated the racialized Other. Despite the continuing presence of Indigenous Americans in northern Wisconsin, Michigan, and Minnesota, Indigenous people were largely absent in the white slavery controversy, in part, because the American imaginary placed Indigenous populations in the far West, a space that needed to be conquered and tamed. The assumed whiteness and masculine possibility of the Northwoods constituted white slavery as a startling disjuncture.

Bushnell created an image of northern slavery as both in isolated open space and confined entrapment. She depicted northern Wisconsin as "forest" and "wilds." Slaves were held, according to Bushnell, in "places buried deep in the dense woods." One newspaper described, "These hell-holes were allowed to go on, drawing in the innocent, demoralizing the camps, and spreading disease and death in all quarters, as if we were living in a land without law."[71] The isolation not only made escape nearly impossible but also evoked a sense of uncivilized lawlessness that tainted the possibilities of the "new north."

Spatial dislocation also appeared in Bushnell's evocation of "home," a term that held special meaning for the WCTU. While "home" commonly evoked safety and security, Bushnell used the term to convey confinement and entrapment. White women were held in what Bushnell called "dens" or "houses" that were surrounded by eight-foot-tall fences. White slaves were forced to wear short dresses, stockings, and slippers, clothing that prevented women from going into public and, thus, attempting escape. A newspaper reporter recounted the attempted escape of "another victim":

> All around the house was a high board fence which she managed to scale. She knew it would be of no use to attempt to escape by the road, and she endeavored to find her way through the woods to Marinette. She had gone but a mile on her way when she heard the baying of hounds, and knew that the dogs kept at the house were on her trail. Fearful of being torn to pieces by the brutes the girl took refuge in a farm-house, where her pursuers found her.[72]

The confinement of the house was not a site of safety and security, nor was the farmhouse to which the woman fled. The residents of the farmhouse not only failed to protect the escaped woman, but they reportedly laughed at her and turned her away. Detailed descriptions of the space of confinement, as well as the resonance with home, created a stark contrast between the supposed safety of home and the enslavement of white women in Wisconsin.

Dislocation in Wisconsin White Slavery

Fears of white slavery in Wisconsin were rooted in fears of dislocation. The Northwoods existed as a remnant of frontier in a quickly changing nation, and, as such, it was thought of as a predominantly masculine space where white men could tame a virgin landscape. The possibilities for women were limited, and, thus, when unmarried young white women were discovered in Wisconsin's Northwoods, newspapers and activists worked to shape the white women's identities in ways that enabled them to make sense of the seeming displacement. In other words, displacement became written on these white women's bodies. The rhetoric of the controversy assumed away the possibility that these women could have agency in their circumstances and also be good women who were worthy of compassion. Instead, white women were deemed worthy of redemption by virtue of their displacement.

Bushnell's earlier rhetoric from Colorado illustrates a different rhetorical possibility. In Colorado, Bushnell called on reformers to accept prostitution as a complex problem where women exercised agency within significantly constrained circumstances. In challenging reformers to resist a clear dichotomy between whore and victim, Bushnell attempted to redirect attention to the systemic issues motivating prostitution, as well as the biases of the reformers themselves. The dramatic shift in Bushnell's approach to Wisconsin implies that she found a more effective strategy for promoting change, and this strategy was predicated on white women's innocence. If they were innocent, they were necessarily out of place, demanding rescue. This assumption, however, was publicly contested.

Defending the State's "Fair Name"

Reports of Wisconsin white slavery had become so widespread and persistent that the governor needed to act and defend the state's "fair name."[73] Wisconsin governor Jerimiah Rusk responded to the barrage of letters, many of which included newspaper clippings, by writing the district attorney of Marinette County, Hiram O. Fairchild, and including a newspaper clipping about Julia Howden. He wrote, "I think this case demands immediate investigation. As you are well aware, this is not the first complaint that has been made."[74] In his response to the governor (which the governor's office may have leaked to the newspapers), Fairchild wrote, "There can be but little if any truth in the charges." He concluded, "Julia Howden is said to be an abandoned woman and the whole affair is thought to be a baseless sensation as far as she is concerned."[75] The governor appointed James Fielding, a clerk and messenger for the State Board of Charities and former sheriff of Racine County, to investigate accusations of white slavery.[76] A report to the governor soon followed that labeled Julia Howden a "drunken whore" and concluded that there was no problem with white slavery in Wisconsin.[77] Despite the governor's claim to have investigated and closed the case, public outrage only seemed to grow.

Dr. Kate Bushnell, however, was not persuaded by Fielding's report, describing him as the "detective" (including the quotation marks) in her report to the WCTU.[78] She not only publicly accused Fielding of fabricating the report but also confronted him in his office in January 1889 while she was in Madison to testify before the Wisconsin legislature.[79] A few days after that confrontation, on the evening of January 18, 1889, James Fielding was arrested while sitting in his office at the State Board of Charities. Although he was only briefly detained in his office, Fielding was required to report to the Madison municipal court the next day to answer charges of "using obscene language to Dr. Kate Bushnell, an unmarried female, without provocation."[80] After several delays, the charges against Fielding were ultimately dropped because Bushnell said that she did not support the charges and refused to return to Wisconsin for the trial.[81]

It may be tempting to seek the truth in the controversy. Was Julia Howden an unhappy prostitute or an innocent woman? Who was lying—Bushnell or Fielding? Was there white slavery in Wisconsin? However, these are the wrong questions. This controversy is really about who belongs and how we know who belongs. Thus, the more pertinent questions are: what does virtue mean, and whose word counts? These questions of definition and evidence are fundamentally rhetorical.

Virtuous Women

The governor's investigation reveals one of the problems with the white slavery metaphor. The Marinette County sheriff's statement was recorded in a deposition:

> That none of the persons whom he has so arrested or which he has seen in any of said houses were other than confirmed prostitutes, judging as he did, of their character, from their outward appearance, conduct and conversation. That he has never known of a single instance of a virtuous woman being enticed or in any manner procured to go into any of such houses nor has he ever heard of such a thing, except as he has read of such instances in the newspapers during the last few months.[82]

Similar statements were often repeated by officials and investigators, and numerous letter writers insisted that no "virtuous" women were kept in houses of prostitution. Furthermore, an E. R. Pethenck reported to the governor, "Dance-houses are breathing holes for hell, but the fuel that goes into them is generally well seasoned."[83] Another report concluded, "They were not what is generally termed 'innocent girls,' for they were decidedly of a sporting turn of mind."[84] Investigators insisted that those in prostitution deserved to be there.

In a *Milwaukee Journal* report that may have been anonymously written by Fielding, the author described Fielding's interviews with women in a Marinette brothel.[85] In many respects the interviews confirmed elements of other reports—women were detained through unreasonable debts and alcohol addiction. Yet, Fielding concluded that he was "satisfied that no one was held there under physical duress and that the place was simply a house of ill fame."[86] Furthermore, high fences were for the "sake of decency," not, he insisted, an attempt to trap women.[87]

These reports were fairly consistent in building off of a dichotomy between the virtuous woman and the irredeemable whore. The correspondence with the governor suggests that what marked a woman as a whore was clear. An official could identify a loose woman based on "outward appearance, conduct and conversation," and a woman's presence in the dance house or prostitution den marked her as beyond the scope of the virtuous woman.[88] In other words, a woman's presence in a site of prostitution functioned as evidence that she was a prostitute; place was written on women's identities.

Bushnell's rhetoric of slavery attempted to counter these assumptions by explaining presence and clothing through a narrative of slavery and entrapment. To illustrate her point, Bushnell described an incident of two innocent white girls from a small Wisconsin town. While walking together, the girls were accosted by Sid Barlow, a known procurer. According to Bushnell, the girls refused to leave with Barlow, who claimed that he wanted to hire them to work in a hotel. In response, Barlow had the girls arrested for streetwalking, paid their fine, and sold them to a den in Merrill, Wisconsin. After being unjustly charged for streetwalking, Barlow had a legal right to procure the white girls because they were already deemed to be immoral.[89] By questioning their initial immorality and framing the girls as slaves, Bushnell opened the rhetorical space that there were white women who needed saving. Yet, in doing so, she replaced the abject subjectivity of the whore with the equivalently abject slave. In her report to the WCTU, Bushnell went further in arguing that this slavery was not a justified punishment for a woman's past sins, all women should be protected regardless of character.[90]

Public officials commonly responded to the governor's call for investigation and prosecution with apathy, and implicit in the apathy was an assumption that non-virtuous women were expendable. The district attorney of Ashland, for example, stated, "I do not consider it my place to act as detective or hunt up the evidence."[91] A circuit judge explained, "A Judge can do little more than aid the Officers by his moral support," and a county sheriff insisted that he would happily follow up on complaints but "it surely is not my fault if the parties are not convicted."[92] As one official after the other absolved themselves of responsibility, they also naturalized the state of prostitution. The treatment of these women, Pethenck concluded, was simply "according to the fate of the fallen sisterhood everywhere."[93] District Attorney Fairchild emphasized that "public sentiment" does not demand for the closing of houses of prostitution.[94] Neither the slave nor the whore appeared to elicit sufficient investment on the part of officials to lead them to action.

A Woman's Testimony

By January 1889, there were two conflicting reports about Wisconsin white slavery—an official report from James Fielding challenging the existence of white slavery and a report from Kate Bushnell substantiating the existence of white slavery. Both reports were dependent on individual testimony as the primary source of evidence. In addition to Fielding's observations, his report included testimony from men who were traditional sources of authority, brothel keepers, and "citizens."[95] While Bushnell's report consisted of primarily her own observations, she also included testimonial evidence, but her sources lacked traditional markers of authority and were primarily women. Nevertheless, Bushnell was explicit that she personally collected evidence from fifty-nine "dens" throughout the state and 575 "degraded women," and her goal was to "ferret out the real facts" without being guided only by rumor.[96] Bushnell noted that there were many exaggerated and misleading newspaper reports that made conditions seem worse than they actually were, and she expressed concern that these exaggerated reports would damage her credibility.[97]

In January 1889, Bushnell was invited to testify before the Wisconsin legislative assembly, and in her testimony, which lasted more than an hour, Bushnell detailed her conclusions and process of investigation.[98] Newspaper reporters were clear that Bushnell's testimony was insufficient. One report claimed that Bushnell's report "lacked solidity" and was motivated by emotion, citing Bushnell's "unqualified indignation."[99] One newspaper mocked the assumption that firsthand accounts would provide sufficient proof, arguing that it was unreasonable that "women should be accorded the same rights as men, even if their character is notoriously bad."[100] Thus, women were placed in a double bind. Bushnell's testimony alone was considered insufficient, and if she had brought women from the prostitution dens, not only would those women be publicly humiliated, but they also would not be believed.

Legislators appeared to be slower to judge than many of the newspapers. They responded to Bushnell's testimony by calling for a legislative committee investigation and subsequently petitioned the governor's office for the information it had collected. The Committee on State Affairs, however, reviewed the files and concluded that additional investigation was unnecessary.[101] The legislature accepted Fielding's conclusions and decided that there was not a problem with white slavery in Wisconsin.

Some accounts challenged Bushnell's character suggesting that she was simply seeking attention and exercising unjustified "indignation."[102] The quarrel with and subsequent charges against James Fielding for using inappropriate language around Bushnell also appear to have arisen from questions about Bushnell's character. News reports implied that when Bushnell confronted Fielding in his office, he shared rumors that Bushnell's interest in brothels was explained by her character as a fallen woman.[103] In other words, Bushnell's existence in a place of immorality marked her as immoral; place wrote meaning onto Bushnell in much the same way it wrote meaning onto the other women in the brothels. The lawsuit created a further bind for Bushnell because lawyers argued that harm could only occur if Bushnell was offended by Fielding's language.[104] If she did not understand the meaning of Fielding's language, she would not have been offended, but if she did understand the meaning, she was clearly not a chaste woman. Either way, Fielding would have been innocent, suggesting that Bushnell made a prudent decision in her failure to return to Wisconsin for the trial.

On the other hand, there were few questions, beyond Bushnell's accusations, about the veracity of Fielding's report. One reporter explained, "His character for honesty and efficiency has always been above reproach."[105] Fielding reported to the governor that he had visited one brothel and found it operating quietly with no clear evidence of trafficking.[106] However, in newspaper accounts, Fielding claimed to have visited several different brothels in different towns across the state.[107] For Wisconsin officials, Fielding's report was an unequivocal truth that proved that Bushnell was simply sullying the state's good name.

Legislating Prostitution and Protecting White Women

James Boyd White argued, "The law establishes roles and relations and voices, positions from which and audiences to which one may speak, and it gives us as speakers the materials and methods of a discourse. It is a way of creating a rhetorical community over time."[108] Wisconsin legislative attempts at addressing white slavery reveal much about the role of law in creating meaning at the intersections of gender, race, and place. During the height of the white slavery controversy in Wisconsin, in 1887, the state adopted a law to "prevent the abduction of unmarried women," Senate Bill 46 (Chapter 214 of Laws of Wisconsin), and this legislation was amended in 1889 (Chapter 420). While it is difficult to establish causality, the initial legislation was proposed with specific reference to reported dives in northern Wisconsin,[109] and the amended legislation was adopted only a few months after Bushnell's appearance in Madison.[110]

Section 1 of the 1887 legislation stated:

> Any person who shall fraudulently and deceitfully entice, abduct or take an unmarried woman of previous chaste character from her father's house or wherever else she may be found, for the purpose of prostitution or for the purpose of unlawful sexual intercourse at a house of ill-fame or assignation, or elsewhere, and any person who shall in any manner aid, abet or assist in such enticement or abduction for that purpose, shall be punished by imprisonment in the state prison not exceeding fifteen years, nor less than five years.

The object of the legislation was clear, the "unmarried woman of previous chaste character." If a woman had an unchaste character the law suggested that she was not worthy of protection, and by failing to substantiate the source of that character, the state assumed the authority to prescribe a woman's status as chaste (or not). Similarly, married women were excluded from those deemed worthy of protection, even though sex trafficking can function as a form of domestic abuse (although a form of abuse that may not have been recognized at the time). These limitations suggest that the law was not protecting women as much as it was protecting white women's chastity. The language of the law also created an acceptable place for an unmarried woman—her father's house. By including the phrase "or wherever else she may be found," the place of abduction was legally irrelevant, but it functioned to reinforce community norms that chaste white women belonged in their fathers' houses. Women who were out of place, not residing in their fathers' houses, where therefore suspect.

The 1889 amended law did not make many changes. It added additional verbs to expand the impermissible ways in which an innocent woman could be removed to include "entice, abduct, induce, decoy, hire, engage, employ or take" for the purposes of prostitution. Furthermore, the law allowed for the protection of any woman (not only chaste women), but the penalty for violating the law was significantly less if the woman was not previously chaste. While the amendment did not give women additional agency or account for the complexity of prostitution, it did attempt to address reports of women who were lured by job prospects only to become trapped in a brothel. The amended legislation also included language that expanded sites of entrapment to include places that were like brothels and recognized that women could be detained by threats and fear, as well as physical force.

Perhaps the most significant change in the 1889 legislation was related to place and evidence. For the state of Wisconsin, a brothel was legally established as such by demonstrating "a common or general reputation as a house of ill-fame, brothel, bawdy-house or house of assignation, or that such house ... has been or is being promiscuously visited at unseasonable hours." Thus, reputation functioned as sufficient evidence to define the character of a place, and that character of the place could then be legally used to determine if a woman were an "inmate" of that place. In other words, if a place had an unsavory reputation, it could be legally defined as a brothel, and if a woman were discovered in a such a place, she should be defined as a prostitute. Then, according to Section 7 of the amended law, a prostitute could be compelled to testify in court, as long as she was not prosecuted as a result of the testimony. This section, perhaps, responds to Bushnell's concern that forcing women to testify would further victimize them. These women could be compelled to testify despite potential damage to reputation, victimization, or social ostracization.

From Julia Howden's sensational story to various attempts to legislate remedies, the Wisconsin white slavery controversy was about making sense of place and the ways in which place writes meaning onto women's bodies. The case study of white slavery in the Northwoods supports two interrelated conclusions. First, there is value in turning toward the local in attempts to understand the rhetoric and, thus, imagination of place. Places can have unique character and meanings, and, in some cases, we can lose the nuance of those meanings by scaling up analysis to region or nation. Furthermore, when considering small-scale local places, the identities of the place may feel stable and intractable, shaping the possibilities for existing within that place. Second, places contain meanings that can be written onto bodies, shaping the mobile imagination. We often make sense of people by their place. Of course, place should never be read in isolation. We make sense of bodies through race, gender, and a myriad of other markers, but place shapes the possibilities for meaning. When white women moved into the Northwoods, they became out of place, and members of the public and political leaders made sense of that displacement by writing those white women as either irredeemable whores or innocent victims. Because of their place, there was not a readily conceivable alternative. While there continued to be murmurs of white slavery, the controversy was fairly quiet following the 1889 legislation. Nevertheless, white slavery once again became the subject of national outcry, but this time the locus of concern was in 1907 Chicago, a place emblematic of the American city.

CHAPTER 2

Mobility and the Danger of the City

MORAL REFORM IN CHICAGO, 1907–1914

In 1909 Chicago celebrated the centennial of Abraham Lincoln's birth in high style. Mayor Fred Busse proclaimed a week of celebration, business owners decorated storefronts across the city, and bronze engravings of the Gettysburg Address graced the walls of hundreds of schools. During this week of celebration, social reformers from across the nation gathered in Chicago to attend the Conference for the Suppression of the White Slave Traffic. For these reformers, the slavery of white women had emerged as the defining issue of their generation. Indeed, a representative from the Chicago Woman's Club made the analogy to Lincoln explicit stating, "Perhaps a hundred years from today America will be celebrating the birth of some woman wise enough and brave enough and noble enough to be the liberator of women from a slavery far worse than that from which Lincoln freed the negro."[1] The new slavery of the twentieth century meant that "no girl [was] safe."[2]

The choice of meeting location was auspicious, not only because of the association with Lincoln but also because Chicago was becoming known as hub of white slave trafficking and activism to combat that trafficking. A confluence of events moved the specter of white slavery from a somewhat esoteric concern over isolated lumber camps or European cities to a plague of the city in the United States, and Chicago quickly became emblematic of the worst vices cities had to offer. After the turn of the century, social purity and social hygiene activists joined forces to foster public concern and champion solutions to white slavery.

At the beginning of the twentieth century, Chicago, like many American cities, was engaged in a debate over vice districts, segregated areas of prostitution, gambling, drugs, and alcohol. The Custom House vice district became known internationally during the Chicago World's Fair in 1893. By the twentieth century, the Chicago vice district known as the Levee, or the South Side Levee, was particularly notorious, housing the infamous Everleigh Club and run by First Ward aldermen Michel "Hinky Dink" Kenna and "Bathhouse John" Coughlin.[3] Despite being technically illegal, these vice districts were sustained by corrupt politicians, dishonest police, and a general public perception that such districts stopped the spread of vice throughout the rest of the city. The debate over white slavery coalesced opposition to vice districts. Rather than insulating the rest of the city from vice by isolating it to one area, these activists framed the Levee as a danger to the entire city. The city was increasingly imagined as leaky—no longer able to contain vice and those who perpetuated vice.

The case of Chicago and its white slavery crusade illustrates the connections between mobility and containment in public controversy. Writers rhetorically appropriated white womanhood to constitute the city as dangerous, representing both virtue and vice. This image of the city constrained possibilities for white women's mobility, but it also functioned as a tool to inscribe race onto the city. The spatiotemporal rhetoric of the controversy conflated supposed danger to white women with the immigrant and Black population of the American city. For these activists the leakiness of the city was the root of the problem, and they characterized this leakiness through the threats of immigration, the permeability of urban spaces, and the dangers of white women's mobility.

The Second City

In 1907, George Kibbe Turner asked in *McClure's Magazine*, "What forces are there, hidden in American cities, which are dragging them ... into a state of semi-barbarism?"[4] In asking this question, Turner reflected a deep-seated cultural anxiety.[5] By the twentieth century, cities were increasingly seen as sites of danger, and Turner, as well as many others, attributed a significant part of this danger to what came to be known as "white slavery," the assumption that middle-class white women were being coerced and trapped in prostitution. The "image of the city," to use Kevin Lynch's influential phrase, was increasingly associated with threat, especially for white women.[6]

In many respects, the city is a rhetorical construct. Cities gain meaning through perception that is created in the features, organization, and experiences with the physical environment.[7] The borders of the city are constituted, often arbitrarily, by statutory language, and the culture and identities of cities emerge through a variety of rhetorics. There are also invisible borders within cities that are discursively constituted, establishing, for example, lines between the "good" and "bad" parts of a city, as well as invisible borders between neighborhoods.[8] In attempting to understand a city or location within a city, people and place can become metonymically connected, suggesting, for example, that a decrepit place houses decrepit people.[9]

In his exposé, George Kibbe Turner participated in constituting Chicago as dangerous. He asked, "Why have the primary basic guarantees of civilization broken down in Chicago?"[10] While the question circularly assumed that the "basic guarantees of civilization" were absent in Chicago, the article was tremendously influential. *McClure's* was one of the most widely distributed muckraking magazines in the country. Not only did it cover issues of national importance, but it also gained a broad national audience.[11] Turner's article was the biggest commercial success of the year for *McClure's* and proved to be a catalyst for reform efforts.[12] With this article and subsequent literature and activism, Chicago became central to the white slavery controversy in the United States.

Chicago had rebuilt quickly after the 1871 fire that wiped out three and a half square miles of the city. In 1893, the city made a debut of sorts in hosting the World's Columbian Exposition. Planners created a White City to host a World's Fair of unprecedented size and ostentatious display.[13] However, the contrast between the glamor of the White City and the deplorable living conditions of many Chicago residents did not remain unnoticed. William Stead, for instance, published *If Christ Came to Chicago* in which he asked what Jesus would think of the Chicago of 1894.[14] Stead placed the economic and civic life of the modern city in stark contrast to Christian ideals, and in doing so, he traced specific maladies of drunkenness, prostitution, and poverty.

It is, perhaps, unsurprising that Chicago would function as a catalyst for the controversy and the hub of reform efforts. According to one historian, "No large city, not even Peter the Great's St. Petersburg, had grown so fast, and nowhere else could there be found in more dramatic display such a combination of wealth and squalor, beauty and ugliness, corruption and reform."[15] Chicago housed one of the world's first skyscrapers, which stood in stark contrast to the squalid conditions in some parts of the city. The city was emblematic of many of the problems of the new urbanization in the United States. Just one year after Upton Sinclair's publication of *The Jungle*, Turner described the three major industries of vice in Chicago (liquor, prostitution, and gambling) as intimately connected to the city's geography and sustained by politicians and police. He described the stockyards as surrounded by Whisky Row, Bubbly Creek (a heavily polluted area of the Chicago River), and the "bare, gaunt, high-shouldered buildings of the yard."[16] The geography of the city was represented as trapping its residents in vice. While the nation had marveled at Chicago when it hosted the 1893 World's Fair, the city was increasingly represented as the worst of the nation.

Moral Reformers

Concerns over the city catalyzed reformers, particularly around the issue of white slavery. One of the most widely read authors in this controversy was Ernest A. Bell, superintendent and founder of Chicago's Midnight Mission and editor of *Fighting the Traffic in Young Girls: Or War on the White Slave Trade*. Bell was known by some as the "father" of the movement against vice, and one profile even named him as a "modern prophet of a living God."[17] Bell was born in Canada in 1865, and after studying theology at Boston University, he worked as a missionary in India and eventually moved to Chicago.[18] In Chicago, Bell discovered a slowly growing community of activists working to combat vice, and in 1904, Bell and a small group began preaching on the streets of vice districts. In 1906, the Midnight Mission was officially born, with Bell as its superintendent. Alongside a group of missionaries, Bell and others preached on the streets of the Levee vice district.[19] By 1907, crowds of eighty or ninety would gather to listen to the preaching and watch the spectacle, and the group reportedly distributed the Bible in forty-three languages.[20] The Midnight Mission initially focused on reaching men patronizing prostitutes, attempting to educate or shame these men before they spent their money.[21] However, the work of the organization quickly broadened as they employed deaconesses and spoke directly to prostitutes in an effort to save women.

Dive keepers reported losing $300 a night because of the preaching, and the missionaries were certainty not welcomed in the Levee.[22] Bell described incidents such as resorts involved in illicit activity drenching the unpaved streets, forcing missionaries to stand in deep muck, verbal assaults, and thrown objects such as eggs.[23] This harassment, however, made the specific stories of redemption (most typically the redemption of men seeking to patronize prostitutes) even more powerful. Like a true prophet, Bell and his missionaries framed their work as truth in the face of sinful unbelievers. The frequent reports of redemption and mild harassment placed the Midnight Mission on the side of righteousness.

After the success of Bell's *Fighting the Traffic in Young Girls*, there was a push for nightly meetings in the Levee, and Bell became a celebrity among

FIGURE 2. "In the Center of the Inferno. The Rev. Ernest A. Bell is leading a meeting in the heart of the vice district. All about are houses of shame—at the very doors of Hell itself.—Chapter XXI." Image from Clifford E. Roe and B. S. Steadwell, *The Great War on White Slavery or Fighting for the Protection of Our Girls*, 1911.

reformers, traveling the country to talk about white slavery.[24] Bell and other members of the Midnight Mission were active leaders in the campaign against vice in Chicago and nationally. The organization named Bell as responsible for the Mann Act, the 1910 federal legislation against white slavery, although the actual story of the legislation's inception is more complicated.[25] Bell and other members of the Midnight Mission were also active in the Illinois Vigilance Association, which worked with the Federation of Churches to create the political pressure that led to the formation of the Chicago Vice Commission.[26]

The Midnight Mission was one of many moral reform organizations that exercised public influence. During October of 1895, the American Purity Alliance (APA) hosted the first National Purity Congress in Baltimore. The congress was attended by a wide variety of activists and political leaders, primarily from purity and White Cross organizations, and the Woman's Christian Temperance Union (WCTU) was well represented.[27] By the turn of the century, however, the APA was losing its political force, and the organization's president, O. Edward Janney, was struggling to keep the organization viable.[28] At the same time a myriad of purity organizations were gaining influence outside of the APA's New York sphere of influence. In particular, B. S. Steadwell's World Purity Federation and the American Purity Federation were mobilizing action in the Chicago area. Steadwell and Janney cooperated in hosting the well-attended and widely reported 1907 National Purity Conference in Chicago.[29] It was at this conference that activist Sidney C. Kendall declared the "white slave" to be the new term that would propel the movement, and under the banner of white slavery, some of the most notable purity organizations, including the APA, endorsed the creation of a National Vigilance Committee.[30]

While the National Vigilance Committee was a loose coalition, it was a meaningful attempt at unifying regional divisions in the purity movement. The Committee was endorsed by some of the most influential social organizations of the time including the WCTU, APA, National Council of Jewish Women, National Federation of Women's Clubs, and the Society for Sanitary and Moral Prophylaxis, as well as many religious organizations. The inclusion of Prince Albert Morrow's Society for Sanitary and Moral Prophylaxis is indicative of the strong connections between religious and medical reformers. Often considered the founder of the social hygiene movement in the United States, Morrow advocated for a practical solution to vice through medical and sex education. Nonetheless, Morrow, as well as Janney who was also trained as a physician, maintained strong connections between medicine and moral reforms, practicing what some called Christian medicine.[31] The coalition of diverse activists created political pressure for concrete action.

Chicago Vice Commission

In 1910 Chicago mayor Fred Busse, a notoriously corrupt politician, created the Chicago Vice Commission to study the problem of vice in the city and make recommendations. The resulting four-hundred-page report became a model for vice commissions across the nation.[32] The report was influential, in part, because of its attention to complex causes of vice. It listed the causes:

> First, lack of ethical teaching and religious instruction; second, the economic stress of industrial life on unskilled workers, with the enfeebling influences on the will power; third, the large number of seasonal trades in which women are especially engaged; fourth, abnormality; fifth, unhappy home conditions; sixth, careless and ignorant parents; seventh, broken promises; eighth, love of ease and luxury; ninth, the craving for excitement and change; tenth, ignorance of hygiene.[33]

Some of the causes such as lack of ethical teaching were commonly accepted, but the report brought attention to the neglected problem of women's low wages. The report also created comprehensive lists of houses of prostitution and other sites of vice, and it named the police as complicit in sustaining vice in the city. The report advocated the "absolute annihilation" of prostitution and recommended the creation of a morals commission and a morals court.[34]

The same month that the Vice Commission released its report, Chicago inaugurated a new mayor, Carter Henry Harrison. Harrison had already served four terms as Chicago mayor (1897–1905), and his family ran the *Chicago Times*, a staunchly Democratic paper.[35] According to the vice activists, the mayor and city authorities largely ignored the Vice Commission report, and, led by businessman Clifford Barnes, activists formed the Committee of Fifteen.[36] According to its first annual report, "This Chicago Committee is incorporated '*to aid the public authorities in the enforcement of all laws against pandering and to take measures calculated to suppress the white slave* traffic.'"[37] However, by 1913, Barnes and the Committee of Fifteen began to increase public pressure on the mayor's office and expanded beyond their original fifteen members to include notables such as Jane Addams.[38] The Committee began publicly listing names of saloons and brothels, attempting to shame both the mayor and the public into action.[39] In one instance, Mayor Harrison forestalled the committee's report by closing seventeen resorts, including the infamous Everleigh Club, just days before the Committee of Fifteen report was made public.[40] The public pressure appeared to have forced the mayor to act against some of his political supporters, prompting change in one of the most corrupt cities in the nation.[41]

Literature of the Movement

Following the 1907 exposé in *McClure's Magazine*, there was a flurry of publications on the topic of white slavery. In 1913, one publication proclaimed, "Probably one thousand million pages against this iniquity [white slavery] have been circulated in North America in the last five years."[42] While this number is clearly difficult to verify, a myriad of books, newspaper and magazine articles, and pamphlets with titles such as *Chicago's Black Traffic in White Girls* and *The White Slave Traffic in America* sustained public attention with sordid tales of sexual exploitation.[43] Much of the literature drew from the genre of the captivity narrative where innocent white women were trapped and exploited by a seemingly barbarous Other, be it Barbary pirates, Indigenous Americans, or Catholics.[44] This literature may have gained popularity because it allowed upper- and middle-class white Americans to vicariously participate in tales of sex and danger, but regardless, the literature was widely popular. The literature worked to shape the popular imaginary of the city, as well as the meanings and possibilities for people within the city.

Immigration and Danger

By the turn of the century, it was clear that Chicago, like many American cities, was changing. Chicago was the second most populated city in the country, following New York, and the city was home to influential business and political leaders. However, of the nearly 1,700,000 residents of

Chicago, there were many immigrants.[45] Between 1880 and 1920, 2.5 million immigrants came into Chicago, most coming from southern or eastern Europe.[46] By 1890, 79 percent of Chicago residents were either foreign born or children of immigrants, and progressives who expressed concern over high immigrant birthrates fueled fear that immigrants were changing the character of the city.[47]

The increasing presence of immigrants not only altered the spatial landscape, but for some white residents, spatial instability also evoked a nostalgia (a spatiotemporal longing) for an ostensibly less complicated past. Change necessarily entails temporal movement, and when coupled with spatial expectations, it can be threatening. Doreen Massey argued that simply moving through city streets (in a context where the city is ethnically diverse) could seemly transport a person across vast cultural distances by seeing different people, hearing different languages, and smelling unusual smells.[48] Karma Chávez explained that this dislocation can easily be imagined as a national threat,[49] and at the turn of the century, part of that national threat was embodied in the perceived risk to white women. The spatiotemporal rhetoric of the controversy layered different mobile imaginations, which together constituted the city as dangerous.

White slavery reformers often based the emergence of the problem in immigration. As a harbinger of what was to come, in 1896, the president of the National Purity Congress described "steamers passing to and fro so quickly and constantly as an international ferriage" as a fundamental change that necessitated American concern with the problems of the "Old World."[50] White slavery reformers explicitly connected danger and immigration, describing the "dark-skinned, scheming dive-keeper" or asserting that white slavery was sustained by Russian Jews.[51] Seemingly innocent spaces such as coffee houses and fruit stands were represented as particularly dangerous because, as the authors explained, they were run by foreigners.[52] One story described Pedro's "coffee-house" as a typical site of white slave traffic, where attractive white "girls" were employed for light housework, only to become trapped and raped.[53]

This perceived danger was sustained by both a nostalgic memory of the past, as well as a fear for the future. Dr. Jean Turner-Zimmermann, president of the Chicago Rescue Mission and Woman's Shelter, described the spatiotemporal dislocation and, thus, danger supposedly brought by immigration. She noted:

> Please remember, as you read this, that America is becoming more and more un-American every day. Each ship, each train Westward or Eastward bound, is now daily dumping into our Land, . . . thousands of the scum and vice and criminal element of South Eastern Europe, Asia and the Orient, and remember too that a short five-years of residence here converts the filthiest criminal from Turkey, Arabia, Syria, Italy, or of any place else where vice and brutality reign supreme, into an American citizen with the right to vote into office men who will and are sworn to protect and aid in every possible way the Jewish, Russian, French or Chinese whore-master as he rents a shanty and proceeds to fatten on the very life-blood of the young girlhood of this and other lands.[54]

Turner-Zimmermann moved readers through a breathtaking world tour of "scum and vice," asserting a spatial/moral boundary between the United States and immoral, dangerous Others. Sexual exploitation of white women by dark-skinned, foreign men represented a fundamental threat to civilization because these men were assumed to be more brutish and less advanced than white Americans.[55] However, modern transportation, according to Turner-Zimmermann, enabled the most depraved people in the world to enter the United States, which not only put "young girlhood" in danger but also risked the very identity of the country. Within this context, losing white women to slavery was part of a dislocation where the white, middle-class perceived a loss of "their" country as the nation became "un-American." For Turner-Zimmerman, the mobility of immigrants was changing the city and, thus, the nation.

Spatial location also seemed to change immigrants. For example, George Kibbe Turner explained, "None of the folks [immigrant and Black], perhaps, have progressed far along the way of civilization; but under the exploitation in Chicago they slip back into a form of city savagery compared to which their previous history shows a peaceful and well-ordered existence."[56] There are at least two layers of spatiotemporal positioning in Turner's statement. First, civilization was posited as a movement from barbarism to refinement, and racial and ethnic minorities (people from different places) were assumed to be less advanced in this movement. Space of origin signaled temporal placement within a civilizing process, and the progress toward civilization, in turn, characterized the space. Second, the city functioned as a unique space within the supposedly civilized United States. For Turner, the geography of the city moved the racialized Other backward, bringing forth inherent brutishness that would have otherwise remained hidden. Turner's phrase, "city savagery," drew on the imagery of the urban jungle, which further positioned the city as a site of spatiotemporal dislocation. While the United States may have been civilized and temporally progressing forward, the city was temporally moving backward, pulling its residents to danger and barbarism.

Shifting geographic scales amplified the perception of danger. The tall buildings and confined spaces of the city cast both literal and figurative shadows on its residents. White slavery activists commonly referenced "dark corners of the city," the "underworld," and "cesspools" of vice, evoking images of darkness and depravity.[57] The connection between darkness and jungle had already been established in the public imaginary with writing such as Joseph Conrad's *Heart of Darkness*, and, as a result, the darkness of the city reinforced the spatiotemporal dislocation constituted in the barbaric urban jungle. Darkness not only hid evil but also created the conditions that sustained evil. The danger for white women was that they could be hidden or trapped within this darkness. Further, the literal dark spaces, such as dark alleys or saloons, were represented as harbingers of "moral darkness."[58] The rhetorical shifting of scales from the expansive city to the dark corner shifted the meaning of the city by forcing a change in perspective—its "dark corners" came to represent the city as a whole.

The danger left an opportunity for reformers to bring light. Ernest Bell wrote the hymn "Light the Night," which was presumably one of the hymns sung by the missionaries of the Midnight Mission.[59] The *Unions Signal*, journal of the WCTU, proclaimed, "You can pour through the dark places of your cities as a purifying flood of light, and love, and truth."[60] Light, then, was a moral obligation to act in the face of emptiness. Immorality and darkness were understood as an emptiness that needed to be filled. Within this rhetoric, morality and goodness were light, and a lack of morality left darkness.

Vice districts also came alive at night (aided, in part, by electric lights), and the figurative darkness of the night presented acute dangers. Quoting Isaiah, Reverend M. P. Boynton, secretary for the Midnight Mission, asked, "Watchman, what of the night?"[61] The Midnight Mission operated at night because it was considered a time of moral danger, and Boynton framed that operation as a calling from God. Turner-Zimmermann called prostitutes

FIGURE 3. "'For God's Sake, Come and Get Me.' Mildred Clark's frenzied cry that rang out in the night as the Gypsy Smith great parade was passing through the vice district. Chapter I." Image from Clifford E. Roe and B. S. Steadwell, *The Great War on White Slavery or Fighting for the Protection of Our Girls*, 1911.

"women of the night," and these women were a danger to innocent young men.[62] Additionally, the Chicago Vice Commission was particularly concerned with "night children," who sold newspapers or gum at night, putting them at constant risk of corruption.[63] Thus, even if white women were to risk being in public space during the day, they were told by these activists to especially fear darkness.

The spatiotemporal discourse of white slavery activists created a type of map that defined the space of the city. The city was symbolized as darkness and urban jungle and, thus, a site of danger and moral depravity. However, the dangerous city did not just spring into existence. The image of the city was rhetorically created through a spatiotemporal dislocation rooted in a nostalgia for the past and fear of the future as the immigrant Other moved into the space. These immigrants were perceived to exist in a different space-time, which was more brutish and less civilized. The immigrant changed the city, and the city changed the immigrant, making immigrants even more brutal and dangerous because of their dislocation. These layers of spatiotemporal mobility rhetorically constituted the space of the city as a site of danger, especially for white women.

Permeable Urban Space

Much like New York's Tenderloin and New Orleans's Storyville, the Levee in Chicago was one of the country's most notorious vice districts. In many ways the Levee was confined. The boundaries were clear and frequently mapped for residents, tourists, and activists. These boundaries provided a structure for a distinct area within a city, and this district had its own leaders, values, and character. The rhetoric of "district" initially created a sense of topographical separation and insulation. The debate over white slavery coalesced opposition to vice districts. Rather than insulating the rest of the city from vice by isolating it to one area, these activists framed the Levee as a danger to the entire city, and that danger was rooted in geographical and human networks of connection. These connections made mobility dangerous—moving innocent white women to danger and moving danger to the innocent.

White slavery literature depicted the border between safety and vice as permeable with uncertain and hidden paths into vice. Thus, for white women, the city was represented as not only a site of constant danger, but women could inadvertently stumble into that danger by talking to the wrong person or stopping at the wrong ice cream parlor. Dance halls, nickel theaters, and saloons were thought to be particularly dangerous, although enticing amusements for young white women.[64] One newspaper described the enticement of the dance hall: "They [young poor girls] discovered, through the agency of chums, who had made the discovery in their time, the delights of the nickel dances, with the lights and the music and sensuous, dreamy movement and warm companionship."[65] These amusements were thought to open white women to danger of being drugged, plied with alcohol, seduced, or tricked into sexual slavery.

Ernest Bell visually depicted the journey to corruption through the dance hall in his book, *Fighting the Traffic in Young Girls*.[66] In one illustration, a well-adorned white woman appears to pause in front of an entrance labeled "dance hall," which the caption described as the "entrance to hell itself." A man, whose face is obscured by his hat, seems to be leading the woman to enter the room by placing his hand on her arm. Inside the dance hall, well-dressed couples are dancing, but, as with other representations, space is folded such that the entrance to the dance hall is the first step to entering the brothel. The image functioned to warn viewers of the folded space that enabled the journey to white slavery. The mobile imagination of journey or path was common in the white slavery literature. Turner-Zimmermann, for example, depicted "the end of the way" as a squalid brothel, and she was explicit in stating that this was "where young girls, who attend public dances and other places of amusement unattended, are likely to wind up."[67] White women did not just exist in vice, but they moved into vice, although these women may not have fully understood where their mobility was leading.

Bell's image also reinforced the hidden permeability of spaces of vice because the warning signs were subtle. A sign in the illustration advertises "wine" and "café," while another sign notes that hotel rooms are available by the day or week, but the naive young woman could easily miss these signals and simply follow her well-dressed suitor. The folding of city spaces and hidden connections to spaces of vice made the entire city dangerous, but it was particularly dangerous in sites of amusement.

Whereas human connections and networks, such as relationships with businessmen, teachers, police, and postmasters of small-town America, could supposedly protect white women, human connections were represented as dangerous if they occurred in the space of the city. White women were frequently told that danger was always hiding, waiting to prey on innocent women. No one, from the seemingly kind older women to the handsome potential suitor, could be trusted. A writer in the *Union Signal* shared England's warning to "girls" that listed eleven things to never do, including: "Girls should never speak to strangers," "Girls should never stay to help a woman who apparently faints," and "Girls should never take a

Mobility and the Danger of the City | 39

FIGURE 4. "Dangerous Amusements—The Brilliant Entrance to Hell Itself. Young girls who have danced at home a little are attracted by the blazing lights, gaiety and apparent happiness of the 'dance halls,' which in many instances lead to their downfall. (See page 112.)" Illustration from Ernest Bell, *Fighting the Traffic in Young Girls: Or War on the White Slave Trade* (Chicago, 1910). From Special Collections, University of Wisconsin–Milwaukee Libraries.

situation [job] through an advertisement."[68] White women, according to this warning, should avoid virtually all human connection because anyone could be dangerous. Bell warned, "Strangers may be 'angels unawares,' but they may be black angels, and some such are wicked women."[69] Within the space of the city, human networks were represented as a constant source of danger, and the hidden permeability of borders within the city reinforced the danger of the entire space.

The folding of city spaces was not only perceived to put young white women at risk, but also it put all citizens at risk because of the unanticipated and uncontrolled movement of disease. One characteristic of the Progressive Era was a preoccupation with medicine and science. The social-hygiene movement was one manifestation of this focus and introduced a scientific rhetoric to educate the public about the dangers of sex. Scientific advances in preventing and treating sexually transmitted disease along with the increasing popularity of eugenics contributed to the momentum of the social-hygiene movement, which came to have a significant voice in the white slavery controversy.[70]

The spread of disease was named as one of the most significant problems with vice districts. In a literal sense, prostitution did contribute to infection. The Chicago Vice Commission warned:

> Prostitution is pregnant with disease, a disease infecting not only the guilty, but contaminating the innocent wife and child in the home with sickening certainty almost inconceivable; a disease to be feared with as great horror as a leprous plague; a disease scattering misery broadcast, and leaving in its wake sterility, insanity, paralysis, the blinded eyes of little babies, the twisted limbs of deformed children, degradation, physical rot and mental decay.[71]

The characterization of the "leprous plague" rhetorically linked the supposed moral and physiological harms of vice.[72] In the Bible, leprosy represented a physical manifestation of sin—an uncleanliness of both the body and the soul—that could only be healed through Christ's salvation. Yet, disease also spreads to the supposedly innocent, dissolving the boundaries between bodies and spaces. Thus, the real social danger was thought to be for the innocent children, wives, and young women trapped in white slavery who were contaminated with diseases such as syphilis.[73] The fear of "scattering misery broadcast" created unanticipated connections that forced a collapse of the borders that seemed to quarantine vice districts from the rest of the city and a shift in scale from the level of city to the bodies infected because of the proximity to vice. The unpredictable mobility of disease stood in stark contrast to its victims who were rendered paralyzed, deformed, and decayed; disease moved while diseased people became trapped.

There was not a clear boundary between social purity reformers and social-hygiene advocates. Indeed, they worked together in organizations such as the Illinois Vigilance Association and the American Vigilance Association. The language of disease blurred the lines between these groups of reformers. For example, the social purity reformers in the Midnight Mission frequently appropriated a metaphor of disease that was particularly salient because of its correlation to literal diseases often seen in prostitution.[74] Within this metaphor, vice districts were "poison" to the entire city and world, and moral "sickness" would inevitably spread to the innocent.[75] The solution, according to Bell, leader of the Midnight Mission, was to "vaccinate them with the word of God" or call on a "surgeon of the soul."[76] Within this framework, a disease of the soul was just as dangerous and infectious as a disease of the body and necessitated specialized intervention.

Both the moral and physiological danger of disease dissolved the borders of vice districts. While the language of vice "districts," created the geographical image of a confined and distinct space, the rhetoric of disease evoked a mobile imagination that could not be confined, connecting people across geographical space with an invisible thread of danger. Even the baby born to a wealthy family in a seemingly safe place was not immune because disease could move to the innocent. Thus, the vice district, according to activists, needed to be a concern to everyone because its disease could infect anyone.

The rhetoric of disease also involved shifting geographic scales, constantly moving between body, home, and nation. The infection of a single body represented a risk to the home (epitomized by the diseased baby) but also a risk to the nation as a whole. By 1905, the US Supreme Court recognized the national importance of protecting public health and safety in preventing epidemics, allowing for compulsory vaccination and immigrations restrictions.[77] Activists drew on this logic in appropriating the language of epidemic and plague. Thus, when the Midnight Mission called for vaccination "with the word of God," activists were rhetorically shifting scale from the individual to the nation; saving of one individual was construed as necessary to save the nation as a whole. When conceptualized as a disease, vice could not be contained in a geographic district, necessitating that it was a problem with which all Americans should be concerned.

To reinforce the permeable borders between places of good and evil, activists declared "war" on white slavery. War metaphors can frame problems in such a way to provoke an aggressive response. In reference to Lyndon B. Johnson's use of the metaphor in the war on poverty, David Zarefsky explained, "It defined an objective and encouraged enlistment in the effort, it identified the enemy against whom the campaign was directed, and it dictated the choice of weapons and tactics with which the struggle would be fought."[78] In effect, the metaphor reduced the burden of proof necessary to prompt social change because war suggests an imminent and particularly dangerous harm.[79] War, however, is also geographical. War is used to claim or defend places, and the rhetoric of war inscribes not only a difference in people but also a difference in place.

White slavers were depicted as engaging in a war against good members of the American population, and unless countered, the threat was that white slavery would continue to expand, claiming additional space.[80] This war meant that no place was safe and even the intangible soul was at risk of violent takeover. That white slavers were depicted as an organized system is important because it opened rhetorical space for the problem to be understood as a war, rather than a conflict with a few individual criminals. The representation of white slavers as largely foreigners further supported the image of war instead of a simple criminal issue.

The metaphor of war exalts those fighting on the side of good, and in the white slavery controversy, the image of good against evil was enhanced with the language of "crusade."[81] When activists described their actions as part of a crusade, they not only unambiguously assumed the side of good but also framed their actions as moral obligation. When the Midnight Mission called for volunteers, they were both calling on supporters to pray and calling on them to fight. Similarly, a pamphlet created by the Committee of Fifteen, a Chicago organization founded after the Chicago Vice Commission reforms were ignored by city officials, concluded, "WANTED—REINFORCEMENTS ON THE FIRING LINE AGAINST COMMERCIALIZED VICE."[82] In one sense, there was an actual space for which they were fighting—the Levee or Congress Street—physical locations activists were targeting in order to attempt to close locations of vice.[83] These battle lines, however, also assumed a symbolic role because white slavery reformers were not simply battling for a street or district but for the souls of white women. Every closed brothel or rescued white slave represented a slowing of the spread of vice and immorality. In this sense, the rhetoric of war built off of the shifting scales in the controversy. The reformers were fighting not only for topographical space but also for the bodies of white women. Significantly, protecting white women's bodies became a conduit for protecting the morality of the nation.

Stasis of Women

Tim Cresswell distinguishes between movement and mobility, arguing that in US law objects are moved but people are mobile because mobility entails agency, and while mobility may be a right of citizenship, there is not necessarily a legal right to move objects.[84] However, discursive representations may complicate any clear lines between the moved and the mobile. Objects or places may be represented as agents, pushing or pulling people.⁸⁵ Similarly, people can be represented as objects that are moved or trapped. For white slavery activists, white women's mobility in the city would ultimately lead to their entrapment, removing agency. The danger began at the railroad where strangers were thought to prey on young white women either on the train or as soon as they got off the train.⁸⁶ Anecdotal stories described a variety of tricks such as a kind older woman claiming to be sent by a relative or a charming young man who knew of a safe boarding house. In each of these instances, the young white woman would be taken to a brothel, trapped, raped, and broken.⁸⁷ However, the danger was thought to persist anywhere in the city where women could be drugged, tricked, or manipulated into a life of prostitution.

The likely result of white women's mobility in the space of the city was represented as entrapment and degradation. In *Fighting the Traffic in Young Girls*, Bell visually represented the path to women's ruin, which cumulated in a picture titled "'The Gilded Life' as It Really Is."⁸⁸ Although many of Bell's images were illustrations depicting young, attractive, middle- or upper-class

FIGURE 5. "'The Gilded Life' as It Really Is." Image from Ernest Bell, *Fighting the Traffic in Young Girls: Or War on the White Slave Trade* (Chicago, 1910). From Special Collections, University of Wisconsin–Milwaukee Libraries.

white women inadvertently moving into sites of danger, "The Gilded Life" was a photograph of a somewhat disheveled white woman sitting in a dirty outdoor space. She appeared to be in a confined space, and although she was outside, there was not a clear way for her to leave. The dirt and darkness of the woman's surroundings reflected the assumption of this white woman's corruption. Further, the window near her chair had bars, which reinforced the sense of confinement and suggested that stasis was not a choice; the woman was trapped. The woman sat with her knees open, wearing what appears to be loose underclothes or a nightgown that hangs off her shoulder. Thus, what should be private is starkly public while still confined. The woman was trapped, but the stasis was not in the private security of the home.

"The Gilded Life" also reinforced a racialized dislocation. A Black woman (possibly a child) stood obscured by the doorway, and while the caption labeled the white woman a "poor slave," the Black woman was described as a "colored attendant" who "watches" the white woman, inverting the racialized understandings of enslavement in the United States. The Black woman was depicted as participating in the white woman's enslavement by "watching" the white woman and presumably preventing her escape. Further, this image represented white slavery as positioning white women near Black women, and, thus, at risk of sexual corruption.[89] Although labeled as an "attendant," the Black women did not appear to attend to the white woman; she watched and reinforced the semi-dressed white woman as the object of the viewers' gaze. The layered messages of "The Gilded Life" brought together the fears associated with mobility—the wrong type of mobility led to the wrong type of stasis. Instead of being protected by the home, the white woman was both confided and on public display, and inversions of historical racial power divisions elicited a strong sense of dislocation and, thus, insecurity for the white audience.

Once women were trapped in white slavery, women flipped from being mobile to being moved, and this transition is illustrated, in part, through the language of traffic. "Traffic" suggests movement, and in the early twentieth century, it could have a negative connotation implying illegal or immoral activity. The language of traffic in the white slavery controversy promoted outrage because it dehumanized women and associated them with commodities, such as livestock.[90] For example, Dr. Turner-Zimmermann asked if her audience wanted "little girls still to be bought and sold like pigs," and in using this analogy, she attempted to harness anger in order to spur action.[91]

The language of traffic removed agency from women, who were simply "parcels," and constructed a system as having agency. Edwin Sims, US district attorney and secretary for the Chicago Vice Commission, described the white slavery system in detail:

> It is only necessary to say that the legal evidence thus far collected establishes with complete moral certainty these awful facts: That the white slave traffic is a system—a syndicate which has its ramifications from the Atlantic seaboard to the Pacific ocean, with "clearing houses" or "distributing centers" in nearly all of the larger cities; that in this ghastly traffic the buying price of a young girl is $15.00 and that the selling price is generally about $200.00—if the girl is especially attractive the white slave dealer may be able to sell her for $400.00 or $600.00; that this syndicate did not make less than $200,000 last year in this almost unthinkable commerce; that it is a definite organization sending its hunters regularly to scour France, Germany, Hungary, Italy and Canada for victims; that the man at the head of the unthinkable enterprise is known among his hunters as "The Big Chief."[92]

Sims's position of authority (attorney general) and the specificity of his description lent it credibility. The language of a system represented the problem as expansive and multifaceted and, thus, requiring a systematic response, moving the problem from private vice to a public problem requiring a public solution. The flattening of scale was critical to the trafficking rhetoric. Rather than conceptualizing the scale of the body and the scale of the globe as distinct perspectives, the rhetoric of trafficking seamlessly moved between global and individual, forcing readers to view the at-risk bodies of individual young women within a global context.

The language of traffic and systems also enabled organizations such as the WCTU to draw on opposition to white slavery by linking the "white slave traffic" to the "liquor traffic."[93] The language that described the problem of white slavery as a "traffic" sustained by a large "syndicate" not only represented the boundaries of the vice district as permeable but also collapsed topographical distance that separated seemingly innocent white women from danger. Anywhere that the liquor traffic could penetrate so too could the white slave traffic. Furthermore, when white women were understood as objects that were moved, there was no longer space for actual mobility because women were not autonomous agents who had a right to movement.

The supposed danger of white women's mobility led activists to contrast the safety of home in the country with the dangers of the city.[94] Edwin Sims stated, "I can say, in all sincerity, that if I lived in the country and had a young daughter I would go any length of hardship and privation myself rather than allow her to go into the city to work or to study."[95] For white women, mobility was clearly represented as dangerous, whereas the stasis of home ensured safety and stability. When Sims warned against allowing daughters "to go into the city for work or study," he was not only warning of women's mobility and privileging stasis, but he was also warning of white women moving into sites of dislocation—sites of work or study as opposed to home. Sims described the consequence of that dislocation by noting, "The recent examination of more than two hundred 'white slaves' by the office of the US district attorney at Chicago has brought to light the fact that literally thousands of innocent girls from the country districts are every year entrapped into a life of hopeless slavery and degradation."[96] "Innocent girls from the country" functioned as a coded way of referencing white, middle-class women. The city, according to these activists, was a place of danger for white women, and the stasis of home functioned as a site of safety.

The city was contrasted with the safety and innocence of the country. When commentators such as Simms described the country as a site of home and safety, they not only created a border between geographic sites of safety and danger, good and evil, but also limited women's mobile possibilities in the city. Within this framework, home and good femininity did not belong in the city, which is clearly a false dichotomy as plenty of women, particularly working-class and immigrant women, lived within the boundary of the city. Thus, reformers marked women's identities through their position in and movement through geographic space. Because women who existed in the space of the city were constructed as sexually deviant or at risk of sexual deviance, good women were effectively excluded from that geographic space. Women's mobility and, thus, opportunities for independence, education, or employment were limited, but, just as significantly, working-class women who could not escape the city were excluded from legitimate womanhood.

White slavery activists warned white women (and their parents) that home was the only safe place, and, in doing so, these activists infantilized women and trivialized their motivations for leaving home. For example, "Don't lose your temper and leave home. The world is wide, but it is wicked, and it has a thousand traps for the girl who lacks the protection of her family and friends."[97] Within this framing, there was not a justifiable reason for leaving home, the traditional sphere for women. The woman who left home was understood as tempted by simple irrationality, such as temper or excitement. Economic necessity was typically not recognized as a motivation, suggesting that these reformers were most concerned about the welfare of middle- and upper-class white women, not the women who lived in economic uncertainty and were, therefore, most vulnerable. Further, the unstated assumption was that middle- and upper-class white women could get married and, as a result, did not have legitimate economic need to come to the city and seek employment. The common framing of a country woman leaving the security of home and entering the danger of the city almost exclusively referred to white women as "girls," infantilizing women and reinforcing that they required the security of home.[98] The prostitute in contrast was a "public woman," losing the innocence of the "girl" and no longer hidden behind the veil of domesticity.[99]

Fallen Is Babylon

In 1912, vice activists celebrated the official closing of the Levee vice district, prompting Ernest Bell to write, "Fallen is Babylon!"[100] Some members of the Midnight Mission debated their next steps as an organization. "Dr. Van Dyke," for example, "urged the necessity of some one making war on the vice of sodomy."[101] There is not archival evidence that the Midnight Mission adopted this focus. Rather, the Midnight Mission and similar organizations found that prostitution of white women remained throughout the city, and, thus, their work remained relevant.

The case of white slavery in Chicago illustrates the interconnections between space, mobility, and the protection of white women. The city moved through time and space in ways that felt counterintuitive for reformers who appeared to imagine a white nation moving toward civilization. White slavery was understood as a significant threat when the city was imagined as a locus of mobility—fast, uncontrolled, leaky, and persistent mobility. Despite reformers' attempts to contain immigration, vice, and women, each leaked through their constructed boundaries, making the entire city a site of danger, and that danger was thought to be a particular threat to white women who appeared to hold the greatest potential for both virtue and vice. When the city is understood through its mobile imagination, it becomes important to consider who is mobile and who is contained, as well as understanding the nature of the mobility and means of containment.

Even as white slavery literature imaged the space of the city as mobile, changing, and chaotic, reformers in New York were working to wrest the locus of reform efforts from Chicago to New York. Although there were clearly exceptions, New York reform efforts were grounded in a rhetoric of science and objectivity. The supposedly scientific rhetoric imagined the space of the city in a way that was stable, contained, and immutable. This differing image of the city appeared to naturalize alternative efforts for reform, efforts to which I will now turn.

CHAPTER 3

The Science of Social Mobility

JOHN D. ROCKEFELLER JR. AND THE
SCIENCE OF REFORM, 1910–1917

Two years after George Kibbe Turner inflamed passions with his Chicago white slavery exposé, he set his sights on New York, specifically Tammany Hall. He claimed, "In the past ten years New York has become the leader of the world in this class of enterprise . . . under the protection of the Tammany Hall political organization."[1] Turner described in great detail an organized national and international trade in primarily poor and immigrant young women that was intimately integrated into the Tammany political machine. Indeed, Turner claimed that the Tammany Hall building "has come to be the leading headquarters for disreputable dances" where young women were procured for prostitution.[2] He concluded, "Shall New York City continue to be the recruiting-ground for the collection for market of young women by politically organized procurers? The only practical way to stop it will be by the defeat of Tammany Hall."[3]

It is, perhaps, unsurprising that Tammany Hall quickly responded to Turner's accusations, especially considering the possibility that the *McClure's* article impacted the 1909 elections in the city.[4] On January 3, 1910, New York's

Judge Thomas C. O'Sullivan, who was likely a "Tammany man," called a small group of citizens to serve on a special grand jury to investigate accusations of white slavery in New York City, and John D. Rockefeller Jr., the son of one of the nation's wealthiest and most influential men, was called to serve as jury foreman.[5] In order to challenge aristocratic power in the city, Tammany Hall commonly used a strategy of making particularly ineffectual aristocrats figureheads in investigations similar to the white slavery investigation.[6] Based on initial newspaper reporting, Tammany Hall appeared to have their man in Rockefeller, who attempted to be excused from the grand jury on account of his youth, inexperience, health, and business interests. After being reminded by the judge of his "patriotic duty," Rockefeller "stammered" an acceptance of the appointment.[7]

Despite its auspicious beginning, the white slavery grand jury conducted a sweeping investigation that lasted for six months, even though it was initially expected to only last for one month, and Rockefeller told his biographer, "I never worked harder in my life."[8] The investigation began a decades-long commitment to the issue, where Rockefeller ultimately gave about $5.4 million to the cause and fundamentally altered the national response to prostitution and white slavery.[9] Using a scientific rhetoric inflected with Progressive Era values, Rockefeller and other reformers accepted the dangers of New York City, but rather than attempt to keep "good" women from such a place, the reformers focused their attention on reform. Their scientific approach created space for a recognition of environment in the causes of vice, opening possibilities for some women to become redeemed because their evil was no longer assumed to be intrinsic.

Activists identified social mobility as the solution to white slavery and constructed paths toward reform. The mobile imagination extends to social mobility; reformers imagined some people as capable of social mobility and shaped the appropriate paths toward a possible new life. These reformers grounded their mobile imagination in supposedly scientific approaches to reform. This chapter traces the rhetorics of reform and social mobility among these scientifically oriented activists, many of whom were based out of New York. While this scientific rhetoric appeared to open possibilities for social mobility for some women who were deemed worthy and capable, it also reified divisions between the redeemable and abject, divisions that tended to map onto race.

John D. Rockefeller Jr., Investigation, and Reform

By 1910, John D. Rockefeller Sr., Standard Oil baron, had stepped away from most of his business interests, and John D. Rockefeller Jr. was expected to take his place. However, during his grand jury service, the news leaked that the younger Rockefeller had resigned from most of his business roles in order to concentrate on managing the family's philanthropies.[10] While Rockefeller Sr. may have been motivated to develop the family philanthropies through "his religious conviction and the old-fashioned concept of stewardship," Rockefeller Jr. brought a commitment to the Progressive Era impetus that scientific thinking and strong management could solve social problems.[11] He brought these methods to the white slavery grand jury, systematically seeking testimony from political officials, representatives from local organizations doing work on the issue, academic experts, and investigators.[12] Rockefeller also wrote letters to nearly every person who had published on the topic of white slavery asking for "actual facts" and the "sources of information from which they were obtained," often quoting something specific from the publication and asking targeted follow-up questions.[13] While Rockefeller received many responses, the president of the *New York Evening Journal* replied, "You will, of course, find it very difficult—perhaps impossible—to get ACTUAL PROOF."[14] Nevertheless, after about six months, the grand jury concluded their investigation and found what they believed was actual proof.

In June 1910, Rockefeller asked for the grand jury to be dismissed and requested to read a presentment to the court outlining the investigation background, findings, and grand jury recommendations. Justice O'Sullivan ultimately declined Rockefeller's request, and instead summarized the findings, "You report that no organized traffic in women exists in this city," and New York is "the cleanest great city in the world."[15] The grand jury report, however, was more nuanced, concluding that there was a problem in New York, even though there was not an organization clearly facilitating the traffic. After disappointing correspondence with the mayor, Rockefeller and James Reynolds, the assistant district attorney with whom Rockefeller had worked during the investigation, conspired to publish the grand jury report and distribute the report to newspapers.[16]

Perhaps one of the strongest recommendations in the report was the need for a thorough investigation of white slavery and prostitution in

New York, and, thus, Rockefeller began acting on that recommendation after discovering that the mayor's office and court had largely dismissed the report's findings. There is evidence that Rockefeller wanted to begin private investigations right away after being appointed to the grand jury, but there were limitations to the admissibility of evidence.[17] After his service, Rockefeller began funding investigations with the explicit request that he not be publicly connected to the inquiries. An early investigation conducted by Dr. Paul Sandfort was facilitated by Reynolds and involved the opening of a false disreputable house, although Rockefeller later denied being associated with the investigation and directed later investigators to avoid any illegal or immoral activity in the course of their investigations.[18] By December 1910, Rockefeller was convinced that the mayor was unlikely to appoint a commission to study the problem and concluded that a public commission would be of limited utility.[19] Instead, Rockefeller began what would ultimately become the Bureau of Social Hygiene, an organization that worked largely in secret for nearly two years while conducting investigations.

In January of 1911, Rockefeller hired Clifford Roe, the lead investigator of the celebrated Chicago effort to eradicate white slavery.[20] The subsequent report that Roe produced on April 1912 reads like a sensational novel with investigators engaging in elaborate plots, detectives who shifted between different characters, and even a state's witness killed by a bombing before trial.[21] Although dramatic, Roe's investigation resulted in few indictments, and Rockefeller did not continue to hire Roe after one year.[22] Rockefeller's experience with Clifford Roe appears to have functioned as a break from the Chicago white slavery campaigns. While Roe's sentimental language chronicled the infiltration in and movement across spaces, what came to be the New York approach to white slavery utilized scientific language to investigate the body as a site of danger and reform.

This rhetorical shift is evident through three primary approaches to the problem of white slavery in New York, each initiated and supported by Rockefeller. First, Rockefeller, through the Bureau of Social Hygiene, funded and published "scientific" reports of prostitution in New York and Europe.[23] The initial investigators, George Kneeland, Abraham Flexnor, and Raymond Fosdick, became long-term allies in Rockefeller's efforts, and Rockefeller not only funded the investigations but also provided specific direction to the investigations and edits to the subsequent publications.[24] These investigations functioned as the "truth" about prostitution and white slavery, and they were intended to provide a scientific grounding for reform efforts.

Second, Rockefeller funded clinical research beginning with the Bedford Hills Laboratory of Social Hygiene.[25] Bedford Hills was a reform institution for young women sentenced by New York courts. The laboratory functioned as a mechanism to study and treat women in order to enable their reform, and the explicit purpose of the funding was to provide a model of criminal justice reform that could be applicable outside of Bedford Hills. In her proposal to Rockefeller, Katharine B. Davis, Bedford Hills superintendent, argued, "definite knowledge *must* precede concerted action to make it worth while or its results lasting."[26] Indeed, Rockefeller explained:

> Miss Davis told us that while the girls in her intuition are committed there for various crimes, practically all of these crimes were committed as a result of or in connection with their being prostitutes. In other words, her experience would go to prove that the one crime of woman is prostitution. All the other crimes are simply incidental thereto.[27]

The bureau later funded a municipal health clinic that would serve public health needs by reporting and managing venereal disease, while studying those who came through their doors in order to find the most effective solutions to the problem.[28]

While Chicago appeared to work toward shutting down and eliminating prostitution, a strategy commonly described as abolition, Rockefeller situated his work within a pragmatic middle ground between regulation and abolition. Rockefeller described his perspective in his proposal for a mayor's commission. He explained, "Let us draw an imaginary line. On one side of this line let us place" men and women who are irredeemable. According to Rockefeller, the irredeemable consisted of "probably less than 25%" of those involved in prostitution.[29] Following this logic, most people were redeemable, and a scientific study of prostitution could reveal the most effective methods of reform and prevention. For Rockefeller, an appropriate response should not be "sensational or sentimental or hysterical," but instead operate with "deep scientific as well as humane interest in a great world problem."[30] This approach used a scientific rhetoric to navigate the middle ground.

Finally, Rockefeller worked behind the scenes to fundamentally alter the national landscape of philanthropic organizations dealing with issues of white slavery and prostitution. By 1910, there was a dizzying array of organizations working on the problems of prostitution, morality, white slavery, and venereal disease. Rockefeller worked behind the scenes to consolidate, direct, and "modernize" the movement, which ultimately led to the creation of the American Social Hygiene Association in 1913 and a shift in national reform efforts to New York City, away from Chicago.[31] While activists around the country utilized scientific strategies of reform and continued activism against white slavery, Rockefeller appeared to have shifted the center of the movement through his money and influence.

The Progressive Era Rhetoric of Science

While the Progressive Era is generally defined as a time characterized by reform, morality, and public interest, J. Michael Hogan also identified "organization, efficiency, rationality, expertise, and science" as "key terms of progressive ideology."[32] Indeed, the turn of the century was a heyday for social science, the assumption that scientific methods could be harnessed to solve pressing social problems.[33] Scholar activists "launched associations, bureaus, and settlement houses of reforms and contributed to the making or remaking of others, including universities and modern philanthropic foundations," and New York City functioned as a "laboratory" of social science study and activism.[34] Not only was New York City the largest city in the nation, twice as large as Chicago, but also it became a hub of reform, hosting a large variety of organizations. Thus, the scientific approach to white slavery was occurring within a larger context of social scientific study and reform.

Criminology was a particular focus of many Progressive Era activists. Well-educated men and women were increasingly looking for improvements on the nineteenth-century prison system, turning toward innovative reforms while conducting and utilizing scientific investigations to support change.[35] As criminologists studied the causes of crime, they tended to favor theories that challenged biological determinism or intrinsic depravity, instead attributing crime to environmental conditions such as education, family, and economic conditions.[36] This faith in reform helped lead to the creation of juvenile courts and morals courts that offered new responses to crime.

Despite their embrace of scientific methodologies and data-driven solutions, Progressive Era activists were humans and, thus, influenced by their biases and preexisting expectations. Indeed, research on the rhetoric of science has established that despite its neutral tone, the "scientific method is diverse, social, argumentative, and suasory."[37] In short, scientific texts are cultural products.[38] Utilizing John Lynch's tripartite registers of scientific practice reveals that Progressive Era social scientists developed a trained way of observing human subjects, working on the material register by recording observable facts about people. The social register was the developing norms of social scientific research that created trained ways of seeing and collecting data. Lynch describes the rhetorical register as the discursive representation findings, and in the case of white slavery reformers this register includes the myriad books, essays, and other publications that both described studies and prescribed reforms based on the conclusions of those studies. Lynch, however, is clear that it is important to understand the "interanimation" of material and rhetorical registers in scientific rhetoric.[39] Such interanimation is critical to reading the New York white slavery activists because the decisions made on the material register—who was seen—necessarily impacted the discursive representations of studies and prescriptions for reform. Furthermore, the social register provides a vital mediation between both the material and rhetorical because the bourgeoning practices of social science were developing, in part, through these very studies. Progressive Era social scientists not only drew on the social register within material and rhetorical registers, but they were also working to shape the social register of the emergent field of scholar activists; in their doing, they were establishing social norms for others in the field. Considering the registers of scientific practice provides a useful lens for unpacking the scientific rhetoric of Progressive Era white slavery activists.

White Slavery and Scientific Reform Rhetoric

The scientific approach to white slavery, epitomized by the New York efforts, was well documented. In addition to Rockefeller's grand jury report, the Bureau of Social Hygiene published what came to be lauded as the most comprehensive studies of prostitution in the United States and Europe until that date. While sensational novels and news reporting persisted, reporters and activists were increasingly publishing on the problem using a scientific tone, making a case for the most effective means of reform. This chapter analyzes these primary source documents, as well as the extensive archival documents from Rockefeller's grand jury service and the Bureau of Social Hygiene.

I ultimately argue that the New York branch of the movement engaged in explicit definitional work to move the definition of "white slavery" from entrapment to redeemability. In doing so, reformers shifted the ground of reform from spaces of entrapment to the mobile imagination of the body, which may or may not have been capable of redemption. To create the possibility for reform, activists focused on creating a limited mobile imagination for women practicing prostitution. Specifically, they attempted to generate the conditions, resources, and support to open possibilities for mobility into white domesticity. The rhetoric of science functioned as a compass to negotiate the site of the body and determine possibilities for redeemability, and rhetorical analysis can help uncover the ways in which the rhetoric operated, as well as the constructed lines between those who were and were not capable of reform.

Definitions of White Slavery

Definition can be an important persuasive vehicle, altering the terms of a debate, undermining fundamental assumptions, shaping social realities, and foregrounding different ideological assumptions.[40] Much like the Chicago branch of the movement, there was little explicit consideration of the definitions of white slavery among New York activists. Rather, the objects of concern were often assumed into existence through an implicit definition of white slavery. Nevertheless, archival documents reveal some of the underlying definitional assumptions in the New York branch of the white slavery movement. These definitions, often simply stipulated in public rhetoric, were integral to shaping the New York approach and larger direction of the movement. Dr. Sandfort, one of the first investigators employed by Rockefeller, reported that in investigating white slavery he was tasked to "investigate the way the girls of the better classes are brought to moral destruction."[41] Sandfort's definition was consistent with Chicago reformers. "Girls of the better classes" implied middle- and upper-class domesticity and whiteness, and, thus, the distinction also mapped onto spatial dividing lines. The girls, according to Sandfort, are "brought" to moral destruction, suggesting a move from a site of domestic safety to a site of danger where white women had no agency in their downfall. "Destruction" signaled a finality to women's state when they were brought to the wrong spaces; often something destroyed may never be repaired.

While Sandfort was operating under a definition of white slavery that considered the wrong people (the better class of girl) being brought into the wrong spaces (sites of prostitution), the New York reformers appeared to ultimately move in a very different direction situating white slavery as a condition of the body. While public rhetoric was not explicit in this definition, John D. Rockefeller Jr.'s grand jury archives include a document that defines white slavery, and this definition appears to be functioning implicitly throughout much of the public rhetoric. Within this definition, the primary identity of the white slave was characterized as a "female person," while other identity characteristics, such as age or previous chaste character, were explicitly excluded from consideration. Instead, "female person" was modified by the state in which her body existed: "kept behind locked doors and windows," "compelled ... by actual or threatened violence or exposure or the claim of alleged legal indebtedness," or if "money or other valuable consideration" is exchanged for the purpose of using her for "immoral purposes."[42] This definition did not address the race of the "female person," and some Black women and immigrant women appeared to have had access to Bureau of Social Hygiene incentives. However, I argue that reformers shaped the mobile imagination of Black women, often framing them as incapable of social mobility and, thus, unworthy of reform efforts, despite fitting this definition of white slave.

The definition signals an expansion of the term "white slavery" to encompass all prostitution, an expansion the definition document labeled as consistent with common usage.[43] Indeed, a US government investigating official explained to Rockefeller in a letter, "I regard every prostitute in this country more or less of a white slave" because of the existing conditions that made leaving prostitution nearly impossible.[44] Kneeland, one of Rockefeller's investigators, reported in his book published by the Bureau of Social Hygiene that because of her relationship to the "pimp" and "house madame," "the prostitute is not infrequently to all intents and purposes a white slave."[45] The enslavement, however, did not simply occur through force. Kneeland continued, "This does not mean that the girl is necessarily imprisoned behind locked doors and barred windows. But restraint may be thoroughly effective, even though not actually or mainly physical."[46] This expanded definition not only increased the purview of activism away from the innocent girl to encompass all women practicing prostitution, but it also participated in shifting the locus of action to the conditions of entrapment.

While some activist considered abandoning the language of white slavery, instead deploying terms like "commercialized vice" or "traffic in women,"[47] Jane Addams, founder of Chicago's Hull House, wrote:

> Those of us who think we discern the beginnings of a new consciousness in regard to this twin of slavery, as old and outrageous as slavery itself and even more persistent, find a possible analogy between certain civic, philanthropic, and educational efforts directed against the very existence of this social evil, and similar organized efforts which preceded the overthrow of slavery in America.[48]

Addams implied that the slavery analogy provided an important framework for understanding the issue that extended well beyond the naming of the controversy. Rather than emphasizing literal entrapment, Addams's reframing situated white slavery as a moral failing, a social evil, and a problem that could be addressed with persistent effort. Thus, in addition to sidestepping the issue of whether women were literally enslaved, she also answered the objection that prostitution was inevitable, opening space for social activism.

Redeemable Women

When the meanings of white slavery included all prostitution, activists needed to shift from framing prostitutes as common whores to creating the space for women who practiced prostitution to be understood as redeemable women. There were two layers to this shift. Activists framed women in prostitution, including lower-class women, as victims, rather than whores. Second, activists emphasized the possibilities for reform, although this reform often entailed the inscribing the norms of upper/middle-class white womanhood on all women. The shifting perspective was grounded in the collection of data about those practicing prostitution, and Kneeland's study for the Bureau of Social Hygiene was considered to be the most scientific and authoritative.

For people practicing prostitution to becomes victims, it was necessary to remove their agency. According to Kneeland, there were generally four causes of prostitution, all of which removed a significant degree of agency from the women. First, he outlined family related causes that included "neglect and abuse by parents, sternness and lack of understanding, immorality of different members of the family, and poverty in the home."[49] Second were reasons related to marriage. Kneeland explained, "It was usually alleged that the husband persuaded the wife to go into the business: he was practically a pimp. Sometimes, cruelty or criminality on his part is assigned,—again, incompatibility, failure to provide, or desertion where the wife states that she had no other recourse."[50] Both of these categories built on the expectations of women's dependent status. Cultural expectations of good womanhood were grounded in women's role within the home. Even at the beginning of the twentieth century as women were increasingly outside of the home seeking opportunities for employment, education, and civic engagement, cultural standards continued to privilege domesticity. These expectations entailed reciprocal privileges and obligations; while women were expected the maintain a home and properly rear children, they were thought to be owed financial support and a stable home. Thus, women who entered prostitution as a result of their family's failures were situated as victims who were failed by those who were obligated to provide support.

The second two reasons cited by Kneeland were personal and economic. Personal reasons included being "seduced" and "ruined" by a lover, and the economic reasons included the need to support family. Both of these reasons removed agency from the woman. Even with seduction, women were positioned as the objects that were seduced and ruined, while nefarious men were the actors with agency in the situation. As another author explained, "She has not chosen, she has merely fallen."[51] Nevertheless, Kneeland left room for some women who were agents and, therefore, irredeemable. Some women, he explained, enjoyed excitement or were "born bad," and he identified others who "cited in explanation of their conduct the deprivations to which they would otherwise have to submit."[52] These women, however, were the exception. Through these conclusions, Kneeland's study created a scientific basis for shifting attention to environmental causes of prostitution, rather than innate degeneracy.

Even after women entered prostitution, Kneeland continued to frame them as victims who could not leave the profession. He explained:

> Alcohol is needed to keep the inmates to their task; but even more essential from the business standpoint are drugs. The girl must be kept gay and attractive; her eyes must look out upon the world of business bright and unfaltering. She must smile and laugh and sing and dance, or she becomes a "has been," a "poor money maker," and so in danger of losing her "job." Is it any wonder that she becomes a drug fiend as well as a drunkard?[53]

Forced alcohol and drug dependency was not only a tool of entrapment, but Kneeland situated these tools as one of the ways women lose agency—removing both the ability and desire to leave prostitution. Further, the more useful to her enslaver a woman became the less likely she was to illicit sympathy "because good men and women have become convinced of her innate degeneracy."[54] The implication was that the women most entrapped and most in need of saving were the ones most ignored and disregarded by the "good" people who could help them. Thus, pimps and reformers had the agency to entrap or save, while prostitutes were victims without agency and continued to be victimized until they were no longer useful.

An ongoing challenge was that few women were willing to self-identify as a "white slave."[55] The failure of women to publicly self-identify as victims had previously hampered reform efforts, which was especially problematic when attempting to collapse a dichotomy between victim and whore. Kneeland described the problem as rooted in sustained and ongoing abuse. He explained:

> He [the pimp] attends to the business arrangements, even to the collection of her [the prostitute's] money, though when she is "well broke," he allows her to collect her own money and give it to him. Some pimps beat their women, on the principle that that is the only way to make them fear and love them. This may seem a paradox; but it is indeed true that many prostitutes do not believe their lovers care for them unless they "beat them up" occasionally.[56]

While today Kneeland's description would be understood as a form of intimate partner violence, readers at the beginning of the twentieth century were likely to see the passive acceptance of violence as a woman's mental defect. Women's sentimentality, according to Kneeland, created the greatest obstacle to saving prostitutes and, ultimately, put many of these women "beyond the protection of the law."[57] Demoralization, sentimentality, love, and shame were all womanly emotions. Thus, even while accounting for and describing women's false consciousness, reformers inscribed traditionally feminine emotionality onto women who practiced prostitution, potentially increasing perceptions of redeemability. After all, if the prostitute's entrapment was the result of her feminine sentimentality, that feminine nature could be redirected toward her redemption.

Redemption was the goal of many in the New York branch of the movement. One activist argued in a philanthropy journal, "A large proportion of 'fallen' girls have every year been safely married, become mothers quite as good as the ordinary, and had husbands quite as faithful as the husbands of their neighbors."[58] By establishing marriage and motherhood as metrics of success, reformers solidified norms of good womanhood, even while expanding the perceived possibilities of who was capable of attaining that status. Additionally, a University of Chicago professor argued in a letter to Rockefeller that many prostitutes return to villages and back to respectable lives. "To prove this would," he continued, "be a task of doubtful merit, since it is probably best for men generally to believe that a woman who once lapses into professional vice is almost certainly utterly doomed."[59] These writers represented reformed women as indistinguishable from a woman who had never practiced prostitution. While, as the male author suggested, such a prospect may have been disturbing for men who could unknowingly marry a former prostitute, the possibility for reform shifted the locus of change from the dangers of the city to the bodies of women, while also building off a challenge to the dichotomy between victim and whore. Each woman may have a capacity for social mobility, and social reformers were then tasked with determining who was capable of moving from vice to a respectable life.

Assigning Blame

When all (or nearly all) prostitution is framed as white slavery, and all (or nearly all) prostitutes are innocent victims, blame needs to reside somewhere, and in the case of the New York reformers, blame rested squarely on the shoulders of pimps and procurers. With a robust layer of sarcasm, Kneeland explained, "And 'pimps' are usually admirable protectors, masters of the art of 'saving' their women from the hand of the law. They are keen, wise young men, well grounded in the business of exploiting the girls of the street at the least possible expense. Some of them are known as 'gun men,' 'strong arm guys,' 'guerillas,' and do effective work for politicians."[60] Kneeland's description is telling. The primary function of the pimp was framed as subverting attempts to save women. By describing them as "keen" and "wise," Kneeland suggested that these men were tricky and difficult to stop, moving the audience toward understanding trafficking as a complex and powerful system. Furthermore, it was a system supported by violence, as implied by the alternative colloquial names, and political leaders. Thus, even though Kneeland and the previous grand jury report did not confirm the existence of an organized syndicate, Kneeland's explanation reinforced the image of a complex business in the exploitation of women.

By attaching blame to pimps and procurers, activists were not challenging men in general. Rather, they were identifying a unique class of men who violated expectations of decency. Kneeland was explicit in separating these men from American manhood. He explained, "The majority of men exploiters of prostitution in New York City are foreigners by birth. Some of them have been seducers of defenseless women all their lives."[61] Kneeland's explanation was working simultaneously in a couple of different directions. First, he shifted the root of the problem to the foreign Other, absolving American men of the majority of the blame. Second, he implied a fundamental difference between American and foreign men that derived from the place of their birth and, thus, their racial identity. Most men involved in the sex trade may have also been in economically precarious situations, but that economic classification was not as relevant to Kneeland's description as the location of birth, suggesting by associational logic that foreign birth and sexual exploitation were linked. Furthermore, by describing the foreign men as being "seducers . . . all their lives," Kneeland implied that sexual exploitation was an intrinsic characteristic, and thus, the men, unlike many of the prostitutes, were deemed incapable of reform.

While Black women received little attention as victims in need of saving, they were a focus of blame and accused of trafficking white women. In a highly publicized 1910 trial, Belle Moore, a Black woman, was charged with trafficking two teenage white girls. While the girls were represented as young and innocent (a representation that was effectively challenged by the defense), Moore was represented as hyper-sexual.[62] In attempting to convict Moore, prosecutors relied on "racial boundary crossing as a way to discuss sexual trafficking."[63] The Moore trial was not an exception. In his report, Kneeland described a case reminiscent of the trial. He explained that Black women "have white girls conducting the resorts while they, the owners, keep in the background."[64] Indeed, this is just one instance where Kneeland discusses Black women through a narrow lens of whiteness, noting race when the deviant behavior occurred near a school filled with white children or involved white women.[65] This lens appeared to have instantiated itself in police practice. In his reflections as New York police commissioner, William McAdoo identified mixed race sites of vice as the most dangerous. He noted, "All of these mixed-race places in the nineteenth, twentieth, twenty-second, and twenty-sixth precincts have no redeeming quality, are breeding-places for crime, and present disgusting exhibition of the degradation of one race and the worst vices of the other."[66] Of course, for McAdoo, degradation was applicable to white participants in vice because they had space to fall, and, by extension, space to grow, develop, and be redeemed. Black people, on the other hand, were assumed to be intrinsically bad, prone to violent passions, and easily corruptible.[67]

While most of the blame was thought to reside with foreign born men (and occasionally Black women), reformers did not absolve customers from responsibility. Indeed, Kneeland argued, "The necessary counterpart to the prostitute is her customer: she is the concrete answer to his demand. There are prostitutes at different economic levels, because their customers are derived from all social classes."[68] By noting that men of all social classes purchased sex, the author suggested that any man could potentially be culpable in sustaining white slavery. The broadening of culpability also broadened the scope of the problem. In other words, if upper-class men participated in sustaining white slavery, the problem became one in which upper-class reformers should be concerned, not simply out of charity for the poor but also because the men in their lives may be part of the problem.

Reformers represented a lack of proper domesticity as a condition that led men to purchase sex. Although Kneeland identified customers as universal, he specifically highlighted one class: "A numerous but pathetic group is that made up of young clerks who, living alone in unattractive quarters, find in professional prostitutes companion in the company of whom a night's revel offsets the dullness of their lives at other times.... No home ties restrain them; no home associations fill their time or thoughts."[69] Because a lack of home appeared to have contributed to the problem, Kneeland implied that domesticity could function as a solution to customer demand, and this was a domesticity that only women could provide.

The Science of Domesticity

For many, Katharine Davis and Bedford Hills offered the solution to the "girl problem," the perception that girls, especially those from immigrant families, were at risk of sexual promiscuity and prostitution.[70] Bedford Hills was just one of many reform institutions for girls across the country that were increasingly seen as critical to reforming young wayward women. While some of the girls and young women arrested and sent to reform institutions practiced prostitution, others were simply outside of their homes and classified as engaging in a "moral" offense or "public order" offense. Furthermore, the term "prostitute" implied that the offender exchanged sex for money, but it could also include a wide variety of moral offenses that included flirtatiousness or premarital sex.[71] Reform institutions offered a secure and supposedly moral environment that served as an alternative to houses of detention or the bridewell, which were used for violent criminals (and primarily men). Perhaps because of the alternative to imprisonment or because of the perceived seriousness of women's crimes, women and girls were far more likely to be detained and removed from their families than men and boys. Thus, reform institutions operated as sites of training for domesticity and moral purity, opening space for perceived social mobility.

Davis became well known for her work at Bedford Hills, which was lauded as a model reform institution. It utilized a three-step process guided by quasi-scientific assumptions about reform. In his introduction to the Kneeland book, John D. Rockefeller Jr. explained the reform process at the Bedford Hill Laboratory noting, "When the diagnosis is completed, it is hoped that the laboratory will be in position to suggest the treatment most likely to reform the individual, or, if reformation is impossible, to recommend permanent custodial care."[72] The assumption that scientifically objective diagnosis was possible, gave medical professionals the authority to determine who was worthy of redemption. According to Davis, this judgement was not necessarily based in past behavior but instead grounded in a scientific judgment of redeemability. Through the screening, Davis hoped to be able to detect those who were "morally defective" and, thus, incapable of reform.[73] New inmates were asked about their sexual experiences including when they first learned about sex and if their first sexual experiences were consensual, and officials made comments in case files about the inmate's demeanor and personality in ways that were necessarily shaped by norms of sex and race.[74]

Second, reformers argued that there was a need to treat the body, especially venereal disease because, as one report explained, "chances of moral relapse are greatly increased by the discouragement and despair incident to the deferred but finally inevitable manifestation of chronic infection."[75] While grounded in scientific language, this connection between morality and disease implied a long-standing cultural assumption that the condition of the soul could be reflected in the physical condition of the body, necessitating a treatment of both in order for reform to be successful. By 1906, there was a reliable blood test to detect syphilis, and within a few years, newly developed treatments created possibilities for medical treatment and, thus, reform.[76]

After scientific categorization to distinguish between the hopeless cases and those capable of being reformed, as well as treatment of physical disease, activists were tasked with the difficult work of reform. In an essay titled "How to Save the Girls Who Have Fallen," Annie W. Allen explained that effective reform for women embraced a model of domesticity. She described Bedford Hills, a model reform institution, as "more like a boarding school than a prison."[77] "For military procedure," Allen continued, "one substitutes domestic system, mutual convenience and special duties for each individual suited to her development."[78] Similarly, the New York Training School was described as embracing "conditions and spirit of a real home."[79] Because the scientists specifically asked questions and made observations about the domestic experiences of prostitutes, they found lack in that space, a lack that derived from cultural expectations of the norm. By extension, reformers concluded that if the lack of proper domesticity contributed to prostitution, proper domesticity could function as a solution to prostitution and a mechanism of reform. The privileging of domesticity as central to reform reflected assumptions about the causes of prostitution, legitimate alternatives to prostitution, as well as expectations of good womanhood.

Katharine Davis argued that a strong home with a vigilant and present mother was critical to preventing girls from entering prostitution. In her study of Bedford Hills inmates, Davis examined several background characteristics of the women sentenced to her institution including family size, father's income, and nationality. She concluded:

Probably of more importance than the size of the family is the economic position of the mother, particularly during the years of the daughter's adolescence. It is a vital loss if a girl's mother is away from home all day, leaving her after school hours to associates of whom the mother knowns nothing and who may be most questionable in their influence on her developing character.[80]

Thus, a mother's place was thought to be in the home to protect the vulnerable innocence of daughters.

If the lack of a proper domestic model was what was thought to have caused the problem, it made sense that rigorous domesticity functioned as part of the solution. Davis began imposing a middle-class model of white domesticity from the first meeting with new inmates where they were expected to join Davis for tea. The girls were reported to have been awed by the porcelain teacups, silver spoons, chocolates, and conversation of a proper tea, and Davis appeared to attribute the surprise to their previous poor training rather than class divisions.[81] Instead of high fences, Davis claims to have kept the inmates at Bedford Hills by creating a loving home for them that replaced their previous lack, although the absence of escapees may be more accurately attributed to the two hundred acre campus located in a rural area far from the city.[82] Indeed, in her investigation of Bedford Hills, Ida Tarbell reported that of 668 girls paroled "three hundred and ninety-three paroled girls were discharged after having 'done well.' Scores of these are happily married, or are earning sufficient incomes. To many of these Bedford is 'home.' They come back for vacation, for Christmas, for Fourth of July."[83] In other words, the model of a strong home based in middle-class standards of white domesticity was thought to create opportunities for social mobility, specifically marriage and middle-class domesticity.

While Davis foregrounded domesticity and promoted marriage as a possibility for redeemed girls, one study found that Davis was training women for servant positions to respond to a domestic servant shortage in the US.[84] Reform institutions across the country followed a similar script of attempting to uphold Victorian norms of purity and domesticity, while teaching women and girls "useful" skills that would presumably keep them from practicing prostitution.[85] Likewise, the Chicago Refuge for Girls boasted both grammar school and vocational and home training. The girls learned sewing, cooking, cleaning, rug-weaving, singing, and pottery in order to "prepare them to meet the every-day demands so that they can go back into the world better fitted for home duties."[86] Coulter House, also in Chicago, claimed to be a "place of transition for any young woman who

FIGURE 6. "Tending the Cows. A wholesome moral tonic." Image from Ida Tarbell, "What Shall We Do with the Young Prostitute? Reform Her or Neglect Her?," 1912. Courtesy of Rockefeller Archive Center.

wishes to return to the life of normal womanhood" and become "honestly self-supporting."[87] Coulter House reported that of the 166 women received between May 1912 and October 1913, there were twenty-nine white slave cases, but they also reported success in returning girls to relatives (sixty-seven) and finding jobs for women (seventy-one), and thirteen were married after coming to Coulter House. Marriage was clearly a goal for Coulter House, but most women ended up finding jobs that ranged from domestic work to stenography and employment in a department store.

Despite the rosy picture of reform, the quasi-scientific focus on redeemability was grounded in a language of racial absence. Rather than focus on the risk to the white and supposedly virtuous middle-class women, these Progressive Era reformers targeted individual women as the loci of reform. Each woman was thought to be judged based on their objective possibility for reform. The rhetoric of the reformers, however, obfuscated the ways in which the scientific approach was racialized. In New York's Bedford Hills, reform was available to those "who, in the eyes of magistrates, were capable of reformation, and by three years of training—less if possible—[reformers could] send them back to society, physically sound, morally controlled, and sufficiently skilled to be able to support themselves."[88] Ida Tarbell explained, "No woman who ever sat through a session of the Woman's Night Court in New York but has been horrified at the girls between sixteen and thirty among the crowds of repeaters, rounders, and moral imbeciles, whom she felt could be induced to lead respectable lives if they were given a fair opportunity."[89] These judgments of reformability were intimately connected to perceptions of race.

Even as Progressive Era reformers adopted a view of criminality that opened space for reform by focusing on the role of the environment, cultural expectations commonly linked Black women to immorality, filth, pathology, and impurity.[90] As Catherine Palczewski argues, "Given Black women were presumed 'always already sexual,' prostitute was synonymous with Black woman and Black woman with prostitute."[91] Nineteenth and early twentieth century norms of "respectability" and "sexual control" stood in opposition to promiscuity, and just as whiteness gained meaning through an absence of blackness, the mapping of promiscuity onto blackness, set the ideal of "good womanhood" outside of Black womanhood.[92] In some cases the mere presence of Black women in public space made them sexually suspect, leading to arrest on charges of prostitution.[93]

Given these cultural assumptions about Black women's sexuality, it is unsurprising that Black women were being arrested for prostitution in numbers far beyond what would be proportionate for the size of the population. While Black people constituted less than 2 percent of the New York City population, in 1915 about 19 percent of people arraigned for prostitution in New York tenements were Black.[94] Women's court arrest records were inconsistent in reporting race and nationality. However, among what was recorded, Black women accounted for about 15 percent of arrests from 1914 to 1915 and 55 percent of arrests from 1916 to 1917.[95] It is not possible to know what degree the differences in arrest records reflect the numbers of Black women involved in prostitution (given that Black Americans were shut out of many employment opportunities), a discrepancy in arrests of those involved in prostitution, or a tendency to arrest Black women who simply existed in public space.

The assumed deviant sexuality of Black women reinforced "Progressives' belief that blacks alone could not be redeemed from transgressive behavior."[96] The construction of Black women as abject was perhaps most apparent in the attention of reformers. In studies of prostitution, Black women were virtually ignored. For example, "practically no colored women were included among the [studies of] street cases and few in the institutions other than Bedford."[97] Black women's absence in social scientific studies of prostitution operated at the intersections of the social and material registers of research; when Black women were not seen, their place became naturalized and outside of the purview of white slavery reformers.

The abject construction of Black women persisted even when they were seen by reformers and deemed capable of change. Tarbell argued that those admitted to reform intuitions like Bedford were significant to understanding the intuition's success. She noted, "Obviously, what could be done depended largely upon the material received."[98] In the case of Bedford Hills, Davis reported that of 647 cases 62.75 percent were "American white," 13.14 percent were "American colored," and 24.11 percent were "foreign born."[99] Thus, although some Black women were considered reformable enough to be sentenced to institutions like Bedford Hills, a significant number of Black women were represented as not being made of the right material. By 1915, after Davis had moved from her position at Bedford Hills, an investigation blamed the racial mixing in the institution as the cause of its increasing problems, ignoring the massive overcrowding and lack of financial support.[100] Even when they were seen and included in reform efforts, Black women were framed as deviant and incapable of reform.

Social Mobility and Scientific Reform

For Progressive Era activists who embraced scientific reform as a solution to white slavery, social mobility was a solution to the plague of prostitution in American cities. These reformers were empowered by John D. Rockefeller Jr., one of the richest men in the country, who was determined to remove sentimentality from the white slavery controversy and, instead, be guided by supposedly objective facts. Science, however, is never neutral. Activists worked through rhetorical registers to frame white slavery as a problem of prostitution impacting women who were capable of reform. This capacity, however, was shaped by the interanimation of rhetorical and material registers. The women capable of reform were the women who were seen, but racist assumptions of Black women's sexuality precluded them from being seen as capable or worthy of reform. Movement into white, middle-class domesticity was framed as a solution to white slavery, in part, because Black women were deemed abject and not subject to reform; Black women could not corrupt white, middle-class domesticity because it was never available to them.

As the scientific approach to the white slavery controversy illustrates, social mobility is an important part of the mobile imagination. The rhetoric both reflected and participated in shaping perceptions of the appropriate path and mode of social mobility, as well as the destination. The possibility of social mobility was integral to the Progressive Era vision of reform and progress. This imagination opened the possibility that, given the correct resources and assistance, white women could be saved from prostitution, thereby addressing one of the great plagues of the American city. For these reformers, social mobility meant moving women into proper expressions of middle-class white womanhood, and while it appears that many of these women moved to domestic service, the rhetoric established an ideal success as marriage and motherhood. By situating this version of middle-class domesticity as the ideal of social mobility, Progressive Era reformers reinforced this vision of American white womanhood as central to national identity; the national ideal could only be achieved through an ideal womanhood rooted in middle-class white domesticity.

The means of achieving social mobility was just as significant as the destination. The reformers established who they imagined capable of social mobility and the path by which one became socially mobile. Specifically, they constructed a path through a supposedly scientific approach that was intended to teach the right women the right performance of domesticity. By using a scientific rhetoric to reinforce who was capable of reform and how they would get there, Progressive Era activists maintained tight control over the image of the American family and, thus, national identity writ large. If the path toward social mobility was dictated by science, only experts could lead wayward women on that path toward reform. Thus, the rhetoric of reform may have appeared neutral and egalitarian, opening possibilities for vast numbers of women trapped in prostitution, but the scientific rhetoric masked the control that reformers wielded to maintain a white, middle-class ideal of domesticity, while discarding women who were deemed unworthy of meeting those expectations. Even through the promise of reform, this mobile imagination functioned as a tool to maintain the white American social imaginary.

CHAPTER 4

A National Solution

PROTECTING WHITENESS THROUGH THE 1910 MANN ACT

When Representative Thetus Sims (D-TN) spoke before the US House of Representatives in January of 1910, he implored his colleagues to stop "raising up a bugaboo" about constitutionality and pass the White Slave Traffic Act. He argued, "And if we pass this bill and it becomes law, we will prevent, I hope forever, the taking away by fraud or violence from some doting mother or loving father, of some blue-eyed girl and immersing her in dens of infamy."[1] Sims was not alone in his concern about the nation's blue-eyed girls, and in 1910, Congress passed the White Slave Traffic Act, which came to be known as the Mann Act after the bill's sponsor, James Mann (R-IL).

Law does not simply create rules by which to live, but it also works to constitute community.[2] Far from existing as a static and objective truth, law entails contextualized meaning that evolves from construction to enforcement to judicial interpretation. In each of these stages, meaning derives from interaction between the text and the intertextual context, and that meaning works to constitute and materially enforce ways of being within community. It shapes the role of the law in public life, the possibilities and limitations of civic identity, as well as understandings of nation.

This chapter traces the congressional debate and federal enforcement of the 1910 White Slave Traffic Act. The law, which was significantly amended in 1986, proved to be deeply controversial. The legislation led to the development of the modern Federal Bureau of Investigation (FBI) and worked as a mechanism to enforce sexual mores. Much of the criticism of the Mann Act comes down to judicial interpretation that allowed the law to be applied to consensual sex. Indeed, David J. Langum argues that the law was a product of mass hysteria and "a classic example of repression imposed through a tyranny of the majority against a dissident minority, the greatest failing of a democratic state."[3] According the Langum, the law was misguided in that it attempted to address a problem that did not exist, but its greatest harm came from judicial extension of the law beyond white slavery. However, as I have argued in previous chapters, there was not a stable and accepted meaning of white slavery from which lawmakers could deviate. The problems with and implications of the Mann Act were far more complex.

In this chapter, I analyze congressional debates and patterns of enforcement through 1917 to uncover the ways in which the legislation both reflected and worked to constitute community. In particular, I focus on the parts of the Mann Act that applied to movement within the United States, rather than the immigration provisions of the law, which I address in the following chapter. I argue that the prevailing community constituted through the Mann Act was not about sexual prudishness, protecting innocent women, or expanding federal power. Rather, the rhetoric of the Mann Act worked to restrict Black people's mobility, constituting whiteness as integral to national identity.

A Federal Law

Edwin W. Sims, the Republican US district attorney in Chicago, was deeply influential in framing white slavery as a national crisis. He not only initiated high profile prosecutions in Chicago and provided public commentary on the crisis but also, as a friend of US Representative James R. Mann of Chicago, laid the groundwork for the White Slave Traffic Act.[4] As chairman of the House Committee on Interstate and Foreign Commerce, Mann was in a unique position to usher this legislation through Congress. While some reports suggest that Sims was the real author of the legislation, Mann insisted that the idea of using the interstate commerce clause as an enforcement mechanism was his own.[5] Nevertheless, Sims clearly had an important role in the development and passage of the legislation.

The White Slave Traffic Act became law on June 25, 1910, after receiving overwhelming congressional support and being signed by President William Howard Taft. The law, which received only superficial amendments during debate, had eight sections. Section 1 defined "interstate commerce" as "transportation from any State or Territory or the District of Columbia to any other State or Territory or the District of Columbia," and "foreign commerce" was defined to "include transportation from any State or Territory or the District of Columbia to any foreign country and from any foreign country to any State or Territory or the District of Columbia." While this language may appear to be "commonsense,"[6] it notably excluded the object of transportation. Thus, the definition of "interstate commerce" only included a definition of "interstate," without any indication of what "commerce" meant in the context of this legislation.

The meanings of and limitations to the commerce clause have been the focus of significant debate. According to Jack M. Balkin, eighteenth century meanings of "commerce" were akin to "intercourse," connoting social interaction, but more often scholars and courts tend to treat "commerce" as economic interaction.[7] In the Antebellum Era, courts upheld a fairly broad scope to the commerce clause, but Progressive Era courts consistently restricted federal authority to areas of trade and economy where states had no authority to regulate, constructing "police powers" as an inherent limitation to federal power under the commerce clause.[8] Later sections of the Mann Act defined the object of transportation as "women and girls," drawing on understandings of the commerce clause that permitted the regulation of interstate human movement, in addition to trade.

Section 2 established that any "person who shall knowingly transport or cause to be transported, or aid or assist in obtaining transportation for, or in transporting, in interstate or foreign commerce ... any woman or girl for the purpose of prostitution or debauchery, or for any other immoral purpose ... or to induce, entice, or compel her to give herself up" to prostitution, debauchery, or other immoral practices, shall be guilty of a felony. There are a few important parts to this section. First, the person who was guilty of a crime was not the "woman or girl" engaging in prostitution or debauchery, but it was the person who transported or caused the transportation of the woman or girl. The woman or girl was the object of transportation, while the person causing that transportation was the agent and, thus, subjected to punishment. Second, this section established an interesting relationship between time/space and criminality. The legislation did not criminalize prostitution or other illicit sex, but this failure is not because legislators believed that these actions were permissible. Rather, legislators criminalized mobility and acts that enabled mobility that could lead to illicit sex in the future.

Finally, the phrase "the purpose of prostitution or debauchery, or for any other immoral purpose" has been the focus of considerable debate. Langum argues that despite the seemingly broad nature of the language, the legislation was only intended to prohibit forcible sex trafficking, but it came to be applied broadly as a mechanism to regulate perceived sexual immorality.[9] While the eventual broad application of the law is irrefutable, the specific context of "prostitution, debauchery, and other immoral purposes" suggests that intent may not have been as unambitious as Langum claims. Prior to its inclusion in the White Slave Traffic Act, the phrase "immoral purposes" was included in the Immigration Act of 1907. The 1875 Page Act had already prohibited immigration from Asian countries for the purpose of prostitution, but Congress broadened the language in 1907 by prohibiting all women and girls coming to the United States for prostitution and other immoral purposes.

Perhaps not surprisingly, the United State Supreme Court was required to adjudicate the scope of "immoral purposes," which it did in *United States v. Bitty* in 1908. John Bitty was arrested after traveling to the United States from England with Violet Sterling. No one, however, accused Sterling of being a prostitute; rather, Bitty's arrest was based on the accusation that he intended to establish Sterling as his concubine. The question became: was concubinage one of the immoral purposes in the Immigration Act? The US Supreme Court employed *ejusdem generis* as an interpretive principle. Ariela R. Dubler argued:

> When a law refers to something specific—like "prostitution"—and then refers to a more general category—like "immoral purpose"—the general category should be construed to apply to things that are of the same type, or genus, as the specific term. The statutory provisions, in other words, did not apply to all forms of immoral behavior, only sexual immoralities, of which the prostitution was understood to be the prototype.[10]

The *Bitty* decision is significant because it occurred shortly before the White Slave Traffic Act was introduced to Congress, suggesting that Congress knew that this specific language in the legislation would not *only* prohibit trafficking for prostitution but also prohibit any trafficking that violated the social mores of sexual morality.

Section 3 of the Mann Act continued to use the language of prostitution, debauchery, and other immoral purposes, but it shifted the focus to persuasion, inducement, enticement, or coercion. The assumption in this section was that a woman may consent to travel because she has been tricked, and, thus, the section explicitly noted that enabling the transportation was illegal regardless of the woman's consent. Furthermore, this section limited the violation to travel on a common carrier, meaning that persuading a woman to travel by train would be illegal, but persuading her to drive or ride in a car would not be illegal. Section 4 was similar to section 3 except that it applied to any "woman or girl under the age of 18" and doubled the potential fine and jail time. Section 5 established the jurisdiction for prosecution of sections 2, 3, and 4 as being in the location of the violation or any location that the woman traveled from, through, or into while being transported.

Section 6 of the White Slave Traffic Act shifted the focus of the legislation to immigration, specifically prohibiting the "transportation in foreign commerce of alien women and girls for the purposes of prostitution and debauchery, and in pursuance" of US treaty obligations. This section established the commissioner-general of immigration as responsible for investigation and supervision of alien women and girls. This section also reintroduced a provision from the 1907 Immigration Act that required anyone harboring an alien woman for immoral purposes to report to the commissioner-general that they are doing so if it was within three years of the woman's arrival in the United States. Failure to report was made a federal crime while state law retained jurisdiction over houses of prostitution within a state. The version of this provision in the 1907 Immigration Act was decided as unconstitutional by the United State Supreme Court because it overstepped federal jurisdiction. However, the Mann Act situated this provision within a newly signed treaty, assuming jurisdiction under treaty obligations and eliminating the three-year time limitation for deportation. Sections 7 and 8 were largely perfunctory. Section 7 defined "territory" to include areas such as Alaska and the Panama Canal Zone, and it defined "person" to be both singular and plural, as well as including "corporations, companies, societies, and associations." Section 8 named the act as the "White-slave traffic Act."

Debating the Mann Act

As the previous chapters illustrate, by the time the Mann Act reached the floor of Congress in 1909, white slavery was a topic of national concern. Citizens across the country read about the plague of white slavery in newspapers, sensational books, and magazine publications. There had been high profile investigations and enforcement of state laws, and new voluntary associations were being created while others adapted their mission to address the perceived problem of white slavery in the United States. The authors of the act received assurances that they had presidential support prior to bringing it to the floor of Congress, but the proposed legislation proved to be somewhat controversial. The controversy, however, was not about the perceived harm of white slavery, but it was about preserving the whiteness of the nation.

Congressional Support for the Mann Act

In attempting to address white slavery, members of Congress implicitly constructed the meanings and significance of women in the nation. In his committee report, James Mann defined white slavery, explaining, "In short, the white-slave trade may be said to be the business of securing white women and girls and of selling them outright, or exploiting them for immoral purposes. Its victims are those women and girls who, if given a fair chance, would, in all human probability, have been good wives and mothers and useful citizens."[11] Within this definition, Mann connected good women's citizenship to whiteness, suggesting both that woman's role as citizen was to become a good wife and mother, as well as sustaining whiteness as central to the performance of good citizenship. In other words, Mann was not calling on Congress to protect all women and girls. Rather, he was explicit in the need to protect white women and girls because of their citizenship potential.

For the bill's supporters, civilized nations protect women's virtue and purity. For example, Representative Gordon J. Russell (D-TX) was met with applause when he proclaimed, "Let me tell you, gentlemen, no nation can rise higher than the estimate which it places upon the virtue and purity of its womanhood."[12] For Russell and many of the bill's supporters, virtue and purity were markers of white American womanhood, not necessarily womanhood in general. Lest people think that Russell was concerned about immigrants, he implored his fellow congressmen:

> Think of it, Mr. Speaker; think of it, gentlemen of this House of Representatives of the American people, 65,000 daughters of American homes each year conscripted into the great army of prostitutes. Think of the tears and the woe and the shame and the poverty and the disease caused by this infamous band of pimps and procurers, who are preying each year upon American womanhood and girlhood.[13]

The danger to white American women and girls was also mirrored in the bill's penalties; the maximum punishment for the transportation of an alien woman was $2,000 and two years in a penitentiary, while the maximum punishment for the transportation of an American woman was $5,000 and five years in a penitentiary.

Russell's commitment to protecting American whiteness is most clear when he extensively quoted the "remarkable citizen" and former representative of Georgia, Thomas Watson, to support his claim about the need to protect the nation's women. Russell's explicit attention to former representative Thomas Watson is notable because Watson was a well-known white supremacist. While much of the congressional debate drew on tropes of white supremacy, Watson's entry into the Congressional Record was an explicit evocation of white supremacist ideology.

Thomas E. Watson was born in 1856 to a slave-owning family in Georgia.[14] Although the family lost their wealth during the Civil War and Reconstruction, Watson was able to attend Mercer College, and he began his legal career in 1875. Watson entered politics in 1880, eventually being elected to the Georgia House, the US House of Representatives, and the US Senate. He ran for US vice president as a populist on the ticket with William Jennings Bryan, and he made two unsuccessful presidential runs on the People's Party ticket in 1904 and 1908.[15] Watson was also a prolific writer, authoring numerous books (including biographies of Jefferson and Napoleon) and publishing magazines (including *Tom Watson's Magazine*, *Weekly Jeffersonian*, and *Watson's Jeffersonian Magazine*). According to the nonprofit foundation named after Watson that currently manages his historic home, "Focusing on national issues, the Weekly Jeffersonian rivaled the Journal and Clark Howell's *Atlanta Constitution* for circulation and statewide influence [*sic*]."[16] Watson was clearly very well-known and influential, and although he is celebrated by some biographers for promoting racial equality, his writing includes very clear evidence of white supremacy.[17] That this legacy remains largely obfuscated suggests that Watson's ideology was deeply naturalized in American public culture.

While those in Congress implied an association between womanly virtue, whiteness, and civilization, Watson was explicit. He explained in one of his publications:

> Different from the white race in physical and mental structure, the negro differs even more radically in the matter of morals. The typical negro *has no conception of chastity*,—none whatever. The men do not have it, and the women are without it. Of *principles*, of virtue, they are wholly devoid. They think no more of the congress of the sexes than they do of the breeding of the beasts. To yield to a natural appetite of that kind is, to them, no more a vice than to eat when hungry and to drink when dry.... This lack of the sense of personal morality is one of the chief characteristics of the negro *now*! A HIDEOUS, OMINOUS, NATIONAL MENACE![18]

On the other hand, northern European races, Watson insisted, had always been more developed and civilized, which was evidenced by their supposed protection of women's virtue.[19] The pseudo-evolutionary rationale behind Watson's assertions had become widely accepted because they build on cultural assumptions that associated civilization with sexual restraint and whiteness with civilization. By extension, those advocating to prevent white slavery were literally concerned with whiteness because the restrained sexuality embodied by white women was thought to be endemic to a civilized nation. This logic suggested that white women in prostitution were necessarily unwilling and enslaved, while those of supposedly inferior races were hyper-sexual, less moral, and willing prostitutes.

For some congressional representatives, the sexual exploitation of white women was worse than their murder. Representative Sims argued, "Whenever I think of a beautiful girl taken from one state to another... and drugged, debauched, and ruined, instead of being murdered, which would be a mercy after such treatment, retain her there and sell her to any brute who will pay the price, I can not bring myself to vote against this bill or any similar measure."[20] Whiteness was implicit in Sims's characterization of the "beautiful girl," and, similarly, the "brute" was implicitly non-civilized and non-white. Representative Russell, quoting Watson, was more explicit in recounting an apparent instance of a Black Chicago man who "purchased" white women as "wives."[21] In many respects, this story was not nearly as horrific as many, but what made it notable enough to reach the Congressional Record was the threat of Black men's sexual access to white women. In other words, the real threat of white slavery was represented as a racialized threat. This supposed threat to white womanhood and, thus, nation functioned to naturalize Russell's admonishment to his colleagues that there was a clear dichotomy between supporters of the bill and whoremongers who "hate God" and would destroy the nation.[22]

Not only did the legislative debate represent white women as endangered but also it represented those women as objects of movement, rather than mobile citizens. Through situating the Mann Act in the commerce clause, it regulated mobility, not acts of prostitution. In an attempt to reinforce women's innocence and simultaneously regulate their mobility, advocates constituted women as objects to be moved. For example, Representative Sims argued:

> Now, what is the man procuring this woman for? ... To make money. To make merchandise of a human soul. Which is more evil, the deluded, deceived, imprisoned soul that is being carried from one State to another by that scoundrel or the scoundrel himself? The poor deluded female perhaps would not be able to make the trip were it not for the demon, in human form, who is furnishing the money to carry her there, to sell her soul and body into hell, in order that he may have a few more dollars to put in his unholy pocket.[23]

Sims depicted evil men as agents and innocent women as objects of commerce. In his account, women do not "travel," but instead they are "carried," suggesting that they did not have the ability to control their own movement. Furthermore, Sims framed the elements of women's movement through the language of commerce; men "procure" a woman and "sell her soul and body." In this representation, women were innocent objects that were traded by men. This shift in agency was also clear in the Immigration Commission

Report that recorded the "importing and placing" of women, situating the agent as the "importer" and the object as the innocent woman.[24]

Opposition to the Mann Act

Those who opposed the Mann Act were clear that they did not support white slavery. Rather, they expressed concern with federal power and the potential dangers of the bill for supposedly innocent white men. Both rationales for opposition were entrenched in assumptions of white supremacy. By 1910, appeals for state's rights were deeply intertwined with memories of Reconstruction, and innocent men were assumed to be white. States and families, on the other hand, were charged with protecting white women from the threat of Black men, protection that the Mann Act failed to provide.

Opponents of the bill expressed concern over federal power on two levels. First, some opponents made a distinction between federal power and police power, arguing that police power belonged to the states. For example, the report from the Committee on Interstate and Foreign Commerce included a minority comment that stated, "Congress can not in the exercise of police power punish citizens of the States for violating a federal statute made under the pretense of regulating morals with suppressing evils which in the strictest and most literal sense, along with the health, peace, and order, is an affair that belongs to the States."[25] The appeal to police powers appears to be a simple issue of definition: is the legislation an exercise of police power or federal power? However, the second level of this argument, connected the debate to values about the optimal limits to federal power, an issue deeply implicated in racial politics.

The legacy of enslavement and the US Civil War functioned as an undercurrent in the debate over white slavery. Representative William Richardson (D-AL) explained, "The farther we get removed from the great struggle of 1861 to 1865, men's minds are becoming clearer on that subject [of state's rights] and freer from passion."[26] Representative Charles Lafayette Bartlett (D-GA) was even more explicit in his warning:

> If by the pretense of regulating morals or preventing people from going from one State to another for the purpose of preventing immoral practices the commerce clause can be used in a case like this, then it is an elastic shield beneath whose protection you can hide in order to protect yourself from the

charge of violating the Constitution of the United States, and we will have here one great central government, and the confederated government composed of an indissoluble union of indestructible States which survived the greatest internecine war that ever bloodied the pages of history will be no more."[27]

Bartlett's opposition was not to white slavery laws, but it was an opposition to federal power; if the federal government attempted to regulate morality in the states, the union of the country would be at risk.

What were states attempting to protect through claiming jurisdiction over morals? Given the context, it is reasonable to assume that legislators were working to protect their right to engage in racial discrimination. In 1883, the US Supreme Court overturned the Civil Rights Act of 1875 by arguing that the law exceeded federal jurisdiction, and in the years leading up to 1910, racial discrimination and violence, including lynching, was becoming increasingly visible. It is likely that, in opposing the Mann Act, these legislators were attempting to protect their right to discriminate. Some of the opposition arguments support this conclusion. Bartlett, for example, cited *The United States v Gould*, a decision that overturned a law that would make illegal after 1808 the "harboring or buying of slaves brought into the United States illegally an offense, and the court held that Congress could not make such harboring or buying a crime."[28] Essentially, the federal government did not, under this case, have the authority to prohibit slavery. Richardson cited a more recent instance where the State of California passed laws that discriminated against Japanese schoolchildren. He explained, "It was found out that a treaty made by the President of the United States and Senate of the United States, while it is pronounced in the Constitution the prime law of the land, never has been so construed as to annul a law made by any State in the Union."[29] In other words, these legislators maintained that the federal government, through neither legislation nor treaty, had the right to prohibit racial discrimination in the states. If the Mann Act were to pass and the federal government had jurisdiction to regulate morality through interstate commerce, the federal government may have gained jurisdiction to address discrimination and racial violence.

Opponents of the Mann Act also challenged assumptions of women's innocence, and instead based their arguments on an assertion of white men's innocence. According to Representative Richardson, "When a bill like this becomes a law, if a man in a State gives a woman a drink of cold water or a crust of bread, under this bill he is under suspicion, and it may put him in the penitentiary for ten years, with a fine of $5,000."[30] In positioning women as objects that are transported, rather than mobile citizens, the Mann Act placed agency and, thus, criminal penalties on those who transport or aid in transportation. Richardson, however, suggested that innocent men's natural chivalry would place them at risk of prosecution. He continued in a speech a few days later, "Now, under the provisions of this Mann bill, when a man living in a residence in a State is held to be guilty when he buys for one of these women a railroad ticket, where does that lead to? Why, the engineer, the conductor, the train crew, are all amenable to that charge."[31] Richardson asserted that employees doing their jobs could be inadvertently guilty of a crime if they did not properly ascertain a woman's moral character. In both examples he cited, innocent men would be guilty of a crime by engaging in proper masculine behavior.

Some opponents of the act also expressed fear that innocent men could be duped by immoral women. Richardson implied that it would be foolhardy to place a white man's life in the hands of "one of these women," suggesting that trafficked women were in a separate category from good white women. Similarly, Senator Weldon Heyburn (R-ID) argued, "It would be intolerable that the person from whom they purchased a railroad ticket should inquire as to the morality or chastity of that person," framing the crime as the immorality in the mind of the women being transported, rather than the person doing the transporting.[32] Representative Edwin Y. Webb (D-NC) was explicit in stating that women were committing the crime in prostitution, and they needed to be prosecuted if the problem were to be addressed.[33] Taken together, these arguments assert white men's innocence, while implicitly challenging assumptions of women's innocence. The arguments about white women's innocence were grounded in racialized gender norms. Civilized men were thought to protect good women, but prostitutes, some of whom were non-white or having sex with non-white men, were necessarily outside of the category of good womanhood.

Enforcing the Mann Act

When adopted in 1910, the Mann Act did not include a specification about who should enforce the new law, and, thus, the newly formed Bureau of

Investigation assumed the mantle of enforcing the parts of the law related to interstate commerce. The bureau, which was later renamed the Federal Bureau of Investigation (FBI), began in 1908 when Theodore Roosevelt's attorney general created a small unit under the Department of Justice, despite congressional concerns about establishing a national police force, and the next year Taft's attorney general named the unit the Bureau of Investigation.[34] According to Langum, the "Mann Act began the transformation of the Justice Department's police bureau from a modest agency concerned with odds and ends of Federal law enforcement to a nationally recognized institution, with agents in every State and every large city."[35] The perceived need to protect white women from trafficking justified federal funding and a massive expansion of the national police force that was to become the FBI.

The growth of the bureau was spearheaded by Stanley W. Finch, who served as its first director until stepping down to become the bureau's Special Commissioner of the Suppression of the White Slave Traffic in 1912.[36] Finch's strategy involved developing networks of local contacts and placing local bureau officials in strategic locations. He sent circulars to postmasters, police officials, and railroad employees asking for help identifying suspected brothels and white slavery cases. In part based on responses to these circulars, Finch hired local white slavery officers in select cities. These local officers were typically non-trained community members who were hired on a part-time basis to census and monitor prostitutes, and, to do so, they were required to develop relationships with local brothels and police.[37] As Jessica Pliley explained, "Cloaked in their respectability, shielded by the legal authority, and ultimately shored up by federal authority represented by the White Slavery Division badge," local white slavery officers were expected to perform proper manhood by protecting women, resisting the temptations of the brothel, and exercising appropriate discretion.[38]

This unprecedented expansion in a federal investigative force was ostensibly for the purpose of stopping the plague of white slavery in the United States, but especially given the ambiguity of "immoral purposes" in the law, agents had vast discretion. Patterns of enforcement suggest that agents utilized the Mann Act to stop perceived threats to white innocence. The bureau was clear that it was not concerned with what it described as "trivial cases," which included common prostitution, adultery, and other consensual sex between adults.[39] Thus, the bureau invested significant time and resources in creating a comprehensive census of commercial prostitution, looking to identify innocent women lured into the sex trade. In a study of the census records of the White Slave Division during the time period when it operated as a distinct unit within the Bureau of Investigation, one analysis found that in less than two years agents registered about 31,700 different women as prostitutes and 90,000 changes of address.[40] The mobility of individual women practicing prostitution was important for providing some level of protection against exploitation; a woman could leave a brothel and work elsewhere if she was being mistreated, a threat that seemed to encourage humane treatment by brothel owners.[41] However, that level of mobility was perceived as a danger by many bureau agents and other officials. When women were assumed to be objects that were moved, that movement needed to be controlled in order to protect women. Thus, agents looked at each move with suspicion as they struggled to identify the innocent victim of trafficking among a highly mobile population of women involved in commercial prostitution.

Jack Johnson and Regulating Black People's Mobility

The United States has a long history of regulating Black people's mobility. Armond R. Towns identifies a "long-held White mastery over mobility maintained by controlling the movements of people of color of all genders, sexualities, and classes,"[42] and after emancipation, this control was often manifest in segregation laws that regulated how and where Black Americans could move through and exist within public space. In *Plessy v. Ferguson*, the US Supreme Court decided that racial segregation was acceptable in interstate transportation. This segregation was one mechanism of enforcing the color line, the metaphorical border of Black physical and social space that maintained racial separation in all spheres of life. However, after the turn of the century, the appeal of the personal automobile made physical and social mobility more difficult to contain, as Black Americans gained both transportation options and class status by owning cars.[43]

This color line worked to limit both physical and social mobility for Black Americans, and that line could be violently enforced through lynching. Although it is impossible to know the exact number of deaths that resulted from lynching, much less the impact that the threat of lynching had on the Black mobile imagination, there were over three thousand incidents of lynching Black Americans between 1880 and 1930.[44] As Ersula J. Ore argues, lynching is a way to mark civic belonging, reinforcing the "constitutive relationship between democracy and antiblack violence."[45] Furthermore, recent scholarship has determined that lynching occurred throughout the country, not only in the South, becoming somewhat pervasive well before the Progressive Era, and it was a mechanism of racial control for a variety populations, including people of Latin American, Asian, and Jewish descent.[46]

The perceived hypersexuality of Black men, as well as the sexual precarity of white women, came to be used as a common justification for lynching. The social imaginary posited Progressive Era white manliness as an epitome civilization, demanding a combination of strength and self-restraint, and Black men were assumed to be less advanced and incapable of self-restraint. According to Gail Bederman, "The horrors of the unfettered 'Negro rapist' demonstrated to American society what could happen if civilized manliness lost its cultural power. Without manly self-restraint, civilized men would be no better than these vicious savages."[47] While some objected to the brutality of lynching, many Americans appeared to uncritically accept the myth of the Black rapist, and the Mann Act offered a legal mechanism of regulating Black mobility and, thus, sexual threat.[48]

Although the vast majority of early prosecutions for Mann Act violations involved nonconsensual sex, the heavily publicized prosecution of heavyweight boxing champion Jack Johnson is a notable exception. In some ways, Johnson had developed a larger-than-life persona. He traveled both nationally and internationally, consorted with white women, opened a supposedly rowdy integrated bar in Chicago and wore ostentatious jewelry. Johnson appeared to be well aware of the color line as he consistently pushed its boundaries.[49] He became the subject of national attention during a fight with James J. Jeffries on July 4, 1910, when Jeffries came out of retirement in an attempt to defeat Johnson, leading many to label Jeffries as the "great white hope" or the "white man's hope." Indeed, one journalist was explicit that this match was not only about boxing, but it was about racial superiority writ large, noting, "It is now only a matter of hours before the absorbing question of whether a white man or a negro shall be supreme in the world of fisticuffs, which means in this stance the world at large, is answered."[50] After "Johnson's one-sided 15-round knockout victory," masses of white rioters emerged in cities across the country, angered by Jeffries defeat, resulting in about eighteen dead and hundreds injured.[51]

FIGURE 7. Jack Johnson, full-length portrait, 1910. Photographic postcard from Wagner and Caywood, Chicago, 1910. From the Library of Congress Prints and Photographs Division Washington, DC.

Johnson's defeat of the "great white hope" challenged the supremacy of white masculinity in terms of physical prowess, and that challenge to masculinity was furthered by Johnson's open sexual relationships with white women. In September of 1912, after less than two years of marriage, Johnson's white wife, Etta, killed herself with a gun in the couple's apartment above Johnson's bar. White newspaper reporting described her death as unsurprising after she was ostracized by both her white friends and Johnson's Black friends. The *Chicago Tribune* reported that Johnson had violently beaten his wife, and the paper depicted Johnson's grief as a false show while noting that the music and hum of the bar did not stop when Johnson left for the hospital.[52] Nevertheless, the *Chicago Defender* explained that Etta Johnson was loved by the boxer's friends and family, and they chronicled her struggles with mental illness.[53]

Shortly after his wife's death, Johnson once again became the focus of public scrutiny when Mrs. F. Cameron Falconet reported to police and newspapers that Johnson had her daughter, Lucille Cameron, and refused to release her.[54] White newspapers described the brutish pugilist as having a "hypnotic influence" over Cameron, the beautiful nineteen-year-old girl.[55] According to Falconet, when she requested to see her daughter, Johnson picked her up in a car and refused to allow her to see her daughter alone. Throughout the visit, he "leered," and before she left the apartment where Johnson was hiding Cameron, Johnson supposedly "taunted" Falconet, "See she sticks to me. And I could get you just as easy if I wanted you."[56] Falconet responded by having her daughter arrested on charges of disorderly conduct, and Cameron was refused bail because according to one newspaper, "The judge, fearing the young woman might leave town and possibly marry the negro pugilist, refused to reduce her bond or release her on her own recognizance."[57] According to these accounts, Johnson was conniving, evil, and manipulative. If the white papers were to be believed, any appearance of a consensual relationship was a result of manipulation, and the only way to protect the innocent white girl was to confine her to a jail or hospital.

The outcry against Johnson was swift, and it was often couched in concern over Johnson's performance of a Black masculinity that violated the color line. The Chicago city council debated a resolution to revoke Johnson's saloon license because one alderman insisted, "Johnson has brought burning shame to the fair name of Chicago." During the debate, another alderman reportedly stated, "Johnson will get you, if you don't watch out," reinforcing the narrative that Johnson was violent brute.[58] Newspapers reported a national outcry against Johnson that included threats of lynching that white newspapers consistently failed to repudiate. For example, "Sam Sparks, former state treasurer of Texas and president of a local trust company, today proposed that a delegation of 100 picked Texans charter a special train and go to Chicago and 'attend to Jack Johnson.'"[59] Booker T. Washington joined the chorus that condemned Johnson and said, "Chicago is now witnessing a good example of the result of educating a man to earn money without due attention having been given his mental and spiritual development."[60] Johnson violated the color line in the most dangerous way possible, having an open sexual relationship with a white woman. Thus, for many white Americans, Johnson needed to be disciplined and put back in his place. While lynching was one violent means of discipline, prosecutors were able to utilize the Mann Act to respond to Johnson's perceived transgressions.

Cameron's refusal to cooperate with police made successful prosecution unlikely, but investigators found Belle Schreiber, a white woman with whom Johnson had a sexual relationship years before. According to the *Chicago Tribune*, "The Schreiber woman had come under the bane of Johnson's golden smile. She had been thrown aside by him. Incidentally, it is alleged, he had beaten her."[61] Johnson and Schreiber's relationship was described as consensual, and having worked as a prostitute, Schreiber did not fit the model of sexually innocent white girl. Nevertheless, white newspaper reporters appeared to delight in Johnson's arrest that November. While he had been represented prior to his arrest as leering, brutish, violent, and arrogant, white newspapers portrayed Johnson as sobbing and pleading during his arrest. One reporter described, "As the handcuffs snapped around the pugilist's wrists, tears streamed from Johnson's eyes."[62] Reporters explained that two days in jail made previously confident and arrogant Johnson "meek and submissive."[63] After his indictment, Johnson requested to plead guilty and pay a fine, but that request was denied.[64] While Mann Act charges appeared to put Johnson in his place as defined by white racial codes, that adjustment was only temporary because, shortly after being released on bond, Johnson and Cameron married. The marriage thwarted attempts to prosecute Johnson for his relationship with Cameron while reinforcing the racialized threat because, with their marriage, Johnson had legal sexual access to a young white woman.

In 1913, Johnson went on trial for violating the Mann Act by sending Belle Schreiber money to travel to Chicago from Pittsburgh, and from the beginning of the trial, Johnson was represented as a violent menace to white women. The original indictment had eleven counts that included enabling Schreiber's transportation for illegal sexual intercourse, prostitution, debauchery, and crimes against nature. The judge eventually dismissed the charges related to debauchery and crimes against nature, but not before

FIGURE 8. Jack Johnson and Lucille Cameron, 1921. *New York World-Telegram and the Sun Newspaper* Photograph Collection. From the Library of Congress Prints and Photographs Division Washington, DC.

Assistant District Attorney Harry Parkin explained to the jury that Johnson had a history of traveling with white women (sometimes three at a time), beating them, placing them in houses of prostitution, participating in fixed boxing matches, and compelling women to engage in sexual activity that was "too obscene to mention."[65]

Belle Schrieber testified that she met Johnson while practicing prostitution at the infamous Everleigh Club in Chicago, and she maintained a relationship with Johnson, often traveling as Mrs. Johnson. When her relationship with Johnson ended (before the passage of the Mann Act), Schrieber had difficulty finding employment, and after being dismissed from a Pittsburgh house of prostitution, Schrieber contacted Johnson asking for help. She explained, "I didn't have any more friends. I lost all my friends, and he was the only one I could turn to. I suppose I regarded him as my friend, too. I thought it was due for him to see me through my trouble."[66] According to Schrieber, Johnson sent her $75 and told her to meet him in Chicago. Johnson admitted to sending the money but denied that he asked her to travel. The facts of the case came down to the question: On this specific date, did Johnson request that Schrieber travel to Chicago? Lacking specific evidence of such a request, it was Johnson's word against Schrieber's.

Despite the apparently narrow question, it was clear that the case was about much more than whether Johnson requested Schrieber to travel on that specific date. After a short period of deliberation, the jury found Johnson guilty on all counts. Johnson's attorneys appealed the decision on the grounds that the Mann Act was unconstitutional and there was not sufficient evidence for conviction. US attorney James H. Wilkerson responded:

> Marked leniency was shown by the trial judge in dealing with this defendant under circumstances of great aggravation. His parade around the country with this strumpet had been an open, brazen, defiant, bestial spectacle, offensive to public decency and destructive of every sense of public virtue. The fact that it was tolerated as long as it was reflects little credit on our civilization.[67]

Wilkerson's characterization of Schrieber as a strumpet reinforces that Johnson's prosecution was not about protecting Schrieber. Instead, Johnson needed to be punished because of a vague sense of public virtue, and the phrase "bestial spectacle" marked racial difference as the threat to civilization by drawing on language of racial hierarchy.

For prosecutors and many white Americans, the sexual possession of white women was an unforgivable transgression of the color line. In a public statement after Johnson's conviction in May 1913, Assistant District Attorney Harry Parkin was quoted:

> This verdict also will go around the world. It is a forerunner of laws to be passed in these United States which we may live to see—laws forbidding miscegenation. This negro, in the eyes of many, has been persecuted. Perhaps as an individual he was. But it was his misfortune to be the foremost example

of the evil in permitting the intermarriage of whites and black. Now he must bear the consequences.... Money and fame, such as it was, bought white women. One is a suicide, the others are pariahs. He has violated the law. Now it is his function to teach others the law must be respected.[68]

Although Johnson was ostensibly on trial for causing Belle Schreiber to cross state lines for sex and prostitution, the assistant district attorney made clear that his prosecution was a warning that Black men should stay in their place. For this transgression, Johnson was sentenced to one year and one day in the penitentiary and a $1000 fine.[69] Johnson fled the United States for about seven years before returning and serving his sentence.

Black activists recognized the racial motivations behind Johnson's prosecution. Following his arraignment in November 1912, Ida B. Wells-Barnett organized and presided over a "big mass meeting for Jack Johnson."[70] Those present at the meeting adopted the resolution: "Resolved: That we appeal to the public for the presumption of innocence which is every man's due, to the press for respite from this most harmful sensationism, and to the government officials to subordinate prejudice to principle and to try their indictments in the courts and not through the newspapers."[71] For these activists, the problem was not with the Mann Act but its application. Johnson noted, "I am not a slave and ... I have the right to choose who my mate shall be."[72] Despite the reversal of the slavery trope, many Black leaders condemned Johnson's immorality while challenging the racism in the law's enforcement. For example, Reverend D. P. Roberts told the *Defender* that if Johnson violated the law he should be prosecuted, but the law should also be used to protect Black women from moral contamination and exploitation.[73]

Mator McFerrin and Saving Black Girls

While the prosecution of Johnson brought the Mann Act into the national spotlight, there were clear patterns of prosecuting Black men while ignoring the misdeeds of white men who exploited Black women and girls.[74] Indeed, the *Defender* urged its readers on multiple occasions to report violations of the Mann Act in order to protect Black women.[75] There were massive variations in who was prosecuted under the Mann Act, as well as discrepancy in penalties after conviction—ranging from $50 fine to five years in a penitentiary.[76] This degree of variation reinforced cultural assumptions that Black women were hypersexual and promiscuous, while white women were generally innocent, capable of redemption, and needing protection. Cynthia M. Blair argues that the case of Mator McFerrin was symbolically important in challenging assumptions of white vulnerability and Black hypersexuality within the white slavery controversy. She argues, "Through a campaign in defense of one unfortunate girl, middle-class blacks leveled their gaze at the hypocrisy of white municipal authorities and reformers whose neglect of black girls and women imperiled the virtue of black womanhood."[77]

At the same time as Jack Johnson's arrest gained national attention, the *Defender* reported on what they called the "worst scandal in years," where orphaned (or abandoned) Mator McFerrin was found to be pregnant while residing in the tubercular ward of Cook County Hospital in Chicago.[78] Reports of McFerrin's age ranged from fifteen to seventeen, but she was consistently represented as young, innocent, and friendless. Thus, she was available to thirty-three-year-old Frank Chaplin, a white patient in the tubercular ward with McFerrin. The *Defender* not only publicized the case but also raised money for McFerrin, who they called the "little victim" and "unfortunate girl."[79] Even though the Mann Act did not apply to the McFerrin case, her innocence was consistently placed in opposition to the Jack Johnson case. The *Defender* described the women in Johnson's case as adults who had family support, but Chicago's *Broad Ax* took the comparison further, positioning McFerrin's innocence in opposition to the "absolute protection" of white women in the United States, "whether their characters are good or bad."[80] Indeed, the *Broad Ax* continued to insist that Black citizens of Chicago would support action against Jack Johnson if white Americans would "assist the Afro-Americans to prevent White gentlemen in the Southern states and other sections of the country; from outraging and debauching innocent young Colored girls and starting them on the road to shame and degradation."[81] The Black papers represented the white press's lack of attention to McFerrin's case as evidence of Black women and girls' expendability in the United States.

While Jack Johnson was being charged with white slavery, the Black press made explicit connections to the US legacy of enslavement and exploitation of Black women. Frank Chaplin pled guilty to bastardy in the McFerrin case, but the *Defender* described his court testimony as "abusive" and "suggestive," while McFerrin, a "mere child," was described as speaking in a "straightforward way."[82] The *Defender* attributed Chaplin's abuse of McFerrin to his being a "scoundrel suffering from the ravages of the 'white plague' [tuberculosis], brought on from his inheriting the blood of his vile and degenerate parents who thrust themselves upon their enslaved female servants and sold in cold blood their own offsprings for paltry sums of gold [sic]."[83] The paper linked McFerrin's abuse to the legacy of enslavement. Through a reversal of quasi-evolutionary assumptions of Black inferiority, the author posited Chaplin's moral failings as a direct inheritance from those who enslaved people of African descent, establishing a moral connection between the past and present, while also planting a suggestion of an inherent biological link that challenged white assumptions of Black inferiority.

This legacy of enslavement extended well beyond the McFerrin case. While Black men risked violence by appearing to glance at a white woman, newspapers included frequent accounts of how white men treated Black women and girls as "natural and lawful prey."[84] In addition to frequent coverage of white men who raped Black women and girls, the Black press marked the seduction and defilement of Black girls by white men as a rampant problem, particularly in the South.[85] The *Defender* argued that the Mann Act could offer a solution to this exploitation:

> But the United States government should prosecute white men who are importing colored women into the North from the South and buying homes for them, and living with them, it is said, in the summer; is this not a violation of the Mann Act? ... Revenge is sweet and the Mann Act affords the only hope for the saving of our girls from the whites who would use them for immoral purposes.[86]

Another author insisted that Black women should refuse to be concubines and demand marriage from white men, thereby preserving "the standard of womanhood."[87] Just as with white support for the Man Act, womanhood was abstracted in these solutions, placing women as representative of the purity of the race.

While much white slavery activism, especially among white activists and politicians, erased Black women, the Black press challenged the language of white slavery as a way to bring attention to Black women and girls. The *Broad Ax*, for example, reprinted an appeal calling for the term "female slave traffic." The author argued:

> For instance, take a Caucasian slave and a Negro slave in traffic, the one is as much harmful to the good wife and children, if her husband is inclined to be immoral, as the other, whether he is Caucasian or Negro. The noble and virtuous Caucasian women suffered much harm in days of Negro slavery from this very evil; thus we see the result of it to this very day. The body cannot be divided; if one part is decayed it will in time decay the other part.[88]

This appeal constructed cross-racial connections based on morality and the protection of women, while invoking temporal connections between traffic in Black women by using the term "Negro slave" to describe both twentieth-century sex trafficking and the US legacy of enslavement. Similarly, the *Defender* demanded concern for the "black slave" who worked at houses of prostitution as maids or played piano and "spread vice and disease among thousands of innocent girls and boys" through exposure and potential corruption.[89] Attempts to protect white women shifted risk to Black girls, and the language of "black slave" drew contrast between the treatment of white and Black women, while reminding Black readers of what was at risk when they allowed their daughters to take such jobs.

Rhetorical Stoppage and the Construction of Nation

There is no doubt that the Mann Act was a massive expansion of legal moral authority and came to be applied unevenly. Nevertheless, recognizing elements of judicial tyranny and oppressive moralism does not account for the racialization that was imbricated in the law. If, following James Boyd White, law constitutes community, the Mann Act constituted a community of moral whiteness through the mechanism of mobility and immobility.

Tim Cresswell argues that material mobility is often understood as marker of citizenship. In this sense, mobility is constructed as a "geographical indicator of *freedom*."[90] Furthermore, the mobility of citizenship is coproduced in relation to the immobility of the noncitizen; in the United States, citizens are supposed to have a right to mobility, but that right does not necessarily extend to noncitizens. However, the removal of mobility, stoppage, works as one way to mark incomplete citizenship. Lisa A. Flores defines "stoppage" as "both a phenomenon related to the forced immobility of bodies—literal and figurative—as it is also a rhetorical mode of racialization."[91] In a material sense, the federal law worked to limit the mobility of women for immoral purposes, stopping women who threatened to violate moral boundaries and the men who enabled that mobility. Stoppage, however, also functions rhetorically. Flores argues, "Rhetorical stoppage makes race partially through its affective intensities."[92] That is, stoppage is both deployed in ways that are racialized and is inflected with meaning in ways that racialize. Although these layers of meaning are inextricably intertwined, both warrant further development in the context of the Mann Act. As Jack Johnson's prosecution illustrates, the Mann Act was deployed as a means of stoppage against men of color. In terms of material movement, Johnson was prohibited from participating in the movement of white women, and, ultimately, his mobility was restricted through imprisonment. Johnson, however, attempted to express a more threatening mobility by crossing the color line, and the Mann Act worked to disciple that mobility.

Beyond the deployment of the Mann Act in ways that enforced racial boundaries, the rhetoric of stoppage in the Mann Act operated as a form of racialization. The stoppage of women's mobility in the Mann Act was consistently framed by its proponents as a stopping of white women through the affective lens of protection. While women's perceived precarity called for efforts to enclose them in the security of home; regardless of an individual woman's desire to be mobile, stoppage was an act of protection that constituted white women's civic identities through their protective enclosure. In other words, stoppage was used to mark some women as white and, thus, worthy of protection as future wives and mothers of the nation. As the Black press emphasized, this protective enclosure was not available to all women. James Mann was explicit in supporting this legislation that it was designed to protect white women who could be "good wives and mothers and useful citizens" if not for the white slave traffic. Those categories were inflected with race, and through the law's application, some women became racialized as white and, thus, potentially valuable citizens.

Some forms of stoppage had a negative valence. The Mann Act was used to mark some men as deviant or always at risk of deviance, specifically men who failed to conform with the American image of white Christian masculinity. This form of racialization situated white men as protectors against a racialized Other. Some opponents of the Mann Act feared that the law may conflate white protective men with deviant men, unjustly putting white men at risk for simply helping seemingly innocent women. Stoppage in the Mann Act was not simply about morality. Rather, it created a mechanism of racialization through perceptions of moral and immoral mobility, participating in constituting the whiteness of the nation.

CHAPTER 5

White Slavery and Yellow Peril

IMMIGRATION AND TRANSNATIONAL THREAT

In 1910, "double the entire fighting strength of the United States Army" landed on the shores of the United States.[1] The arrivals were not an invading military force but migrants, many of whom were interested in settling in the United States. By the turn of the century, immigration had entrenched itself as a pervasive public issue. As huge numbers of people entered the United States, Americans debated about who should be worthy of entering the country. Indeed, in the first decade of the twentieth century, about eight million immigrants were thought to have entered the United States.[2] Many came from European countries, and, by the turn of the century, most recorded immigration was from Eastern Europe.[3] However, immigration from Asian countries had increased dramatically. Mary Clark Barnes and Lemuel Call Barnes described new trends in immigration noting, "Asiatic elements are much larger than most people think. In the year ending June 30, 1912, more than twenty-one thousand people from Asia landed in the United States." They somewhat ominously concluded, "The Orient is here."[4]

Especially after emancipation in the United States, China was perceived to be a source of cheap and easily exploitable labor, and, therefore, Chinese immigration to the United States was initially encouraged.[5] Large numbers of Chinese migrants arrived on the West Coast of the United States, and many worked in mining and other manual labor. However, the welcoming of immigration from Asia was short lived, and by the 1870s, anti-Chinese sentiment was on the rise, especially in California. Many critics of immigration framed Asian migrants as a unique threat. These critics accused Chinese men of bringing "drug use, prostitution, and gang activity" to the United States, while Chinese women were often assumed to be prostitutes and thought to cause "moral and racial pollution."[6] Following the Chinese Exclusion Act of 1882, other Asian immigrant populations, such as Japanese citizens, began to immigrate to the United States in increasing numbers, and many of the same concerns about Chinese immigrants were transferred to other Asian immigrant groups. Some public figures identified clear differences between migrants from different countries, noting, for example, that Japanese immigrants were supposedly more civilized than immigrants from China.[7] However, opponents of immigration tended to be less nuanced. There were many instances where opposition to Asian immigration escalated to violence against people of Asian descent and communities with large immigrant populations.

Immigration opponents tied the white slavery controversy to fears over immigration as foreign men, especially those from Asia, were thought to enslave women. This concern led some activists to warn against the danger of entrapped Asian women in the United States, which they called "yellow slaves." While Asian women were posited as endangered, the largest threat to Americans was represented as the moral contamination and physical risk to white womanhood through Asian men supposedly sustaining white slavery. The Orient, Edward W. Said argued, has a long history of being figured against the West.[8] The supposed civilization and moral superiority of the West gained meaning through its opposition to the Orient, and, thus, the danger of sexual deviance, such as sex slavery and polygamy, was often described by westerners through associations with the Orient. In other words, part of the way that Americans were to know that polygamy in the United States was immoral and dangerous was by associating it with assumed practices in Asian countries. Within this context, Asian immigration was not simply a problem of surplus labor, but it was a spatial problem where immorality and barbarism were thought to be invading an otherwise civilized country. The Orient was imagined to be moving into America, and spatial folds threated the neat dichotomy between the civilized West and the heathen Orient.

To illustrate the imagined movement of space, I consider the relationship between the white slavery controversy and Asian immigration through perceptions of Chinese slavery, marriage fraud, and the supposed enslavement of white women in American Chinatowns.

Immigration is not only an expression of material mobility, but it is also rooted in the imagined possibilities of movement and the cultural meanings of those possibilities. The controversy over white slavery, yellow slavery, and immigration functioned to remove the imaginative possibilities of Asian women's mobility. Not only were women from Asia typically prohibited from immigrating to the United States, but the rhetoric explicitly removed immigration to the United States as a legitimate possibility. It removed the imagined possibly for a "good" type of immigration for Asian women. In doing so, Asian men in the United States were not future citizens, but, instead, were deemed transient workers and potential contaminants who were both disposable and dangerous. Rhetoric of the white slavery controversy attempted to flatten the folds that brought Asian immigrations into American space.

Federalization of Immigration and Protection of the Border

As the nineteenth century expansion of the United States illustrates, national borders are not stable, and as Americans were grappling with the meanings of immigration, they were also attempting to understand the meanings of the national border. Anssi Paasi argues, "Rather than neutral lines, borders are often pools of emotions, fears and memories that can be mobilized apace for both progressive and regressive purposes."[9] Rhetorical research on borders has established that national boundaries are critical sites that shape not only national space but also national identity.[10] As Lisa A. Flores has argued, rhetoric influences meanings of the border and implicitly constructs meanings of good citizenship, and that construction is often racialized such that the border functions as a means of protecting the nation from racialized threats.[11]

At the end of the nineteenth century, Americans wrestled with two competing understandings of the border: porous borders and secure borders. For much of the nation's history, there were not federal immigration laws, and the United States had a fairly open border and greater acceptance of porous-border ideologies. However, it is an oversimplification to think that the United States simply had porous borders and then moved to secure borders. Rather, there was an ongoing deliberation about the role of the border in national identity.

A porous border ideology accepts that immigrants will come into the nation, and many immigrants come for good reasons. This does not entail an absence of xenophobia, but the ideology tends to accept immigration as an immutable reality that comes with opportunities and challenges.[12] Therefore, a significant debate occurred about the responsibilities to the immigrant for safety and Americanization. For example, in her recommendations to the Immigration Commission, Frances A. Kellor, the general director of the Inter-Municipal Research Committee of New York, argued, "The duty of the general Government, while necessarily somewhat limited, covers the supervision and protection of the arriving aliens up to the actual time of their settlement within a State and then the duty of that particular State commences with respect to such citizens in embryo."[13] Kellor insisted that the government had a duty to immigrants, in part, because, if given the appropriate resources, immigrants would become true Americans.

Even within the porous-border ideology (or sometimes central to expressions of that ideology), some activists and politicians assumed that there was a definitive American identity, and social workers, activists, or the state had an obligation to move the immigrant from their previous identities to fully American. Theodore Roosevelt, for example, praised some groups of immigrants as having the potential to enrich the United States, but that potential necessitated full assimilation. Roosevelt specifically chastised German Americans for hyphenating their allegiance, which symbolized a failure of full American assimilation.[14] Of course, not all immigrants had access to this American identity because it was imbued with whiteness. Thus, even some activists with porous-border tendencies questioned immigration from Asia because of assumptions that Asian immigrants could never assimilate. As KC Councilor notes, metaphors of digestibility were prominent in the Progressive Era United States.[15] Rather than restrict or accept all immigrants, these activists sought immigrants that could be effectively digested into the American polity.

In opposition to porous borders, a secure-border ideology represents the border as security from those on the outside. Karma R. Chávez explains that those represented as threats to the national family are considered strangers, and borders work to unify the polity against strangers.[16] In doing so, this type of border rhetoric can work to constitute a sense of national identity through opposition to an outside threat.[17] That delineation is bound up in racialized logics of belonging, logics that continue to be articulated through metaphors of contamination, pollution, and threat.[18] Within this framework, the problem of immigration is often defined as one of leakiness of the border.[19] While the United States has definitively embraced a secure-border ideology in the twenty-first century, this way of conceptualizing the border has a long history. Between 1835 and 1860, groups calling themselves "Native Americans" (or "Nativists") and "Know-Nothings" gained national recognition in their opposition to immigration, particularly Catholic immigration.[20] By the turn of the century, immigration law and enforcement focused on protecting the United States from the contamination of immorality. Immigration officials exercised mechanisms to protect the United States from corruption, restricting immigration and enabling deportation, and while immigration restrictions defined the parameters of who was believed to be worthy of entering the country, deportation was a mechanism of enforcement to regulate the behavior of immigrants.

The immense possibility of immigration, for many, threatened to irrevocably shape the character of the nation. Theories of Darwinism had become influential in the United States, positing that some races were superior because they reflected different states of human evolution. Not only could immigrants bring crime and harmful practices to the United States, but some feared that they could contaminate future generations with racial inferiority.[21] Even those who saw value in porous borders may have accepted Darwinist beliefs, and some advocated eugenics as a means of ensuring national progress. For example, according to Prescott F. Hall:

> Although the value of artificial selection in breeding animals, and producing seedless fruits and new grains—in fact in nearly every department of life—is now generally recognized; and although some advanced persons talk of regulating marriage with a view to the elimination of the unfit *for other purposes than mere survival*; yet most people fail to realize that in the United States, through our power to regulate immigration, we have a unique opportunity exercise artificial selection on an enormous scale.[22]

Thus, it is not surprising that the earliest immigration laws in the United States were explicitly racialized, and even though future immigration legislation retained an appearance of race neutrality, they were grounded in racialized logics that would become apparent in enforcement practices.

Immigration Law

Prior to 1875, the US federal government had little involvement with immigration, and states like New York, California, and Louisiana had their own immigration laws.[23] However, widespread concern about immigration, as well as an 1876 US Supreme Court decision, motivated federal control over immigration. While the first general immigration law did not pass through Congress until 1882, the Page Act, often considered the first federal restrictive immigration legislation, was adopted in 1875.[24] This law prohibited the importation of prostitutes and "coolie" laborers from East Asian countries (although it primarily targeted Chinese immigration), and it required women from East Asian countries to obtain certification that proved that they were not immigrating for "lewd or immoral purposes."[25] The implication was almost complete exclusion of Chinese women from the United States, despite a treaty with China that affirmed a right to voluntary migration.[26]

In 1882, the United States passed the Chinese Exclusion Act, which dramatically restricted Chinese immigration by prohibiting all but a few categories of migrants, such as students and merchants. The act deliberately excluded Chinese laborers, and it had the effect of further restricting the immigration of Chinese women to the United States because few Chinese women fit within the allowed classes.[27] Although wives and children were eventually allowed to join permitted Chinese immigrants, women were required to prove that they were indeed legitimate wives, and the status of husbands were conferred on their wives, which meant that the wives of laborers already in the United States were not permitted to join their husbands. The Geary Act extended the Chinese Exclusion Act and created a precursor to the federal passport system.[28] In 1902, the Chinese Exclusion Act was extended, and it was made permanent in 1904.[29] The United States entered into a "gentlemen's agreement" with Japan in 1908 to enact similar restrictions without an exclusion law.[30]

In 1882, Congress also adopted the first general immigration law that taxed immigrants entering the United States and prohibited some classes of immigrant, such as convicts, "idiots," and those likely to become a public charge.[31] This law was amended in 1891 to exclude additional classes of immigrants, such as polygamists, and it created the office of Superintendent of Immigration, which became the Bureau of Immigration of Naturalization in 1906.[32] In response to demands for additional action on immigration, Congress passed the Immigration Law of 1907. This law added "women or girls coming into the United States for the purpose of prostitution, or for any other immoral purpose" to the list of restricted migrants, and immigration inspectors were permitted to deport women who engaged in prostitution or immoral activity within three years of entering the United States. The 1910 Mann Act built off the 1907 language, adding a prohibition on importing that class of women and lifting the three-year time limit to deportation.

Immigration Enforcement

To enforce immigration laws, immigration inspectors were stationed at the borders and in strategic locations across the country. They were permitted to refuse entry to immigrants who were not permitted into the United States, and they were also tasked with identifying and deporting immigrants who violated laws while in the United States. A 1909 confidential circular explained, "It is desired that this active and stringent enforcement of the immigration laws with regard to the 'white slave' trade, be given every precedence in the work of your office over less important matters, and that every effort be exerted to make the Bureau's activity in this respect of the greatest possible effect."[33] White slavery was well established as a national concern in 1909, but the connection to immigration was buoyed by the official investigation of Special Immigrant Inspector Marcus Braun.

Marcus Braun migrated to the United States in 1892 from Hungary.[34] In the United States, he became a journalist and eventually ran his own newspapers in both English and German languages. By 1898, Braun was a stringent supporter of Republican Theodore Roosevelt and helped organize support for Roosevelt, especially among New York's Hungarian community. After Roosevelt's election to US president in 1900, Braun appealed to Roosevelt for a job. Braun turned down Roosevelt's initial offer of Ellis Island immigration inspector because he felt that the pay was too low, and Roosevelt eventually responded by appointing Braun Special Inspector for Immigration.[35] Braun received considerable attention for his early work at the Immigration Bureau when he claimed to have identified fraud and labor trafficking in European immigration to the United States. In 1908, Braun was tasked with investigating the white slave traffic in the United States and its relation to immigration.[36]

Over several months, Braun traveled the United States investigating foreign-born women who were thought to practice prostitution, and he insisted on the significance of white slavery as a focus for the Immigration Bureau by comparing it to the bureau's enforcement of the Chinese Exclusion Act. He explained, "What is the clandestine importation of a few hundred Chinese or Japanese, or a gang of men under contract to perform certain labor, or of some people with one or another ailment, in comparison to the importation of Daughters of Eve, the sex of Mother, Wife, Daughter, Sister for the purpose of Prostitution? Why to me, it seems to be absolutely insignificant."[37] According to Braun's "conservative estimate," there were over fifty thousand foreign-born prostitutes in the United States and ten thousand pimps and procurers.[38] However, because of the three-year limitation for deportation at the time and a lack of official immigration records, it was difficult to determine how many of those were in the country illegally, and, according to Braun, the well-organized networks of pimps and procurers made capture very difficult. Braun also made some sweeping claims about migrant women in his report. He asserted that most immigrant women were prostitutes, a majority of alien prostitutes in the United States were French or Belgians and Russian or Polish Jewish women, and 90 percent of Japanese women in the United States were prostitutes.[39] In other words, most immigrant women were suspect, at least to some extent.

Because all migrant women were suspected of prostitution, immigration inspectors were tasked with interviewing women attempting to enter the United States and preventing the entry of prostitutes and supposedly immoral women. While immigration officers shared photographs of known prostitutes and procurers that could be used to identity and prevent entry into the United States, immigration inspectors had to primarily rely on surface impressions and interviews with women. The interviews with women were often invasive and aggressive such that some inspectors were reprimanded by higher-up officials. For example, Commissioner John Clark reprimanded US inspectors in Winnipeg for asking one woman sixteen similar questions that included, "You are a prostitute yourself, are you?"; "Just after your husband left, didn't you practice prostitution?"; "You will admit that you are a prostitute?"; "You are absolutely decent, decent in a every way?"[40] In a letter the following day, the commissioner continued to explain to the officers in Canada that he wanted the law to be "thoroughly enforced" but was concerned by the excess of "zeal" shown by some officers in questioning women.[41] The commissioner advised that women should not be questioned about sexual matters without evidence, but evidence could include suspicious appearance or actions.[42] Presumably, immigration officials could discern immoral women by their clothing and behavior.

Immigration inspectors had vast discretion in determining who they would question and the aggressiveness of the questioning. While officials in Canada, who processed primarily white, European immigrants, were admonished for being too forceful, aggressive questioning and long detention was the norm for women immigrating from Asian countries to the west coast. In 1910, an expansive immigrant detention facility opened on Angel Island off the coast of San Francisco. About 70 percent of arrivals were detained at Angel Island, and, according to Erika Lee and Judy Yung, "Of the 300,000 detainees ... there were [about] 100,000 Chinese, 85,000 Japanese, 8,000 South Asians, 8,000 Russians and Jews, 1,000 Koreans, 1,000 Filipinos, and 400 Mexicans."[43] Race, gender, ethnicity, and international relations shaped decisions to detain, the nature of questioning, the length of detainment, and the conditions of detention. In particular, Asian women could be subject to months of interrogation even if they provided copious documentation and hired legal representation.[44]

The second responsibility of immigration officers was identifying immigrants who were in the country illegally and arranging for their deportation. As Flores argues, deportability is "a global practice of regulation and surveillance that produces climates of vulnerability and exploitability," marking some as never fully belonging and always needing to prove their worth.[45] By 1909, immigration officers across the country were given special duty assignments to identify and deport "alien immoral women," as well as supporting the prosecution of those who procured and harbored such women. The Bureau of Immigration and Naturalization called for simultaneous "zealous, unflagging efforts" to address the white slave trade in the United States, and although the deportation of prostitutes was an important part of the immigration officer's job, they were to be especially attentive to the "apprehension and punishment of those who do the importing and harboring."[46] Prior to the Mann Act, these immigration officials had a nearly impossible task of determining if a prostitute arrived in the United States within the last three years, thus making them eligible for deportation. Marcus Braun argued that the prostitute should have the burden to prove that they had arrived more than three years prior, but the lack of official paperwork made enforcement challenging.[47]

The 1910 Mann Act removed the three-year limit to deportations, making all migrant women at risk of deportation if they engaged in behavior perceived to be immoral. Immigration inspector Daniel Leonard explained that authorities could determine which prostitutes were not citizens, and therefore subject to deportation, by their "broken English."[48] However, the threat of deportation could be wielded against all immigrant women. For example, on December 31, 1909, the Bureau of Immigration and Naturalization issued an arrest warrant for Paraskowja Posouch (also known as Pauline Postach) on charges of prostitution.[49] Posouch had given birth to a child out of wedlock after arriving in the United States, but the question for immigration investigators was if she was immoral enough to be deported or if she was seduced with a promise of marriage. During the investigation, Posouch and her attorneys provided evidence that Posouch was moral and steadily employed as a laundress or domestic since arriving in New York. She explained that she entered into a relationship with Foma Sicka and became pregnant after promises of marriage. When Sicka then refused to marry her, she had him arrested on charges of bastardy to compel him to support the child.[50] After several weeks of investigation, the Bureau of Immigration and Naturalization concluded that Sicka charged Posouch with prostitution for retaliation and in an attempt to avoid supporting the child. As a single immigrant woman in New York, Posouch was already vulnerable, and she learned that upsetting the wrong man could not only damage her reputation and be physically dangerous but also lead to her deportation. However, official discretion was shaped by perceived connections between race and morality. While Posouch was given the benefit of the doubt, Juana Pares was not as fortunate. When she admitted to immigration officials that she had engaged in premarital sex as a teenager prior to attempting to immigrate from Mexico to the United States, she was denied entry, even though the immigration officials admitted that she was young and vulnerable at the time.[51] While both women engaged in similar behavior, Posouch's racial and ethnic background gave her access to moral womanhood in ways that Pares could not access.

Yellow Slavery and Asian Immigration

In the Progressive Era United States, there were strong connections between the national home and the familial home.[52] It was supposed that a strong nation was built on a specific understanding of manliness that necessitated support and protection of the heterosexual nuclear family. Becoming American necessitated assimilation into this image of manliness. Some critics argued that the differences between white Americans and Asian immigrants were simply too great, preventing Asian immigrants from assimilating into American culture. For example, "Altho [sic] these [Oriental] races may not be considered in any way inferior to ourselves, it is a fact that they are materially different: that they are not so easily assimilated as are members of the European races; that they do not readily marry with our people nor our people with them."[53] This author implied that assimilation was an unqualified good; a strong nation included unified people, and ideally that unified population would be white. Indeed, Professor Edward A. Steiner speculated that Americans conflated Asian immigrants with the "qualities and proportions of the Negro problem."[54] In other words, the problem with Asian immigrants was that they were not white, and the US Supreme Court formalized this perception when it decided in 1917 that people of Japanese descent were not white, regardless of the actual tone of their skin.[55] The racialization of Asian immigrants as non-white helped perpetuate the inscription of these migrants and their decedents as perpetual foreigners.[56]

Chinese Slavery

Prior to Chinese Exclusion in the United States, Chinese laborers were actively recruited as docile but hard workers who seemingly accepted exploitative working conditions. This assumption of Chinese labor was built from decades of global trafficking that included both willing migration, often through indenture, and unwilling migration, known as the coolie trade.[57] Indeed, some Southerners attempted to import Chinese labors in response to the abolition of enslavement following the Civil War.[58] While Chinese labor in California may have been initially encouraged, it was not long before significant anti-Chinese sentiment developed among the white population. A common concern was that Chinese labor took white

American jobs and pushed white workers into low-wage, exploitative working conditions in order to compete, a concern that was often represented as emasculating.[59] Frank Julian Warne, a critic of immigration, explained the significance of immigrants supplanting white American jobs, "In a democracy like ours it is impossible to dissociate the worker from the husband, the father, the citizen, the church member, and so on. . . . Thus higher wages to the worker means greater power to guard himself and family against poverty, to support a higher standard of living, and to secure larger opportunities to benefit from democratic institutions."[60] Warne represented an association between working, masculinity, and citizenship, and he framed immigration, especially from Asia, as a threat to white manliness and, thus, democracy.

The supposed Chinese threat was not isolated to labor. Chinese immigrants were remaining in the United States, settling in communities, and attempting to establish families (or reunite with families) in the United States. The immigration of women enabled the expansion of Chinese communities through procreation, and it created space for Chinese men to perform masculinity by residing with their families and serving as head of the family. Yet, US immigration law made it virtually impossible for Chinese women to immigrate to the United States, and the law, along with constructions of Chinese culture, figured nearly all Chinese women as enslaved. Claims of Chinese women's enslavement circularly reinforced perceptions of Chinese barbarity.

Politicians, moral reformers, and journalists tended to represent all Chinese women as existing in one of three categories of "yellow slaves:" prostitutes, wives, and girl servants. These categories were often collapsed together in the public imaginary into an image of the yellow slave.[61] Prostitution was thought to be endemic to Chinese migrants, and according to Mary and Lamuel Barnes:

> It is believed by those who are most fearful about them on the Pacific Coast that they introduce vices which are characteristic of their low standards of morality, and which draw not a few Occidentals into their vile currents. The "white slave traffic" is a somewhat metaphorical phrase, but the yellow slave traffic has been literal. It has been conducted on a large scale and with written bills of sale.[62]

Comments such as these represent two common assumptions: those of Asian descent were inherently immoral and the use of the term "slavery" in Asian prostitution was not an exaggeration of actual practice.

The supposed evils of Chinese slavery became well publicized during a 1901 California legislative inquiry into accusations of San Francisco police corruption. A federal inspector and translator explained that he had met and participated in the rescue of many Chinese prostitutes, noting, "They all tell the same unhappy story. Many have been lured from their homes and forced to lead lives of shame by their owner. They are brutally treated and intimidated. I have often seen signs displayed announcing girls for sale."[63] The *New York Times* vividly described the sale of Chinese prostitutes in San Francisco at public auction, "as publicly as if they were in Canton, where human slavery is a recognized institution." The paper continued to describe the auction, explaining how the girls "stood stolidly as if they were accustomed to such proceedings" and the auctioneer "enumerated their good points."[64] The description created a clear parallel to the memory of auctioning of enslaved people of African descent. This slavery of Chinese women, according to the *San Francisco Examiner*, was "flourishing under the very noses of the police," who accepted bribes to turn a blind eye.[65] Not only were most Chinese women assumed to be prostitutes, but missionary workers insisted that all prostitutes were enslaved. Miss Cameron from the Presbyterian Home lamented, "It does seem sinful that we have no law to save these poor girls from signing their own moral death warrant. Poor things!"[66] For this missionary worker, prostitution was a form a moral death, and Chinese women were incapable of deciding to practice prostitution. If a Chinese woman failed to attest to her enslavement, missionary workers framed that failure as evidence of the women's mental and moral subjugation.

Chinese wives were also frequently represented as enslaved. Critics assumed that marriage fraud was pervasive among Chinese immigrants, and writers shared frequent reports of Chinese women being tricked into coming to the United States for marriage and then being sold into prostitution. For example, an article in the *California Illustrated Magazine* supposedly included the testimony of a sixteen-year-old girl who explained that arranged marriages were common in China, so she believed that she was meeting her husband in California until she was forced into prostitution before escaping to the rescue mission.[67] Similarly, when Lee Kan was detained for prostitution in San Francisco, she explained that she came to the United States to marry Soo Hoo Lam Wong, but she quickly learned that he was already married. She explained to immigration officials that he and his mother forced her into prostitution and claimed her earnings, effectively ensuring that Lee Kan was trapped.[68] Stories such as these perpetuated the assumption that Chinese immigrants did not value marriage and that most Chinese marriages were ruses to import prostitutes, which was used as evidence of Chinese racial inferiority.

Critics also challenged cultural differences, using them to undermine some marriages and block women from entering the United States. While marriage norms vary across the world, for Americans a monogamous union with a male head of household was the only accepted form of legitimate marriage. However, Chinese cultural norms were different; some Chinese men had multiple, hierarchical wives or concubines. The United States did not recognize these marriages and classified these relationships as illicit. In order to protect against illicit sex, Chinese women were interrogated and had the burden to prove the legitimacy of their marriage. In San Francisco, immigrants were detained in a shed at the wharf prior to building the Angel Island Immigration Station in 1910, and these facilities allowed for longer detention of more immigrants. Questioning of Chinese women who were detained in Angel Island could last for several days and result in forty or fifty pages of testimony, but there are records of some women being detained for over a year.[69] Husbands and wives were typically questioned separately and were expected to have matching answers to esoteric questions about the husband's ancestral home that could include the number of chickens or the direction the house faced.[70]

Even if a woman was deemed to be a legal wife, Chinese wives were often represented as perpetual slaves. An article in the *San Francisco Chronicle* described the "slavery" of Chinese wives, explaining that all wives were owned, but, it continued, "If he has grown wealthy enough to live in good style he buys a small foot woman to add a distinguished air to his name and establishment."[71] By the twentieth century, Chinese women had unprecedented opportunities in the United States, and many were involved in their families' economic and social lives.[72] However, the popular imagination continued to represent Chinese women as isolated, trapped, and inherently different from their white counterparts.

The final category of "slaves" were servant girls. The 1901 California inquiry issued a final investigative report finding, "That Chinese women and Chinese girls (mere infants, frequently,) are bought and sold as chattels in Chinatown in violation of a vital principle of our national life—a condition of affairs that is a disgrace to the great State of California."[73] While the infantilization of prostitutes was common, people in some areas of China also practiced a type of selling of girls called *mui tsai*. This practice was often considered to be a type of charity where poor families would sell their daughters to work as domestic servants until they were old enough to be married. Judy Yung concludes that this practice was certainly abused, especially because *mui tsai* had no legal recourse if they were harmed or sold into prostitution, but it was also a commonly accepted form of charity that elevated the status of wives in both China and US Chinatowns.[74] However, Americans consistently associated the *mui tsai* system with prostitution. For example, missionary worker Mary Grace Charlton Edholm explained, "All little girls bought for illegal purposes in Chinatown are made to work and act as servants until old enough to be inmates of the [prostitution] dens."[75] Edholm makes explicit the comparison to the United States' legacy of enslavement, and, perhaps, that legacy was so bound with sexual exploitation that the *mui tsai* system was unintelligible, despite similar systems of adoption in the United States.

Picture Brides and Marriage Fraud

Americans valued marriage; it figured relations between both the members of a family and the family and the state. Marriage functioned as a mechanism of regulating womanhood while empowering men as representatives of the family. The figuration of marriage within the American civic imaginary was so important, in part, because "women's bodies functioned as symbolic containers of American values."[76] Thus, American public policy often worked to promote and protect an American concept of family and home. For example, in 1907, the US Supreme Court insisted that there was "both a national and international interest to [maintaining] marital unity."[77] In practice, however, the value of marital unity was deeply racialized.

The Supreme Court clarified in the *Bitty* decision that sex outside of marriage qualified as one of the immoral purposes that could be used to prohibit immigration. Marriage was the line between licit and illicit sex, and this "marriage cure," which made something otherwise illicit acceptable within the context of marriage, applied to a variety of areas of law, including rape and domestic violence.[78] Even while marriage could function as a cure for particular cases of illicit sex, immorality, especially in the context of immigration, was often perceived as a threat to marriage as an institution, leaving judges and immigration officials with the task of evaluating which marriages were legitimate (and therefore protecting the morality of the nation) and which marriages were illegitimate (and therefore endangering marriage and, thus, the nation). Marcus Braun amplified this threat when he reported that the easiest way for a prostitute to enter the United States was by traveling as the "wife" of an American citizen.[79] Thus, women had the burden to prove that their marriage was real, rather than the state having the burden to prove that the marriage was false.[80]

When Japanese immigration began to increase in the United States, the fear of illicit sex shifted to "picture brides." A picture bride was essentially a woman in an arranged marriage. The Japanese migrant in the United States would send their picture to someone in Japan who would then find a potential wife. If the man in the United States approved of that potential wife, they were officially married in Japan, and the woman traveled to the United States to join her husband and meet for the first time. Because the couple was married by Japanese law, the wife was allowed to enter the United States. The practice held danger for many Japanese women who arrived in the United States to find that their husband had provided an old picture, exaggerated his wealth, or was otherwise an undesirable husband.[81] Critics in the United States insisted that picture brides were not real wives because the marriage was arranged and occurred by proxy. Marcus Braun further asserted that picture brides were simply a way to disguise the entry of Japanese prostitutes, and he estimated that 90 percent of women who entered the United States as picture brides were prostitutes.[82]

Even for those who believed Japanese women to be moral, the practice of picture brides was a cause for concern. According to one author who supported Japanese immigration, the large increase in women after 1908 indicated a "greater tendency among Japanese to settle in this country."[83] Although the desire to settle in the United States could seem like a desire to assimilate and become American, it was common for those opposed to

Asian immigration to reframe US settlement as a threat. For example, a State of California report quoted Daniel J. Keefe, US commissioner general of Immigration, from a 1912 report:

> This practice [of picture brides] must necessarily result in constituting a large native-born Japanese population—persons who, because of their birth on American soil, will be regarded as American citizens, although their parents can not be naturalized, and who, nevertheless, will be considered (and will probably consider themselves) subjects of the Empire of Japan under the laws of that country, which holds that children born abroad of parents who are Japanese subjects are themselves subjects of the Japanese Empire.[84]

That report continued to explain, "No matter how many successive generations of American-born Japanese there may be, none of the children born in America are relieved of allegiance to Japan unless the parent has renounced allegiance to Japan *and had his renunciation accepted by the Japanese government.*"[85] The supposed inability to assimilate framed Asian immigrants as foreign invaders rather than embryonic citizens. For white immigrants, settling in the United States was a sign of assimilation, but for Japanese immigrants, settling in the United States was a sign of invasion.

There were few paths for women, especially women from Asia, to enter the United States. Gender norms and immigration laws made immigration difficult. The cultural narrative of marriage fraud made migration virtually impossible for Asian women. Nearly, every woman from Asia was marked as immoral, and she had to prove her morality to US officials and the general public. However, marriage was systematically removed as evidence of morality through claims that marriages were ruses designed to import women practicing prostitution or simply illegitimate unions designed to circumvent US immigration law. Without marriage as a path to immigration, Asian women had little access to the United States, effectively removing mobile possibilities for many women across the globe.

Chinatown and Geographies of Danger

Rhetorical borders do not always correspond to official national boundaries. Topography can be rhetorically folded and nested in ways that connect locations, shaping the mobile imagination and, thus, national identity. The supposed threat of Chinese immigration was often articulated spatially; white national space was being invaded by settlers of a different race. Chester H. Rowell, editor of the *Fresno Republican*, described the "yellow peril":

> The Pacific coast is the frontier of the white man's world, the culmination of the westward migration which is the white man's whole history. It will remain the frontier so long as we guard it as such; no longer. Unless it is maintained there, there is no other line at which it can be maintained without more effort than American government and American civilization are able to sustain.[86]

By invoking a sense of a geographic tipping point, this author posited nonwhite immigration to the United States as a threat to the entire country. For Rowell and others, migrants from Asia were an inherently different race than white Americans. A US Immigration Commission report explained that they were following the most commonly accepted scientific classification of races by dividing immigrants into one of five categories: "Caucasian, Ethiopian, Mongolian, Malay, and American, or, as familiarly called, the white, black, yellow, brown, and red races."[87] Immigration from China (and other Asian countries) threatened to shift the population of the United States from what was implied to be the most civilized race, thus putting the entire nation at risk.

By the turn of the century, Chinese migrants had spread across the country and began to settle in Chinatowns. However, San Francisco's Chinatown was the largest and most established and, thus, a target of anti-Asian sentiment. Perceptions of "stench, filth, crowding, and general dilapidation" became associated with San Francisco's Chinatown, and charges that Chinese were introducing foreign diseases helped fuel anti-Chinese attitudes that were used as evidence of inherent racial difference.[88] In arguing in support of Chinese Exclusion, Rev. William Rader argued, "Chinatown furnishes the best argument against Chinese immigration from the moral standpoint. Its odors and filth, its prostitution and slavery, its opium joints and gambling dens, its unsanitary conditions and atmosphere of secret sin—these convince the nostril, influence the eye and turn the stomach!"[89] The conflation of

FIGURE 9. "The Foreign Element in New York—The Chinese Colony, Mott Street. Drawn by W. Bengough.—[See Page 214]." Image from *Harper's Weekly*, February 29, 1896. From the Library of Congress Prints and Photographs Division Washington, DC.

material and moral cleanliness was common. Images of squalid living conditions often functioned as evidence for Chinese depravity, disregarding discriminatory housing policies and poor pay that pushed people into substandard living conditions.

The designation of a place as a Chinatown was a shifting designation to reflect where Chinese migrants were located in a city. The bodily presence of those migrants remade the space into a supposedly "self-contained and alien society" that, according to Nayan Shah, was used to justify "policing, investigations, and statistical surveys that 'scientifically' corroborated the racial classification."[90] A Chinatown was often constructed as separate and non-American. For example, Rowell of the *Fresno Republican* explained, "The Chinese live both by preference and by compulsion in 'Chinatown,' where they conduct their own affairs, independently of our laws and government, such as they do in China." He continued to described Chinatowns as "simply a miniature section of Canton."[91] In other words, Chinese migrants settled in the United States and created Chinese space that defied US national map space.

The racialized body remade the space, transforming the United States into part of China, and in turn, the space remade the body. The British activist Lady Somerset described her visit to New York's Chinatown, "I saw an American girl lying senseless in an opium den, surrounded by the heathen authors of her shame; herself, their fellow victim, in the toils of that relentless vice."[92] For Somerset and others, Chinatown had a corrupting influence on the surrounding areas, and it was especially dangerous for white women who could be trapped in vice, threatened with Chinese gang violence, drugged with opium, or moved outside of the reach of US law because they were in another world. In other words, Chinatowns threatened to make white women and girls into white slaves. Even the New York police commissioner argued, "Chinatown is a plague spot that ought not to be allowed to exist. It is a constant menace to the morals of the children of the neighborhood, and a cover for desperate criminals," even though he admitted that conflicts within Chinatown rarely spilled outside of its borders.[93] The very existence of Chinatown in New York was represented as a danger to the entire city, challenging perceived scales of transnational threat. There was, however, at least one woman who dedicated herself to protecting the United States from that supposed threat.

The Angel of Chinatown

In 1913, a "wonderful woman" began traveling the country to speak in support of woman suffrage.[94] Rose Livingston was unlike the typical suffrage speaker of the time because she spent most of her days and nights roaming New York's Chinatown in order to rescue "white slaves," earning her the title, Angel of Chinatown. A profile that was reprinted in newspapers across the country explained, "If you see a black-haired, black-eyed, rather sallow little woman, who looks about 30 and doesn't weigh over 100 pounds, her face quite free from paint and her clothes those of a poor dressmaker who aims to be comfortable instead of stylish in any detail, you can recognize Miss Livingston in Chinatown."[95] According to Livingston, her work to save white women and girls from forced prostitution made her a fierce advocate of woman suffrage and a popular suffrage speaker.

Livingston began a high-profile speaking tour in support of suffrage rights for women after being discovered by New York suffragists Harriet Burton Laidlaw and James Lee Laidlaw. One newspaper described Livingston as "a very petite woman, of strong character and purpose and the possessor of an indomitable will."[96] Still another insisted, "The grammar of Rose Livingston is not good and her manners are not polished, but the record of what she has done dignifies human nature and shows that the world is yet blessed with souls fiery for the right and counting it a privilege to give their lives, if it shall be necessary for others."[97] Audiences were riveted by stories of her own escape from white slavery in New York's Chinatown, and her ongoing mission of rescuing white girls despite persistent danger to herself.

Livingston was entering a suffrage movement that seemed to be regaining momentum after numerous stalled state referenda. In 1912, Oregon, Kansas, and Arizona adopted woman suffrage, and the 1913 Washington, DC, suffrage parade on the eve of Woodrow Wilson's inauguration revitalized the push for a constitutional amendment. Although there were exceptions, the suffrage movement remained dominated by upper-class white women, which was especially true of the principal national suffrage organization, the National American Woman Suffrage Association (NAWSA). The national organization and other branches of the movement had a long history of exclusion and ignoring the needs of working-class women and women of color, and the national organization had previously embraced a "Southern strategy" that emboldened racism in the movement to win Southern support. Thus, for some women in the suffrage movement, Rose Livingston appeared to be a novelty.

The New York suffragists, especially the Laidlaws, appear to have taken Livingston under their wing. James Laidlaw managed expenses for Livingston, and she was often described in correspondence as a "little girl." In reporting on Livingston's Ohio speaking tour, an Ohio suffragist commented, "Well dear little Rose has come and gone having stirred up the entire town and doing more practical good for suffrage than any one other speaker of whom I have known."[98] And, she did this good despite what the writer perceived as Livingston's lack of education and tendency toward hysteria. George Hugh Birney of Cleveland was impressed enough by Livingston to write a general recommendation for her as a speaker, but he cautioned, "Miss Livingston is little more than a mere child, in her intellectual development and is quite temperamental and therefore, should be closely supervised if she is to be used as a speaker for suffrage."[99]

Rose Livingston's background came under scrutiny when she publicly accused the New York police and mayor of accepting graft, being complicit in white slavery, and failing to protect Livingston as she did her work saving girls in Chinatown. In response to this attention, the mayor appeared to collect evidence that Livingston was a fraud, and he dismissed her accusations.[100] Before sending her on a woman suffrage speaking tour, James Laidlaw conducted his own investigation. He gathered testimonials from doctors, including the physician who helped Livingston recover from drug addiction, and missionaries, who testified to Livingston's good work.[101] Laidlaw became confident that Livingston was doing good work. Nevertheless, Livingston's background remained murky. The most widely circulated profile of Livingston explained that she came to New York from Wyoming six years prior, and she began rescue work after learning about the magnitude of the problem.[102] However, while speaking in Ohio, she claimed to have been kidnapped from rural Ohio at the age of ten, and "she remained the property of her first purchaser for nearly 15 years, guarded in a room by Chinamen, both day and night. She was rescued by the officers of the Home Missionary society and has since devoted her life to rescuing others."[103] This was the narrative that was promoted by suffrage activists.

A heavily circulated profile of Rose Livingston began:

Sometimes, but very rarely, there happens into the dead prose of modern life a figure clothed in chivalry and romance; and the figure many be so prosaic, the romance so common, that none know it through all the passing years. Such a figure has appeared in Chinatown, in New York. It is the figure of a modern Bayard; but a woman Bayard, without fear and without reproach. Her name is Rose Livingston. She will probably be murdered. But, so far, she lives, although often wounded. She is the woman who is fighting New York's police, procurers and thugs for the immortal souls of the city's young girls, innocent still or already ruined.[104]

In comparing Livingston to the legendary knight, the author posited her as a brave warrior who eschewed simple comforts in fighting for a higher purpose. Livingston's public persona as a fearless warrior and martyr became critical to her advocacy for suffrage, even while it naturalized Chinese barbarity.

Nearly every account of Rose Livingston in newspapers chronicled the injuries she received in attempts to rescue white girls in Chinatown. According to the *Brooklyn Eagle*, she has "been stabbed three times, arrested, shot at, had her jaw and arm broken and her hip dislocated by being thrown from a roof of a house during her experiences in the rescue of white slaves."[105] An account of one of her Ohio speeches included the explanation, "She spoke earnest but with evident difficulty which was doubtless due to the diseased condition of her throat and face, caused by a blow given her by a New York 'pimp,' thereby necessitating a recent operation when eight broken bones were removed."[106] Livingston often emphasized in her speeches that her work was such a threat to Chinatown prostitution that there was a price on her head and she was at constant physical risk.[107] Livingston had her sacrifice written on her body through persistent injuries, signaling that she would sacrifice her body for other women's souls.

The physical violence against Livingston, especially in the context of her small stature, both undermined the masculinity of the men who supposedly enslaved women and represented Livingston has a martyr. Norms of manhood posited men as having an obligation to protect women, but that obligation was inflected by race and class. While a prostitute or a Chinese woman may not have been represented as worthy of manly protection, Livingston was a petite, white, social worker, and a failure to protect her was a failure of manliness. Livingston's fearlessness in the face of violence and threats stood in contrast to the physical safety of men who refused to act, and, thus, her injuries were a sign of the failure of white manhood.

Throughout her speeches, Livingston framed her actions as those of a soldier. In a speech to the Labor Lyceum, she proclaimed, "I hope they will not kill me until the women of this State get the ballot that they may carry on the work that I have started and I regret that I have but one life to give for the children of my country."[108] In paraphrasing the supposed last words of a Revolutionary War hero, Livingston framed herself as a hero in a war of independence. Rather than fighting for the independence of a country, she was fighting for the independence of women and girls when she patrolled New York's Chinatown. Livingston told a reporter, "I am going to be killed I don't see how I can avoid it."[109] The recognition and acceptance of her death positioned Livingston as a martyr and a hero.

Livingston was direct that blame rested with white men, not the women in prostitution. For example, she asked:

> Can any of you men live on $3 a week? I have tried it and it is impossible, and it is that which has driven the girls to a life of prostitution. Many of the "cadets" have the protection of the police and they will not make arrests. This is not a thing to be treated lightly, for you men never know when it will touch your home. There are now 350 white girls in Chinatown and 6,000 girls were lost last year in the United States. The "cadets" have beaten me and broken my bones, but they have found that it does not scare me, so now they have put a price of $500 on my head, for they know they will have to kill me to get rid of me. I will have an American flag put on the coffin of a white slave, for, like the soldier, she has laid down her life, if not for her country directly, for the protection of our decent women.[110]

Within this meandering argument Livingston challenged the performance of white American masculinity. She began by refuting assumptions that women practicing prostitution were inherently immoral, and she did this by explaining poor wages as one of the factors that pushed women into prostitution. She prompted identification by explicitly telling white men that their daughters could face this same danger, which both humanized women practicing prostitution and made the threat present for the men in the audience. Then, she explained the danger to her life that came with doing rescue work, and while this may appear disjointed, it implied a question to the men in the audience: If Livingston were willing to risk her life to stop white slavery, why were men not willing to risk their lives to protect their daughters? In concluding with the image of the American flag on the casket of a white slave, Livingston alluded to the sacrifice that the US military made overseas, most recently in Central America and the Caribbean, while little was done to protect women at home. Livingston's framing posits the death of women practicing prostitution as a sacrifice that fulfilled an insatiable need for American white girls. Thus, white women were sacrificed in a war located in Chinatown, while she implied that white men failed in their duty to provide for and protect white women.

If this challenge to white manhood were not enough, Livingston was often direct in her expression of who was to blame. At a speech in the Metropolitan Temple she said, "Please don't put the blame on the Chinamen for the conditions. It's the white man, the cadet, the voter, who sells the girls to the Chinese."[111] Livingston appeared to naturalize the violence of Chinatown and the supposed barbarity of Chinese men. Chinatown was a place apart and a site of danger, and Livingston blamed white men for failing to fulfil their obligations to protect white women from that danger. The only way to keep white women safe from Chinatown was suffrage, and men were failing once again by refusing to adopt woman suffrage.

Chinatown and the Racial Imperative for Suffrage

For Progressive Era activists, Chinatowns were not simply neighborhoods within a larger city. They were represented as a transnational threat—a folding of space that brought China into the heart of the United States. These racial geographies were inscribed with gender. The threat of Chinatown was represented as a moral threat that could disrupt the fundamental national character, and nothing better represented this supposed moral national character more than white womanhood. White womanhood was used as a container for national virtue, making the threat of Chinatown a danger to the nation as a whole. Through Rose Livingston, suffrage activists harnessed the perceived threat of Chinatown, insisting that men failed in their duty to provide for and protect women. Only through suffrage rights could white womanhood be safe from the danger of Chinatown.

A critical examination of the white slavery rhetoric of the woman suffrage movement points to the significance of a transnational optic in the analysis of US national social movements. As American women attempted to reposition themselves in the US national imaginary, their civic identities became interwoven into a folding of transnational space. Women's coverture, the legal principle that placed women under the cover of male head of household and, thereby, justified limited legal and political rights necessitated a neat spatial division of the world.[112] Like concentric circles, if home was nested within the nation and the nation nested within the larger world geography, women could be safely protected (and covered) within the home. The racial geography of Chinatown disrupted this neat organization. Women could no longer be protected if China was folded into the nation and creeping into the American home.

Just as the male solider was tasked with protecting the external national borders, Rose Livingston worked to frame her role as a soldier for the nation's morality. She assumed the identity of full citizen through sacrifice for her country. This framing of women's identity was prescient because as the United States entered the First World War, transnational space became folded in ways that had a dramatic effect on the nation. In finally agreeing to support woman suffrage, Woodrow Wilson spoke of suffrage as a war measure that reflected women's vital service.[113] The folding of transnational space meant that the geographic imagination of coverture was untenable.

Rose Livingston continued her work in New York's Chinatown, although there were tensions between Livingston and some other activists. Livingston appeared to drift away from the Laidlaws, and in 1926 Harriet Laidlaw wrote a diplomatic letter explaining, "As a Director of such Organizations as the American Social Hygiene and the Florence Crittenden League, and as one who is anxious to see such cases go through the hands of such organizations, I nevertheless do realize that Rose Livingston's work has its place and I know that the money that she raises is used to good advantage."[114] Livingston remained active with her rescue work into her seventies.[115] In 1929, after receiving a gold medal from the National Institute of Social Sciences, Livingston, who was "visibly touched," said, "I never expected recognition in my lifetime. . . . I had only hoped to receive my reward when I was called to rest. . . . [This] medal is not given to me, it is given to God."[116]

We do not know if Rose Livingston exaggerated her background, if she "saved" as many girls as she claimed, or if the women she saved actually wanted saving. It is also extremely unlikely that there were masses of innocent white middle-class girls kidnapped into sex slavery in the United States; women's agency is far more complex. Nevertheless, Rose Livingston and the rhetoric of white slavery in the suffrage movement worked to fold transnational space in ways that built off racist fears—reinforcing both women's vulnerability and their potential strength. For suffrage advocates like Livingston, women's ability to vote was a necessary tool in the war against white slavery.

Spatial Mobility and National Belonging

While immigration and the security of the border is often articulated through a language of jobs and material resources, rhetorical analysis of controversies surrounding Asian immigration reveal an underlying commitment to racial differentiation rooted in assumptions of civilization and sexual morality. Americans situated the United States as a critical boundary between the heathen and civilized worlds, and perceptions of white women's sexual activity functioned as the core of national morality. White women were tasked with preserving the sanctity of the home, and the influence of the home radiated outward to community and nation. US immigration law defined Asian women outside of the scope of moral American womanhood, enforcing perceptions of an irreparable divide between two worlds.

Turning to early immigration laws helps uncover the centrality of white womanhood to national identity. Chávez describes "alienizing logic" as "a structure of thinking that insists that some are necessarily members of a community and some are recognized as not belonging, even if they physically reside there."[117] Significantly, Chávez argues that alienizing logics are not binary, and, thus, someone can belong within some contexts and not others or move in and out of belonging. The development and enforcement of federal immigration law was grounded in an alienizing logic that placed heightened scrutiny on women, especially women from Asian countries. Regardless of actual immigration status, women were acceptable if they performed the appropriate type of womanhood. However, that performance of womanhood was deeply racialized. Women from European countries, especially Western Europe, needed to prove that they were married or offer other evidence of virtue, but other women faced an impossible burden. For example, if a Chinese women showed evidence of marriage and domesticity, she was deemed a "yellow slave" wife, but if she was not married, she was labeled as a "yellow slave" prostitute. For many women, successfully entering the United States was not sufficient to be accepted by the United States.

Racialized womanhood functioned as a container for national space. There continues to be a national interest in regulating performances of womanhood, and US immigration law was developed as a mechanism of that regulation. Moral women were deemed necessary for a moral nation, and by defining Asian women outside the scope of legitimate womanhood, their presence threatened to contaminate the rest of the United States. The movement of China into the spatial boundaries of the United States was represented as a threat to white womanhood and, thus, the entire nation.

CHAPTER 6

White Slavery and Transnational Flow

INTERNATIONAL SEX TRAFFICKING ACTIVISM BEFORE WORLD WAR I

In 1876, British activist Josephine Butler identified an invasive species that threatened England, noting, "This Continental system is the full-blown poison flower of the evil root of State-regulated prostitution which our legislators have silently planted in our English soil."[1] The British had a long history of exporting their culture and planting themselves in other countries, but, as Butler explained, the deep interconnections of the world also meant that England could not insulate itself from outside influences, even objectionable influences that put English women at risk. The world was changing. In the decades preceding the First World War, the world had entered into an age of globalization where vast spaces were becoming increasingly connected and interdependent, people and information moved relatively quickly, and networks of social relations often extended across national boundaries.[2] Gregory Blue has called this a second period of colonialism, and while the transatlantic trade in enslaved people was no longer the driving force for empire expansion, many European countries saw colonialism as a military and economic necessity in the globalized world. As a result, Blue explains, "The colonial order at the beginning of the twentieth century constituted a diversified system involving many different types of states in a complex hierarchy of domination that spanned the globe."[3]

At the same time as fears over white slavery were touching small Wisconsin towns, white slavery controversies operated at a global scale, challenging national boundaries, organizing power relations across colonizers and the colonialized, and prompting international coalitions and conflict. White slavery, and by extension white womanhood, functioned as a synecdochical representation of both national strength and precarity for many European countries who constituted "their" women as symbolic of their civilizing influence, while simultaneously recognizing that globalization made it virtually impossible to protect white women from outside threats. As the controversy slipped into different contexts, it moved in ways that made it intelligible to different audiences, opening space for both global connection and conflict.

This chapter shifts to the transnational scale of the white slavery controversy. It considers the moments where the controversy over white slavery slipped across national borders, prompted international coalitions, and became implicated in the increasingly globalized world. However, even as white slavery worked at a transnational scale, it was consistently pulled into statist logics, which led to conflicts between nations that supposedly shared the same goals. In protecting white womanhood, European nations, along with the United States, were reifying their boundaries and national identities at a moment when territorial boundaries may have felt unstable in the face of globalization. Following Raka Shome's conclusion that whiteness is a discursive formation that travels in ways that are used to sustain global Western power, I argue that white womanhood was used to shape national identity through controversy within a nation, and it also functioned as a tool to define nation in opposition to others within a global context.[4]

This analysis of the white slavery controversy begins in England and moves to international white slavery organizing that cumulated in a set of international treaties that attempted to combat the problem of the white slave trade. It would not be possible to truly consider the global without removing complex context and flattening the controversy in ways that oversimplify and exclude. Thus, rather than attempt to consider the global at large, I focus on the movement and slippage between different localities that become visible through a transnational optic.

My decision to begin in England and move outward is deliberate. Britain was the largest empire in the world, and London was the center of that empire, operating as a significant political and commercial hub.[5] At the same time, English activists often placed themselves at the center of international sex trafficking activism, describing English leadership as propelling international movements. The historical reality is, of course, more complex. Different countries, both inside and outside of Europe, had various understandings of the problem and activism relating to sexual exploitation and trafficking; it is inaccurate to say that activism originated with the English. Furthermore, centering England in historical analysis risks reifying the West as the global center, marginalizing those outside of the center. Nevertheless, white slavery is a rhetorical construct that is distinct from a material history of sex and sex trafficking. It is not possible to understand the rhetoricity of the white slavery controversy without interrogating the ways that white slavery was constituted in England to understand prostitution and sex trafficking. Beginning with English activism is important to uncovering the ways that white slavery rhetoric participated in shaping transnational space. Nonetheless, in its rhetorical movement, the controversy changed, and activists in different localities found rhetorical agency in their appropriation of and responses to the controversy.

The New Slavery in England

In 1864, Britain passed the first of a series of Contagious Diseases (CD) Acts. Although similar laws had been in place throughout the continent, Britain adopted specific sites of state regulation of prostitution in order to address incidents of sexually transmitted disease among members of the military.[6] Initially framed as a military readiness issue, the slow expansion of the CD Acts eventually spurred public opposition in the 1870s.[7] English opposition brought together diverse national and international coalitions, to address white slavery and promote abolition of legal prostitution in England, British colonies, and the continent of Europe. Even after the repeal of the British CD Acts in 1886, international organizing continued to increase as activists worked to address a problem that failed to remain bounded by national borders. By uncovering the abolitionist tropes in the early anti-regulation movement, I identify the seeds of white slavery that took root with the later purity reformers.

Although there were variations in laws that regulated prostitution, most European regulation laws required that prostitutes register themselves and undergo regular screening for sexually transmitted diseases. If a woman were found to be infected, she would typically be housed in an official capacity, often in a location called a lock hospital that was called such because women were confined (or locked in) until they showed no signs of disease. This system depended on women's registration and inspection, and many cities tasked police with identifying unregistered prostitutes. In England, women identified by the police had to either undergo an inspection or prove their innocence to a magistrate. Likewise, in France the *police des moeurs* utilized what critics identified as aggressive and dishonest measures to register women, regardless of whether the women identified themselves as prostitutes. Once registered, women became official "public women" or, in England, "Queen's women."[8]

After a series of slow CD Act expansions, in 1869 English activists formed the National Association for the Repeal of the Contagious Diseases Acts, often known as the National Association. Women were initially excluded from the National Association meetings, leading some women to form the Ladies' National Association for the Repeal of the Contagious Diseases Acts (LNA), and Josephine Butler was almost immediately brought into the movement.[9] Butler quickly emerged as an outspoken leader of the movement to challenge regulation. Butler was born in 1828 to a family with "aristocratic connections" and had an evangelical Christian upbringing.[10] Her family had a long history of activism related to issues like poverty and enslavement of people of African descent, and she continued to be active around issues of enslavement and women's rights after her marriage to George Butler in 1851. Judith R. Walkowitz argues that Butler displayed two somewhat contradictory tendencies in her activism. She celebrated women's moral virtue, engaging in uplift and rescue work, but, at the same time, she advocated for gender equality, even insisting that women who practiced prostitution had the right to sell sex without police abuse.[11] Her outspoken activism made her a natural choice to work as leader of the incipient movement.

Christian morality was deeply ingrained in the opposition to prostitution. However, the rhetoric of morality operated differently in the National Association from what was common in the United States. For example, Butler argued, "Our race is suffering largely from a species of moral atrophy,—from a fatal paralysis of the sense of justice. Many literally do not know what justice is."[12] Christian morality, for Butler, was grounded in principles of justice. She continued to explain, "I have ever maintained that the principles which underlie all just law—respect for the human person, for the personal rights of all, for the claim to liberty of all who are not legally judged and condemned as criminals, for the equality of all—rich and poor, man and woman—before the law, are principles which have a divine origin."[13] While rooted in Christian morality, Butler's argument was not an opposition to sex or a demonization of prostitution. Instead, she insisted that governments should not exploit poor women for the benefit of others, and the basic premise of justice helps explain the nearly seamless movement that Butler and similar activists made from the abolitionist movement to what they came to call the new abolitionist movement.

The language of white slavery was apparent early in opposition to regulation. A French advocate explained:

> This is what is passing in the 19th century in a civilized country, where, perhaps, we would not find a single partizan [sic] of negro slavery. We tolerate, we protect, we approve of white slavery. Indignation is expressed against the private harems in Turkey. In France the police maintain public harems. They keep prisoners in them behind iron gratings; they provide the prisoners; they guarantee to the consumer the good quality of this merchandise which they prepare to serve the appetites.[14]

The rhetoric is strikingly similar to that which would emerge in the United States. White women were represented as slaves who were physically trapped in prostitution and traded as products. The key difference between the later American rhetoric and this French account is the agent. While Americans blamed pimps, procurers, and traffickers, European activists represented government officials as the root of the problem in countries with regulation. According to this author, the police kept white women trapped in prostitution and actively sought to register new white women to maintain the supply of prostitutes. According to the National Association, government sanction was the central moral failing. "Wickedness and vice," they insisted, "ought not to be regulated, fostered, and made easy and healthy by Government."[15] The argument is based in a chain of logic that frames government regulation as implicit government endorsement. Regulation made prostitution "healthy" by attempting to mitigate the risk of disease, but this mitigation, according to the National Association, worked to encourage vice by eliminating a possible deterrent to illicit sex.

For many advocates, ending regulated prostitution was an issue of justice for women. According to the National Association, "Men are as dangerous to society in this respect as are women, yet the Acts referred to deal *with women only*."[16] The laws subjected women to regulation to protect men, demonstrating that the law was not only rooted in a double standard of morality, but also a law that applied only to one sex who happened to be the sex that could not vote. The targeting of women through regulation reflected an assumption that women who practiced prostitution were expendable. Although white womanhood was often lauded as epitomizing the virtue of nation, women practicing prostitution were defined outside of the category of good womanhood. Activists against regulation countered this assumption by reinscribing women, although for many activists only white women, who practiced prostitution within the category of legitimate womanhood, making them worthy of justice and protection.

The abstract concern for justice was consistently supplemented with a concern for good white women who risked being trapped by the law. According to one pamphlet, "The provisions for compelling women to register themselves as prostitutes are so unfair, harsh, and crafty, that any poor and friendless woman, even if virtuous, is in constant danger of being drawn into the net."[17] There were frequent stories of the white girl who made one mistake, an innocent white woman who was taken by police while walking home from work, or the upper-class white lady who was arrested and kept overnight until claimed by her husband.[18] Furthermore, once a woman was registered as a prostitute, she had little hope of regaining respectability. Through registration, a woman's public status was irrevocably changed.

While stories of innocent white women being mistaken for prostitutes worked to generate fear in the minds of the audience, Butler's frequent accounts of inspection as physical violation angered audiences. The National Association explained:

> What is this "examination?" As the Acts are silent it can only be stated as a fact, that it is instrumental, indecent, degrading, and indescribable. To an unwilling patient it is neither more nor less than PERSONAL VIOLENCE—an outrage—which, if perpetrated in any district where the Acts are not in force, women render the perpetrator liable to punishment for felony.[19]

The introduction of the speculum made exams particularly invasive because they involved looking inside of women to assess health. In a letter to London physician James John Garth Wilkinson, Butler recounted the experience of an inspection that would be applied to all suspected prostitutes, even the "delicate girls of 15":

> It is such awful work; the attitude they push us into first is so disgusting and so painful, and then these monstrous instruments,—often they use several. They seem to tear the passage open first with their hands, and examine us, and then they thrust in instruments, and they pull them out and push them in, and they turn and twist them about; and if you cry out they stifle you with a towel over your face.[20]

With this description, Butler moved inspection from a medical procedure to state sanctioned rape.

Butler and other British activists were caught in a tension between white slavery as a transnational phenomenon and nation-based logics of understanding and responding to problems. Early in response to the CD Acts, British activists positioned themselves both apart from and leaders for the rest of Europe. Compared to other European countries, Britain adopted regulation late. Indeed, many countries had some form of regulation since Napoleon, and Butler represented regulation as a European importation. Furthermore, she described English women as spurring the international movement. For example, in a public letter to supporters of the movement, Butler explained that she received letters from across the continent. In one pamphlet, she quoted Countess de Gasparin and reported that the countess "urges all Christian people throughout Europe should league themselves together in order to get rid of this 'patented leprosy,' the regulation and protection of prostitution; and she appeals first to the *women of England* to inaugurate this movement."[21] By having the demand come from the countess, Butler situated her action as a calling to which she must respond. Within this framing, the women of England must act to save not only their country but also the rest of the world.

The interconnections of the problem became most evident after the emergence of a series of reports that white women from England were being lured to and trapped in countries like Belgium for prostitution. Alfred Dyer became a vocal advocate for reforming British law to save English girls who were being lured to Belgium with promises of marriage or employment. He explained that, after hearing reports of English girls imprisoned in sex slavery, he investigated and confirmed these accounts. Dyer concluded:

> It is beyond doubt that a large and well organized traffic exists in supplying licensed houses of debauchery on the Continent of Europe with English girls, young, good-looking, and whenever possible, innocent and virtuous, for these can be sold for the most money. All manner of devices and stratagems are resorted to, the most frequent being proposals of marriage with persons of wealth, or offers of lucrative situations. It may be said that girls are silly to listen to such offers. No doubt they are. But girls in the best ordered families are not very wise at the age of seventeen; and it must be remembered that the victims of this infamous traffic are mostly in unsheltered positions, away from home, and oftentimes orphans.[22]

For Dyer, English girls were valued for their purity and innocence, the same characteristics that made them an easy target for procurers. However, the British had an obligation to protect them because, according to Dyer, these white women were British subjects and, therefore, have "a right to be protected from a state of bondage."[23]

As National Association activists recognized the intrinsic transnational nature of trafficking, they formed the British, Continental and General Federation for the Abolition of the Government Regulation of Vice in 1875, which was renamed the International Abolitionist Federation in 1898.[24] One journal published an account of their 1877 congress in Geneva, noting, "Without entering into more painful details, we may say that they [prostitutes] are traded from country to country by infamous agents, that the houses in which they live, the *maisons tolerés*, are often . . . veritable prisons from which escape is impossible."[25] By positing prostitution as a trade that defied national boundaries, abolitionist organizers worked to develop transnational coalitions with the united goal of abolishing state regulated prostitution.

The organized response to regulation in Europe had two significant implications on the development of the white slavery controversy. First, it planted the seeds of "white slavery" as the language of sex trafficking. Many of the early opponents of the CD Acts were veterans of the international abolitionist movement. They drew on the existing coalitions and language to develop a case against the regulation of prostitution. Specifically, the language of white slavery appeared to emerge from the shift in legal status that occurred with regulation. Once a woman was registered, it was virtually impossible for her to regain her previous status as a private woman; she was meant to provide sexual services for the benefit of the nation. As the CD Acts were repealed in Britain and the movement developed stronger international connections, the language of white slavery appeared to slowly shift to a focus on mobility and trafficking. For example, at an 1899 international conference, the organizers defined white slavery:

> To make known the nature of the White Slave Traffic by which is meant the purchase and transfer from place to place of women and girls for immoral purposes, who are, in the first place, inveigled into a vile life by the promise of employment in a foreign country, and, thereafter, are practically prisoners, and who, if they really desire to escape from a life of shame, cannot do so."[26]

The meaning shifted from one based in legal status to one of movement and entrapment, and this shift coincided with the increasing dominance of purity reformers in the European movement.

The second major implication of the early movement was a recognition of white slavery as a transnational problem. Activists came to acknowledge that borders could not protect white women. Moral contamination seeped across national boundaries, and women were physically moved between nations, limiting the ability for any one nation to address the problem. Eventually, in an attempt to protect "their" white women, many European nations developed international systems of coordination, but this organization only occurred once the problem moved from being about state regulation of prostitution (an issue with which there remained significant disagreement) to entrapment of innocent white girls.

The ways in which white slavery emerged as a transnational phenomenon reflects one of the ways that white womanhood travels. The European nations most active in combatting white slavery were also colonizers that had long histories of exploiting women.[27] For example, the National Association worked to distribute a report from John Pope Hennessey, governor and commander-in-chief of Hong Kong, who explained, "These Chinese women have a dread and abhorrence of foreigners, and especially of the foreign sailors and soldiers. Such Chinese girls are the real slaves in Hong Kong."[28] Dutch women, who maintained a commitment to abolition even while the rest of the continent was shifting to purity reform, also worked to address prostitution in the Dutch East Indies.[29] Nevertheless, there was little popular support for addressing the exploitation of women in colonialized nations because non-European women were not understood as white slaves who needed protection. Indeed, regulation of prostitution in colonialized nations was often represented as necessary to protect white women because under regulation European soldiers were thought to be less likely to transmit disease from foreign prostitutes to white women at home.[30] Furthermore, assumptions of moral degeneracy among supposedly less advanced people were used to justify their regulation, rather than embracing the possibility for reform.[31] The International Abolitionist Federation remained committed to complete abolition of regulation, but, as the locus of power shifted to purity reformers, women in colonialized countries often became either expendable or invisible.

The Maiden Tribute of Modern Babylon and International Purity Reform

In 1885, William T. Stead sent shockwaves through England with the publication in the *Pall Mall Gazette* of a multi-part investigation titled, "The Maiden Tribute of Modern Babylon." Stead became editor-in-chief of the *Pall Mall Gazette* in 1883, and he is credited with spearheading several innovations in tabloid journalism.[32] He was also active in England's social reform movements, and when the Criminal Law Amendment (CLA) Act stalled in the House of Commons, Stead utilized his paper to mobilize popular support and prompt action.[33] The CLA Act is best known for increasing the age of consent for girls in Britain from thirteen to sixteen, but it also restricted prostitution and criminalized sodomy. The law passed the House of Lords after an 1883 British investigation found strong evidence of English girls in Belgium brothels (an investigation prompted by Dyer's reports), but it was not until Stead's exposé that prostitution, especially juvenile prostitution, became a topic of national concern. Publications ranging from the medical journal the *Lancet* to the *Methodist Times* praised Stead's investigation and demanded immediate action. The Salvation Army collected thousands of signatures supporting the CLA Act, and the law passed through the House of Commons within weeks of the "The Maiden Tribute" being published.

Although Stead received support for the exposé, he also encountered a barrage of criticism for publishing lurid details of sex, violating norms of Victorian propriety. Stead was eventually convicted and served jail time for purchasing thirteen-year-old Eliza Armstrong (who was called "Lily" in the story), though he maintained that his actions were only intended to prove that a thirteen-year-old could be purchased for sex in London. Although "The Maiden Tribute of Modern Babylon" continues to be recognized for its journalistic innovations and for motivating significant social change in nineteenth century England, the United States, Canada, and continental Europe, its rhetorical power comes, in part, from mobile transformations of white womanhood. Stead's exposé refigured urban space and the possibilities and meanings of white women's mobility, while also dislocating the relationship between the public and illicit sex.

On July 4, 1885, readers of the *Pall Mall Gazette* were greeted with a "frank warning." The CLA Act appeared to have been abandoned, and, as the editor explained, they were compelled to publish their special report to inform the public of the urgent need for such legislation. However, Stead continued, "The story of an actual pilgrimage into a real hell is not pleasant reading and is not meant to be."[34] What followed was a four-part series. The first part of the investigation came two days later. It highlighted the problem of juvenile prostitution in London and was punctuated by the purchase of thirteen-year-old "Lily" from her mother. The second part, published on July 7, outlined the processes of tricking and procuring juvenile prostitutes. The third part focused on the role of the current law in enabling juvenile prostitution, in addition to offering accounts of very young white children who were raped by men. On July 9, the *Pall Mall Gazette* explained that police and the city solicitor were attempting to block distribution of the paper, and the final installment was published the following day. The final part of the report included an indictment of the London police, explanation of the international trade, and specific coverage of the resumed debate over the CLA Act.

As suggested by the title of the series, the Greek myth of the Labyrinth of Crete operated as an organizing mechanism to conceptualize the entrapment of girls in London vice. Stead explained, "Maidens they were when this morning dawned, but to-night their ruin will be accomplished, and to-morrow they will find themselves within the portals of the maze of London brotheldom."[35] By introducing the image of London vice as a labyrinth,

Stead disrupted the neat spatial mapping of London that divided the city into the upper-class, respectable West End and the poor, dangerous East End. Instead, the "maze of London brotheldom" became superimposed on existing geography, forcing a reimagining of known spaces, as well as revealing the hidden "chambers and underground passages" of the labyrinth.[36] In order to emphasize this disruption, Stead's exposé moved between brothels on the East and West sides of London.[37] This travel through London vice, according to Stead, "seemed a strange, inverted world."[38]

Much like the labyrinth of Crete, Stead represented London vice as nearly impossible to escape. He described the "network of snares and wiles and 'plants,' intended to bring in fresh girls."[39] These girls may have worked in a factory or as governesses, been from the English countryside or another European country, and they may have become entrapped by a supposed friend or their own mother. No white girl in London was safe because there was an insatiable demand for virgins, and a network of procurers, brothel keepers, and midwives worked to fill that demand. Once a girl became entrapped, escape was nearly impossible. One woman told Stead that, although girls may not understand what was happening or may change their minds, attempt to revoke their consent, or fight off the man, "she repents too late when she repents after crossing my threshold."[40] Once a girl entered the brothel, her property may have been taken, and she often accumulated debts that prevented her escape. Furthermore, London brotheldom was represented as a vast international network, and London was one part of the diffuse market for international sex trade. Stead explained:

> Prostitution in England is Purgatory; under the State regulated system which prevails abroad it is Hell. The foreign traffic is the indefinite prolongation of the labyrinth of modern Babylon, with absolute and utter hopelessness of any redemption. When a girl steps over the fatal brink she is at once regarded as fair game for the slave trader who collects his human "parcels" in the great central mart of London for transmission to the uttermost ends of the earth. They move from state to stage, from town to town—bought, exchanged, sold—driven on and ever like the restless ghosts of the damned, until at last they too sleep "where the wicked cease from troubling and the wearily are at rest."[41]

In other words, the only escape, for many women, was death.

Just as the people of Athens were thought to have sacrificed maidens to the Minotaur, Stead represented the white girls trapped in prostitution as innocent victims who were sacrificed because of greed and lust. Stead described white juvenile prostitutes in ways that emphasized their youth and innocence, explaining, for example, that one girl was a "loving and affectionate child,"[42] while another had "baby eyes."[43] He also compared white girls to animals, like hunting grouse, explaining that the young grouse was better protected than the thirteen-year-old girl.[44] Stead spent several nights "prowling" the streets of London, and noted, "the deep and strong impression which I have bought back is one of respect and admiration for the extraordinarily good behavior of the English girls who pursue this dreadful calling."[45] While the white girls were innocent in Stead's account, men and police were the villains and posed the greatest danger to English white girls.

While Stead refigured the space of London, he also worked to dislocate middle- and upper-class readers, moving them into intimate and illicit spaces. This dislocation is part of what leads Greta Wendelin to label "The Maiden Tribute" as a rhetoric of pornography by its moving of the reader into the space of the forbidden. Perhaps the most striking example of this dislocation is the story of "Lily," who was later revealed to be Eliza Armstrong. Stead described how he purchased thirteen-year-old Armstrong from her mother, and, although the mother was aware of her daughter's fate, the child thought that she was moving to a respectable job. Stead walked readers through Armstrong's inspection by the midwife to confirm her virginity, and he concluded the first part of "The Maiden Tribute":

> She was taken up stairs, undressed, and put to bed, the woman who bought her putting her to sleep. She was rather restless, but under the influence of chloroform she soon went over. Then the woman withdrew. All was quiet and still. A few moments later the door opened, and the purchaser entered the bedroom. He closed and locked the door. There was a brief silence. And then there rose a wild and piteous cry—not a loud shriek, but a helpless, startled scream like the bleat of a frightened lamb. And the child's voice was heard crying, in accents of terror, "There's a man in the room! Take me home; oh, take me home!"
>
> * * * * * *
>
> And then all once more was still.[46]

The vivid description of Armstrong's cry brought the reader into the room, and the break in the narrative, symbolized by a line break and six asterisks running across the column, led the readers to imagining the rape of a child. The reader was moved from sympathizing with the plight of the child to voyeuristically witnessing the child's rape.

Walkowitz argues that "The Maiden Tribute" demonstrates the connections between melodrama and pornography as literary genres.[47] Stead moved between investigative reporting (listing witnesses to support the facts of his reporting), melodrama (eliciting sympathy for the apparently innocent girls), and the urban explorer (voyeuristically observing those different than himself). These orientations worked together to disrupt the position of the reader as entirely separate from the problem of juvenile prostitution, leading some critics at the time to label "The Maiden Tribute" as obscenity and attempt to block its distribution.

The CLA Act passed in August 1885, and Stead worked to create the National Vigilance Association (NVA) to support the enforcement of the new law. The agenda for the organization quickly grew to the general promotion of purity and suppression of vice.[48] The NVA was led by William Alexander Coote, an Evangelical Christian who came to Stead's attention after leading a social purity rally following publication of "The Maiden Tribute," and Coote led the NVA to become the dominant organization in the international movement against white slavery.[49] Rachael Attwood argues that the NVA had a "statist outlook" that led them to work closely with national governments.[50] At their first international conference, which prompted international organizing under the leadership of the British NVA, a Professor Stuart argued, "This traffic is one of the blots on modern civilization; there is nothing conceivable worse in the whole range of international relations than the fact that these international relations and commerce include within their borders, a commerce in human beings, a commerce in the most unprotected portion of human beings—in our young women and girls."[51] For Stuart, white slavery was at its core an international problem that necessitated an international solution. Yet, the risk was to "our" women and girls. Stuart maintained a national frame of protecting the white women and girls of England, and international mobility meant that the only way to protect English women was through international networks of activism. Indeed, the NVA led the international community by developing the basis of two international agreements. The first was largely procedural and signed by most European countries in 1904, although the United States did not affirm the treaty until 1908. The treaty of principles prohibiting the white slave traffic was eventually adopted in 1910.

One implication of the NVA's statist approach was a shift away from antiregulation activism toward multilateral government cooperation on addressing sex trafficking. Perhaps not surprisingly, Josephine Butler was highly critical of the NVA approach. In an 1897 pamphlet, she insisted:

> We have learned that it is not unusual for men and women to discourse eloquently in public on the subject of personal domestic, and social purity, of the home, of conjugal life, of the dignity of womanhood, of the duties of parents, and yet to be ready to accept and endorse any amount of inequality in the laws, any amount of coercive and degrading treatment of certain classes of their fellow creatures, in the fatuous belief that you can oblige human beings to be moral by *force*, and in so doing that you may in some way promote social purity.[52]

Nevertheless, the NVA became the driving force in international activism, definitively shifting international organizing toward stopping a mobility-based understanding of white slavery.[53]

White Slavery and International Politics

In 1909, after completing an exhaustive investigation of prostitution in the United States, Marcus Braun arrived in Europe to follow up "in those countries on such clues as you have already discovered during the course of your investigations in the United Sates and with the object of obtaining as full information as possible regarding the operations of dealers in alien women of the class mentioned and the shipment to this country of such women from the countries named."[54] While he was warmly received in England, he expressed dismay at the lack of cooperation he received visiting other countries. For example, he was told by a French official that he was not permitted to conduct any investigation in France. Furthermore, Braun reported that this French official expressed a fundamentally different interpretation of the 1904 agreement than Braun. He explained:

> Mr. Hennequin ... told me plainly and bluntly that the French Government is not here for the purpose to assist the United States in the detection of infractions of the U.S. Immigration laws. He further informed me that prostitutes have a perfect right to travel and to circulate freely from and into France; he gave me to understand that he is not at all in sympathy with the U.S. Immigration laws, which prohibit a prostitute to go into the United States if she desires to lead a decent life there, nor does he see his way clear how it is possible to prevent the travelling of any woman who desires to go the United States for some other immoral purpose ... he does not see why that should be objectionable and how this Government can prevent it ... [He said,] "this has got nothing to do with the international agreement for the repression for trafficing [sic] in white women."[55]

Additionally, Hennequin insisted that if a woman were lured to the United States, Americans "have no right to treat them as a prostitute," and simply deporting the woman is a violation of the international agreement.[56] Although Braun disagreed with the French interpretation of the agreement, Hennequin spoke with authority as both the official French contact regarding the white slave agreement and a delegate at the 1904 conference.[57] Nevertheless, Braun proceeded to create an international incident when he decided to continue his investigations in France, despite being prohibited by French authorities.[58]

Based on his correspondence, Braun clearly believed himself to be in right. He was, after all, attempting to protect white women in accordance with existing international agreements. One reading of the disagreement between Braun and the nation of France (as well as several other European countries) could be read as a conflict between international agreement and national sovereignty. However, there appears to be fundamental differences in the ways that nations interpreted the white slavery agreements, and these differences come back to the constructed relationships between white womanhood and nation. Robert Asen identifies such complex polysemy as characteristic of public policy rhetoric because multiple authors work to generate public policy. In the case of the white slavery treaties, it is impossible to know if the ambiguity was strategically built into the text to generate agreement or if some audiences engaged in what Leah Ceccarelli calls resistive reading as a way of generating meanings that were never intended by the authors.[59] The polysemy of the treaties enabled an unprecedented international agreement, but it also opened space for later disagreement on application. Braun's experience was just one example of that disagreement.

The official versions of both agreements were heavily based on drafts created at the NVA's conference in Geneva in 1902. The 1904 Agreement for the Suppression of the White Slave Traffic focused on logistics for international cooperation, specifying norms of communication between contracting countries and the obligation to monitor the movement of women and girls. Most European countries signed onto this agreement during the 1904 conference in France, but the United States did not sign on until 1908.[60] The 1910 International Convention for the Suppression of the White Slave Traffic was more contentious and required longer for the signatory countries to reach agreement. This convention specified that someone who trafficked a woman or girl could be punished, even if the offense crossed international boundaries.

These agreements provided the basis for treaties that extend into the twenty-first century, establishing who should be protected and for what purposes. Although some attendees at the convention advocated modifying the language to "traffic of persons," rather than "white slavery," that change was rejected, and the language of white slavery (*traite des blanches*) became an organizing framework for the agreements. The commitment to protecting white womanhood was significant because signatory countries used the treaty as a mechanism of protecting "their" women, and they were marking their women as white. Increasing transportation networks meant that white women were perceived to be at risk because once they left their home country, a nation lost control of their women and had no mechanism of protection other than an international treaty. As a further indication that signatory countries were primarily concerned with their own white women, individual counties could decide if the treaty applied to their colonies, and many countries decided that there was no urgent need to protect colonialized women in the same manner as white European women. Conference participants spoke European languages, employed European standards of womanhood and morality, and treated colonies as an afterthought.

Despite agreement to a groundbreaking treaty that was eight years in the making, the 1910 White Slavery Convention was significantly ambiguous, especially in regard to issues of consent, innocence, and protection. A major issue of disagreement hinged on the legality of prostitution in general. Article 2 of the 1910 agreement came closest to a definition of white slavery, utilizing language that remains in contemporary trafficking agreements, referring to the use of "fraud, or by means of violence, threats, abuse of authority, or any other method of compulsion, procured, enticed, or led away." However, there was disagreement about if a woman could consent or if any move into prostitution was evidence of fraud or compulsion. In an apparent attempt to clarify the issue of consent, Article 1 stated: "Whoever, in order to gratify the passions of another person, has procured, enticed, or led away, even with her consent, a woman or girl under age." While this section may appear to prohibit all prostitution, which satisfied some representatives like the Italians, the French insisted that Article 1 applied only to those who were under the age of consent and Article 2 applied to women over the age of consent. Jean Allain argues that this ambiguity was deliberate, and the conjunction "or" in both Articles 1 and 2 were conjunctions of continuation, not alternation. In other words, the French interpreted Article 1 as "a woman under age" or "a girl under age," while Article 2 referred to women and girls who were over the age of consent. Significantly, there was substantial disagreement about the age of consent, and, while the signatory countries never agreed on a consistent age of consent to be included in the treaty, they agreed on a nonbinding protocol document that set the minimum age of consent at twenty.[61]

At the 1910 Fourth International Congress for the Repression of the White Slave Traffic, delegates attempted to clarify some ambiguities surrounding existing treaties. For example, in answer to the question "What is the best definition of the term 'White Slave Traffic' (Traies des blanches)?" the congress passed a resolution stating that "any person who shall cause with a view to monetary profit, a woman or girl to lead a life of debauch, shall be considered a white slave trader."[62] Significantly, the definition only clarified the meaning of "white slave trader," failing to address the ambiguity around who qualified as a white slave and was, therefore, "protected" by the treaty. The same congress noted that they believed "that the legal dispositions now applicable to those who trade in minor girls or women should be equally applicable to those who trade in girls and women having reached their majority."[63] However, this clarification was nonbinding, and it did not specify the extent that the treaty applied to all women regardless of age. The statement appeared to gesture toward moral clarity while sustaining official ambiguity.

The 1910 white slavery treaty was groundbreaking because it recognized sex trafficking as a transnational problem. As white women and girls moved across national boundaries, reformers drew on international networks in an attempt to create a single standard for white women's appropriate mobility. However, even within Europe, reformers were confronted with conflicting understanding of womanhood and morality. While ambiguity was, perhaps strategically, built into the international treaties, every nation could claim success without acquiescing to moral standards outside of their national frame. In other words, every participating nation could claim to be protecting their women, without international agreement on what that protection meant in practice.

Colonialism and White Slavery

Even as Europeans created international coalitions to protect their white women, such sentiments rarely extended to colonies. Histories of colonialism are complex and multifaceted, but there is widespread agreement that the development of colonialism was dependent on the exploitation of labor, particularly the enslavement of people of African descent.[64] As European sentiments shifted away from the explicit support of the transatlantic trade in enslaved people, colonialism was no less implicated in labor exploitation, but that exploitation often occurred under the guise of protection. Liat Kozma argues:

> Colonial prostitution was also affected by segregation and the hierarchic logic of empire, as the legal status of prostitutes was differentiated by race, and they were often separated from the more "respectable" parts of society. As the regulation of prostitution was increasingly controversial in Europe itself, it was maintained in overseas colonies because it enabled colonial authorities to protect their soldiers and settlers from venereal disease, and at the same time monitor interracial encounters.[65]

The colonial regulation of prostitution was a mechanism of regulating racial mobility and sustaining colonial authority. Just as protecting white women appeared to shore up a sense of national identity, the sexual exploitation of colonized women shored up empire. Colonialized women became materially contained through regulation, and the regulation system was often used to contain different cultural expressions of womanhood. According to Kozma, in Egypt for example *'awalim* were a type of refined female entertainer, but colonial regulation imposed European norms of white womanhood on Egypt, leading *'awalim* to eventually become classified as prostitutes.[66] In this sense, the traveling of white womanhood worked as a means of containment. While there were pockets of resistance to colonial regulation of prostitution, Kozma argues that there was not meaningful movement on this issue until in the interwar period with the creation of the League of Nations' Advisory Committee on Traffic in Women and Children. By this time, state regulation of prostitution became increasingly viewed as inconsistent with the civilizing mission of colonial countries.

Well before the legal shifts that occurred in the interwar period, there was activism that attempted to address sex trafficking in colonies, and India appeared to have been a locus of activism. Regulation and registration of prostitution had existed in some form in India throughout most of the nineteenth century, but these rules became formalized with the Cantonments Act of 1864 and the Indian Contagious Diseases Act of 1868.[67] When the Indian acts were repealed in 1888, the Indian press largely celebrated the repeal, but cantonment rules continued in India, leading to little practical changes in regard to prostitution.[68] Opposition to regulation continued, and in 1890 the British branch of the British, Continental and General Federation for the Abolition of the Government Regulation of Vice was renamed the British Committee for the Abolition of the State Regulation of Vice in India and throughout the British Dominions.[69] This organization believed that despite legal change, registration and regulation continued in British colonies. Thus, when Americans Dr. Katherine Bushnell, known for her exposure of white slavery in Wisconsin lumber camps, and Elizabeth Wheeler Andrew, a temperance advocate and widow of a Methodist minister, visited Josephine Butler in England prior to a world tour for the World Woman's Christian Temperance Union, Butler implored them to uncover the truth about practices in India.[70]

Andrew and Bushnell arrived in India in December of 1892, and, in their report that was made public in 1893, they explained that they arrived in India without knowing the languages spoken, having contacts, or knowing who they could trust, so the women put their faith in God to guide them. In 1899, their report was published as *The Queen's Daughters in India*. The American women represented themselves as missionaries, and, without asking for official permission, visited *chaklas* (government sanctioned brothels) in ten different cantonments (military stations) throughout the country, interviewing 395 people with the help of a translator. Much like Bushnell's account of the Wisconsin lumber region, Andrew and Bushnell represented themselves as called by God to undertake this unpleasant task.

Andrew and Bushnell's report received considerable attention and was reportedly critical to the creation of the 1893 official committee of inquiry in England.[71] A careful analysis of their report reveals temporal and spatial flows that become evident through a transnational scale of analysis. Recall that prior to Bushnell's work as National Evangelist for the WCTU, she relied on a rhetoric of identification to call on Colorado WCTU members to respect and accept women who practice prostitution in order to fulfil their larger mission. In her work in Wisconsin, Bushnell's rhetoric shifted toward saving those she represented as innocent victims, inviting her audience to see themselves as rescuers of women different from themselves. By being Americans outside of British colonialism, Andrew and Bushnell worked in both rhetorical directions simultaneously.

Andrew and Bushnell begin their report by positioning Indian women as "sisters" and "Queen's daughters," and in doing so, they collapsed the distance between England and India, creating bands of connection based on sex. By reminding their audience that Indian women were also British subjects, they planted seeds of identification and moral obligation. However, they pushed the identification further by explicitly calling on their audience to imagine themselves in the place of women in India. They wrote:

> Imagine yourself the one apprehended, and the case assumes a different aspect. A policeman comes to your door and reads a warrant for your arrest as a common prostitute; you ask on what authority; you are informed that the name of the informant is not made public, because if a man can be induced to help trace out diseases—it being regarded as a "point of honour" to inform other men where danger lurks—his confession must not be made known, it would injure his reputation.... You contend that you have right to your good name, and that is a principle of justice that no one can be punished on secret and unproven evidence.... You are then informed that unless you go at once without any trouble, you will be taken out of the town in which you live, set down as a common vagrant by the roadside, and if ever again found within the limits of the city in which your parents, brothers, and sisters live, you will be arrested and put in jail. What will you do?[72]

In this scenario, Andrew and Bushnell erased race, representing the figure in the scenario as an innocent woman trapped by unfair laws and corrupt officials. By removing race, they invited their white audience to imagine themselves in this situation, and that identification was punctuated by the short question: "What will you do?" The question worked simultaneously in two directions. It prompted the audience to consider the impossible choices that trapped many Indian women in prostitution, but it also prompted the white English audience to consider what they would do to fix this problem in their colony of India.

The evacuation of race, however, is a privilege of whiteness. By attempting to bring white European women into the experience of Indian women, Andrew and Bushnell also erased the complex power dynamics of colonialism. Indian women could not forget this disparity. Andrew and Bushnell narrated one experience, "They blessed and thanked us over and over. We told them, 'We are your sisters'; they replied, '*We are your slaves.*'"[73] This quote removed the whiteness characteristic of white slavery rhetoric, and, instead, it used the trope of sisterhood to do similar rhetorical work, highlighting a disjuncture between slavery and the white audience.

Even while Andrew and Bushnell worked to create identification with their English audience, they also differentiated the Indian women, constructing them as less civilized and in need of saving. They represented the Indian women who practiced prostitution as naive, unsophisticated, and immature, calling them "little women." According to Andrew and Bushnell, "In the simplicity of their faith and lack of practical knowledge, several of them had ventured to intimate that we might go to England and see the Queen, and tell her their troubles."[74] The supposed immaturity of the women made their saving even more urgent and emphasized their intrinsic innocence, despite practicing prostitution.

Even as critics of the British colonial practices, Andrew and Bushnell appeared to affirm Christian moralizing as a justification for colonialism. The problem for the authors was not British colonialism, but it was that the English were failing in their moral duty to civilize the Indian population. In offering their critique, they drew on a rhetorical parallel to Bushnell's work in Wisconsin. In her Wisconsin white slavery investigation, Bushnell created an association between southern enslavement and slavery "up North," and, in *The Queen's Daughters*, the authors created an association between southern enslavement in the United States and British colonial practices in India.

Andrew and Bushnell insisted, "Life in India does not tend to the elevation of British morals.... The industrial conditions are all against good morals, and are closely analogous to the conditions that prevailed in the Southern States of America before the Civil War. Wages are so low in India as to constitute the native the virtual slave of the Anglo-Saxon."[75] They continued, "England virtually owns a whole nation of slaves in her control of India, and the effect of this fact upon the morals of that country will depend wholly upon whether she rules to redeem her subjects or to enrich herself. The worst feature of all in slavery is the appropriation of women by their masters."[76] In establishing connections between the American legacy of enslavement and prostitution in colonialized India, Andrew and Bushnell challenged the moral superiority of the British through the rhetorical flows of the white slavery controversy.

White Slavery and Transnational Flows

A transnational optic brings attention to rhetorical and material flows that move beyond national boundaries, and the white slavery controversy entailed multiple levels of flow that were bound up with white womanhood. White womanhood operated as representative of national identity for European and American countries. In many respects, the virtue of nation was bound up with the perceived virtue of a nation's women, even when meanings of virtue varied among different cultures. Activists went to great lengths to paint a picture of the world where a nation's women could not be protected because they could easily be moved across borders, necessitating international cooperation and apparent agreement on the meanings of white womanhood. Because of perceived dangers to white women, European and American countries constituted white womanhood as valuable, fragile, and endangered.

However, white womanhood travels, especially in the context of colonialism. White womanhood as a symbolic construct is distinct from white women as mobile humans. The movement of white women was perceived to endanger a nation while the movement of white womanhood functioned as a mechanism for national expansion and colonial control. Colonizers often imposed policies that positioned native women as tools that could be used to protect white womanhood. By naturalizing the sexual exploitation of native women, colonializing countries both exercised a form of domination and, with regulation policies, protected their own white women from disease and contamination.

Activists such as Bushnell and Andrew attempted to challenge the sexual exploitation of women under British colonialism. Yet, in doing so, they reinscribed white womanhood as a universalized frame, marking Indian women as the oppressed Other in need of saving. The layers of power that emerged in attempts to save Indian women exemplify Gayatri Chankravorty Spivak's argument about why the subaltern cannot speak.[77] The complexity of Indian women's lives was unintelligible to Western European and American women, and attempts to save Indian women often solidified the power of white womanhood and, thus, the reach of empire.

Conclusion

The rhetoric of white slavery, much like its contemporary counterpart "modern-day slavery," was insidious. It could be wielded as a rhetorical tool to meet a variety of needs within a particular time and place. When white slavery emerged as an issue of international concern in the Progressive Era, there was a common fixation on protecting the purity of white womanhood, constituting an image of white women's precarity that was only tangentially connected to the realities of women's lives. In this sense, white womanhood was about much more than individual women; it symbolized national identity, values, and future possibilities. Yet, when activists were referring to the protection of women, they were inscribing only some actual women into the symbolic category of white womanhood. Only some women fit, and the capacity to fit was dependent on racialized performance of womanhood that aligned with the national values of a given time. Inscribing some people within the category of womanhood while keeping others out was a way of keeping control over national identity and future possibilities.

By the 1880s, the purity of white womanhood appeared to be in danger. Activists feared that white women and girls were being tricked, manipulated, and sold into a slavery worse than death. The real danger, however, was not for the individual girl who left her safe home looking for adventure, but white slavery was constructed as a crime against the nation. The rhetoric worked at different scales and shifting contexts to reinforce the whiteness of the nation. White womanhood symbolized purity, morality, and domesticity. It seemed to ensure the future of the country that could only come to be through white women's reproduction, and in this sense, white womanhood was sacred. If the purity of a white woman was sullied through white slavery, she could no longer function as an appropriate vessel for reproducing future citizens. Thus, in attempting to stop white slavery, activists were attempting to protect a national imaginary imbued with whiteness. White womanhood was a tool to shape national identity.

To uncover the stakes of the white slavery controversy, I have turned to an analysis of the mobile imagination within the rhetoric. Sex trafficking rhetoric was about a fear of mobility—a mobility that endangered white women's purity. As a result, the rhetoric of white slavery was an articulation of the mobile imagination. The mobile imagination is a way of understanding the possibilities at the intersection of space and time, and, by elucidating the mobile imagination, we can reveal deeply engrained assumptions about national identity and belonging. The mobile imagination includes conceptions of who can move, how mobility occurs, and what meanings of mobility circulated. Sex trafficking is about movement, but the rhetorical constructions of that movement (the mobile imagination) shape understandings of national identity and belonging.

First, the mobile imagination constitutes who can move and what meanings of the movement exist. Across the scales of the controversy, white women were thought to belong at home. White women's immobility (stasis) within the home was represented as stability, safety, and economic supremacy for both white women and the nation writ large. On the other hand, white women's mobility was represented as consistently placing them in danger, although that danger shifted based on the various scales of the controversy. In 1880s Wisconsin, that danger was found in the Northwoods, a site perceived to be at the edge of civilization. After the turn of the century, the American city became a liminal site of civilization, as the city threatened to move backward, regressing in the face of massive immigration. As evident in international treaties, if women moved outside of their country, it became nearly impossible to protect them, because they were moving within a supposedly barbaric underworld and exposed to the fetish of the uncivilized. Spatiotemporal understandings were embedded within these perceptions of danger. Implicit within perceptions of space/time was a sense that the protection of women's purity in the home was a marker of whiteness and, thus, advanced civilization. In contrast, wilderness settings, immigrants, Black Americans, and residents of colonized countries were represented as barbaric, and, through white slavery, these groups were constituted as a threat to white womanhood and a threat to the spatiotemporal status of the nation.

The mobility of migrants, people of Asian descent, and Black Americans was often represented as a danger to white women and, thus, to the nation. Their stoppage was enforced through social, legal, and scientific means that included Mann Act prosecutions, deportations, and colonial practices. In other words, an analysis across scales reveals the ways that the prosecution of Jack Johnson and the maintenance of India *chaklas* existed within a spatial network that was maintained through the supposed protection and precarity of white womanhood. In this sense, the white slavery controversy generated multiple levels of immobility, but that immobility had different purposes and affective valences for different groups of people. The affective associations, along with material means of control, shaped subjectivity within national space.

Second, the mobile imagination shapes perceptions of how mobility occurs, constituting meaning for different paths and modes of mobility. In one sense, white womanhood was an identity that shaped possibilities for mobility, but it was also a vehicle for mobility. For some reformers, the proper performance of white womanhood could move women out of white slavery, but only some women had access to this vehicle. White womanhood, as a symbolic construct, was wielded as a tool of containment that traveled. Black women were often represented as outside of the scope of social mobility, and Black Americans were often constituted as a danger to white womanhood. Racial scripts, according to Natalia Molina, "highlight the ways in which the lives of racialized groups are linked across time and space and thereby affect one another, even when they do not directly cross paths."[1] Through these racial scripts, the purity and precarity of white womanhood operated relationally to reinforce the promiscuity and disposability of Black, Indigenous, Asian, and migrant women. Poor women were taught to correctly perform moral white womanhood to avoid indefinite confinement in prisons or reform institutions, migrant women in the United States had to perform white American womanhood to avoid deportation, and reformers implicitly drew on white womanhood to justify colonial control under the guise of its civilizing influence.

In addition to the modes of mobility, the paths were just as treacherous. The paths of dangerous mobility were often represented as hidden, permeable, and moving, creating an image of public space as inherently threatening for white women. Cities like Chicago were characterized as dangerous because innocent white women could easily fall into the traps of white slavery. Seemingly innocuous paths seemed to all lead to the brothel. Likewise, William Stead represented brotheldom as a hidden labyrinth that transcended national borders, constituting the space of white slavery as distinct from clearly defined map space.

Finally, consideration of the mobile imagination calls for attention to the potential for movement. Through the rhetoric of slavery, reformers removed agency from women they purported to protect. The needs and desires of actual women were largely irrelevant. Moral women were passive (they were moved, not mobile), and by extension, the rhetoric of the controversy reified women's status as private, controlled, and protected. Women who violated these norms could be dismissed as unworthy of protection. While reformers certainly drew on problematic norms of innocent victims and external saviors, my argument extends beyond this observation.[2] The configuration of agency within the mobile imagination is part of what rhetorically constitutes how moral women were thought to move. This is part of the network of associations that shaped how womanhood could be used to reinforce white national space. For instance, by removing agency from white women, reformers placed agency on non-white populations who were represented as insidious threats to white womanhood and, thus, the nation. Rhetoric matters and works in complex ways, and attention to rhetoric can help us understand identity, place, and belonging.

Modern-Day Slavery

While white slavery was the defining issue for many activists at the turn of the nineteenth to twentieth centuries, at the turn of the most recent millennium, human trafficking re-emerged as an issue of massive global concern. Nevertheless, there is little consensus about the scope of the problem. Quantifications of contemporary human trafficking range from the United Nations estimate of 2.4 million people to the nongovernmental association Free the Slaves' estimate of twenty-seven million people.[3] A 2003 study sponsored by the US federal government estimated that about six hundred thousand to eight hundred thousand are trafficked yearly between national borders, but this study did not address the number of people trafficked within a country.[4] Additionally, the International Labor Organization (ILO) estimates that 12.3 million people are trapped in a form of slavery.[5] These dramatic discrepancies may be due, in part, to the difficulties of studying illegal activity. However, much like white slavery a hundred years earlier, there continues to be little consensus on the definitions of trafficking. Practices that fall under the scope of modern-day slavery can include "debt-bondage, serfdom, servile (arranged) marriage, and child servitude," in addition to forced labor and sexual exploitation.[6] Maggy Lee argues that there are six conceptual approaches to understanding contemporary human trafficking: "(1) as a modern form of slavery; (2) as an exemplar of the globalisation of crime; (3) as a problem of transnational organized crime; (4) as synonymous with prostitution; (5) as a migration problem; and (6) as a human rights challenge."[7] These different conceptualizations can overlap, contradict, and change over time, but as Lee explains, the different ways of understanding the problem entail different possible solutions.

For many contemporary activists against trafficking, forced labor, and modern slavery (TFLS), TFLS is a form of literal slavery that has become pervasive in the United States and around the globe.[8] Kevin Bales, cofounder, and former president of Free the Slaves, is one of the most prominent voices in the modern-day slavery framework for conceptualizing human trafficking. Free the Slaves is a US offspring of British Anti-Slavery International, an organization that began in 1839 to end the enslavement of African people.[9] Nevertheless, Bales has argued that current slavery is not marked by complete and permanent ownership but entails debt-bondage and forced labor.[10] As with "white slavery," the term "modern-day slavery" is evocative, especially because the language of slavery evokes moral repugnance, demanding decisive action to save innocent victims.[11] Celebrity activists often draw on these perceptions of moral certainty when advocating against modern-day slavery. For instance, in his opening statement to the Senate Foreign Relations Committee on Ending Modern Slavery and Human Trafficking, actor and activist Ashton Kutcher explained, "I've seen video content of a child that's the same age as mine [two years old] being raped by an American man that was a sex tourist in Cambodia. And this child was so conditioned by her environment that she thought she was engaging in play."[12] It is easy to see the horrific rape of a young child as a clear harm against an innocent child. Stories such as these have coalesced opposition to human trafficking as an unambiguous evil.

While the rhetoric may be effective at eliciting public outrage, Annie Hill argues that the framework of modern-day slavery reifies a hierarchy between innocent victim and hero.[13] Most sexual exploitation, however, is more complex, and few humans can fit within this model of innocence. Much like the Wisconsin lumber camps, innocence can too often be predicated on a complete absence of agency, and potential rescuers can determine who is worthy of assistance. Modern-day slavery emerges from a mobile imagination of innocent people who are trapped and have lost all potential for mobility, and, thus, the solution may appear to be rescuing the innocent victim. However, people engaged in sex work often work in conditions of structural violence and precarity, and yet many find moments of agency, albeit in ways that may be restricted and contested.[14] Agency is not zero-sum.

Perceptions of agency are also inflected by racism in ways that can blame people for their own victimization. For example, Chrystul Kizer was sixteen years old when she began to be abused and trafficked by thirty-three-year-old white man named Randy Volar, and she was seventeen when she killed Volar in June 2018. Months before Volar's death, the police had investigated him and found evidence that he was abusing and trafficking multiple Black girls, some as young as twelve years old. Yet, he remained free to continue his abuse. Legally, children cannot prostitute themselves, so criminal responsibility should be placed on the adults engaging in the transaction. A child that is deemed too young to consent to sex is legally a victim, not a sex worker engaged in criminal behavior. Nevertheless, the lead investigating officer described one of Volar's fifteen-year-old victims as "prostituting herself out," suggesting that she was not a real victim.[15] Similarly, Kizer initiated contact with Volar and maintained contact because she reported that he was nice to her. Black girls, like Kizer, are often characterized as hypersexual, a perception that can be used to justify their abuse and exploitation, and class appeared to further naturalize perceptions that Kizer benefited from Volar and, thus, deserved her treatment. Volar's victims did not fit the mythology of the innocent girl held against her will, and the mythology of what innocence looks like can be used to validate (or at least ignore) sexual exploitation. The hierarchy between hero and victim constitutes a racialized and sexualized model of victimhood that marks some people as expendable.

Annie Bunting and Joel Quirk also argue that the rhetoric of slavery is problematic because it "aggregates very different problems under the rubric of a fictive global struggle."[16] Current rhetoric combines different problems under a single banner (labor, marriage, prostitution), but while all these issues are serious, they tend to call for different material solutions. Conflating forced migrant labor with domestic child sex trafficking, for example, may seem persuasively expedient, but it also risks flattening the complexity of the different problems and foreclosing meaningful solutions.

Lee's second framework for understanding trafficking is as a form of globalized crime. As the world seems increasingly connected by technology that spurs the flow of people, ideas, and communication, some people also identify these connections as vehicles for crime, especially human trafficking.[17] The movie *Taken* is a popular example of this framework. In this film, retired CIA agent Bryan Mills (Liam Neeson) is tasked with rescuing his daughter Kim (Maggie Grace) when she is forced into prostitution in Paris. Casey Ryan Kelly argues that *Taken* represents the purity of white womanhood as endangered by a foreign Other, in this case Arab men, and the "film also reinforces whiteness by normalizing white masculine violence as protective and necessary to the proper function of global law and order."[18] Just as Edwin Sims and Ernest Bell warned Progressive Era girls to stay home and not seek adventure, Kim's desire for adventure left her vulnerable to supposedly dangerous foreign men. The interconnectedness of the world made all public space seem potentially dangerous to innocent white women because the paths into danger were represented as ubiquitous and seemed to defy map space.

The third approach of understanding trafficking as a form of transnational organized crime is exemplified in the 2000 United Nations Convention against Transnational Organized Crime and its supplemental Trafficking Protocol.[19] Lee argues that this protocol is at the heart of most contemporary approaches to trafficking and supposes that tactics used to address organized crime can be effectively transferred to human trafficking. The search for an organized cabal was a fixation for some white slavery activists, and thus, when John D. Rockefeller Jr. concluded his grand jury investigation by noting that there was no evidence of an organized traffic in white women, some people, including the judge, interpreted Rockefeller to be saying that white slavery was a myth. However, Rockefeller's conclusion was more nuanced because he found evidence of trafficking through unorganized and informal channels. For some, the search for a cabal of human traffickers continues. For example, right-wing group QAnon captured the imaginations of hundreds of thousands of people by claiming that Democratic politicians were either complicit in or explicitly organizing child sex trafficking rings.[20] Calls to save children from sex trafficking have not only terrified some families who have been unwillingly appropriated, but apparently well-meaning people have flooded government and nonprofit agencies, diverting resources from those who need assistance. These claims of trafficking have also motivated several crimes by people who claimed to be protecting children.[21] The rhetoric that ties sex trafficking to organized crime not only risks flattening a complex issue but also has been harnessed as a tool to supposedly protect white American national identity.

A fourth conceptualization of human trafficking roots the problem in prostitution. Lee argues that, with modern-day trafficking now and with the white slavery controversy then, "trafficking narratives and counter-trafficking campaigns have relied heavily on the paradigmatic images of female powerlessness, sexual purity, and the spectacle of transgressive bodies."[22] Within this frame, all (or nearly all) prostitution is a form a trafficking, and women practicing prostitution need to be saved. The documentary *Rape for Profit* is an example of this frame. A *Seattle Times* review of the film recounts one scene that could have come directly from Ernest Bell or William Stead: "'I was so hungry to be wanted by somebody,' a tearful young woman named Darly confides, that when a woman she soon discovered was a madam told her she would protect her, Darly thought she was being 'saved.' By the time she learned the truth, her supposed savior had her working the streets."[23] The film follows white men, much like those in Ernest Bell's Midnight Mission, as they attempt to shame men purchasing sex and save women selling sex. As with white slavery, contemporary concern with prostitution rarely considers the lived experiences of actual people who engage in sex work, instead treating the prostitute as a symbol of women's vulnerability and exploitation. One implication is that some sex trafficking initiatives have made sex work more dangerous, diverting attention from HIV prevention and the empowerment of sex workers.[24]

Human trafficking has also been understood as a migration problem, most often a subset of illegal immigration that necessitates increasing migration controls.[25] This migration framework supports the frequent assumption that trafficking is a problem with other countries, and robust borders can protect the United States.[26] The *New York Times*, for example, followed Jason Frank, a QAnon "influencer," while he patrolled the US/Mexico border looking to supposedly save migrant children from trafficking.[27] Of course, most scholarship distinguishes trafficking and smuggling, but Frank and others like him seem to slip seamlessly from smuggling to sex trafficking, representing their protection of the US border as heroic. A similar rationale was evident in early immigration laws. The laws were framed as necessary to both protect migrants and protect American from immigrants. Immigration restrictions marked some migrants as inevitably sexually promiscuous and dangerous to white American women, and danger was frequently associated with race, justifying that less desirable populations be restricted. In the context of human trafficking, protecting people at the border often seems to be a pretext for using the border to protect Americans from non-white migrants.

Lee identifies the final conceptualization of human trafficking as a human rights framework. Human rights may be the most capricious of Lee's frameworks, because, although the language of human rights has become pervasive, there is little consensus on the meanings and political applications of human rights. For instance, some theorists argue that human rights are protection against the state, securing negative rights for people.[28] Yet, within the context of human trafficking, a human rights approach tends focus on structural power, rather than individual coercion and exploitation, suggesting that human rights entail specific positive rights.[29] Alison Brysk, a vocal advocate for a human rights framework, argues, "Slavery is not an accident or an atavism; it is a predatory strategy of commodification of fellow human beings in privatizing world."[30] As a result, she calls for solutions that foreground empowerment instead of protection.

Although prominent anarchist Emma Goldman's perspective on white slavery was not completely in line with most vocal advocates of her time, her 1910 essay on the topic was very similar to contemporary human rights activists. She was explicit that sex trafficking was not a moral problem, but rather she insisted that sex trafficking was a problem of women's rights within systems of economic exploitation.[31] Among the more vocal advocates within the white slavery controversy, Frances Willard, Josephine Butler, and Katherine Bushnell may be closest to utilizing a human rights rhetoric because each challenged the ways that laws and social norms burdened women.[32] Bushnell challenged power dynamics that trapped women in prostitution, and Butler argued that women should not lose their bodily autonomy if they have sex outside of marriage. However, Willard, Butler, and Bushnell never abandoned their commitment to protection, and Butler explicitly called for an abolition of state regulated prostitution, while some contemporary human rights advocates insist that state regulation of prostitution may be necessary to empower sex workers and, thus, alleviate sex trafficking. Across these differences, human rights (and similar Progressive Era rhetoric) consistently draw on conceptions of agency, and, within the mobile imagination, agency is rooted in the power to determine mobility (or immobility). However, beyond opening future possibilities for mobility, there are important practical questions that remain even within a human rights approach to trafficking. As Michael Ignatieff explains, despite the universalizing language of human rights, it is important to consider the political questions of who is represented and what rights are limited.[33]

It is not unusual to identify connections between historic and contemporary issues. However, the commonalities between the white slavery and modern-day slavery controversies are particularly salient. First, these controversies illustrate that the language of slavery is problematic. Slavery is certainly evocative, and some contemporary activists insist that it is a factually-accurate description of the situation with some human trafficking. However, rhetoric does not exist in a vacuum, and slavery, especially in the United States, remains tied to the legacy of enslavement of people of African descent. While scholars have done important work documenting resistance and agency among enslaved populations, the popular imagination is not as nuanced.[34] If enslaved peoples are understood as abject and devoid of agency, few people will self-identify as slaves, and the rhetoric of slavery tends to empower the rescuer of an innocent, while entirely disempowering the person being trafficked. This dichotomy not only fails to recognize the complexity of people's lived experiences but also can add an additional layer of harm to those already experiencing a form of trafficking. With temporal distance, it may be easier to see how the rhetoric of white slavery weaponized a victim/whore dichotomy, and attention to twenty-first-century manifestations of those threads then help us attend to the ways that the rhetoric continues to be weaponized against those that activists proport to help.

Commonalities between white slavery and modern-day slavery can also illuminate how trafficking rhetoric is not only about protecting people but also works to constitute identity and belonging. By turning to the mobile imagination constructed within the white slavery controversy of the Progressive Era, I have argued that womanhood was symbolically appropriated to reinforce the whiteness of nation. Likewise, there are larger ideological assumptions at work in the current modern-day slavery controversy, and a critical engagement with the rhetoric may help uncover the larger cultural work. This engagement can help us better understand the limitations, possibilities, and exclusions of the community being constituted by contemporary trafficking rhetoric. Specifically, contemporary calls to protect women and children work in conjunction with racialized national identity. The rhetoric of white supremacy is adaptable, but uncovering how white womanhood was appropriated to shore up the whiteness of nation in the white slavery controversy can help make the threads of white supremacy more visible in modern-day slavery rhetoric.

White Slavery and the Problem with Progress

Robin E. Jensen has identified an "irony inherent in much Progressive Era communication that included sexist, racist, classist, and xenophobic appeals" despite a purported commitment to reform and public deliberation.[35] Indeed, there was a wide diversity among progressives who disagreed on issues ranging from labor to immigration to war.[36] Daniel T. Rodgers has concluded that it is not possible to identify a unified progressive movement, but rather historians now recognize the multiplicity of perspectives during the era.[37] Yet, Glen Gendzel aptly notes that it is significant that a wide group of reformers during this time period called themselves progressives, despite their significant differences.[38] While Gendzel identifies positive statism as a commonality among progressives, I turn to the metaphor of progress to understand the ideological commitments and contradictions evident in the white slavery controversy of the Progressive Era.

Progress is a metaphor of mobility used to conceptualize a linear spatiotemporal movement of a people with a culture. The country was moving, and progressives were responding to perceived changes and attempting to shape the future. Indeed, what we now call the Progressive Era was steeped in the spatiotemporal metaphor of progress. Gail Bederman explains, "Human races were assumed to evolve from simple savagery, through violent barbarism, to advanced and valuable civilization."[39] This framework allowed for linear movement, either forward or backward between savagery and civilization. In writing about the need to address white slavery, Jane Addams argued, "Secure in the knowledge of evolutionary processes, we have learned to talk glibly of the obligations of race progress and of the possibility of racial degeneration."[40] For her, the previous generation's elimination of Black enslavement was progress, but failure to address white slavery risked that evolutionary progress. Even rhetors who worked to challenge racial and gender norms of the era tended to employ this framework of progress, perhaps shifting the timelines, criteria, or definitions of progress.[41]

In the Progressive Era, progress was a central trope of the mobile imagination. It reflected a spatiotemporal logic that constituted a sense of national identity, belonging, and possibility. The white slavery controversy is just one example of how activists worked to protect the supposedly forward progress of the nation. Reading the mobile imagination can help uncover the overlapping ways that mobility (or immobility) shape national space. The forward progress of the nation was thought to require people to exist within space in different ways. White women needed to be protected within their sphere of the home, and the nation needed to guard itself against any perceived threat to white womanhood. During this period, progressives were not questioning "imperialist white supremacist capitalist cisheteropatriarchy;" rather they were operating within a spatiotemporal logic that naturalized their understandings of a civilized country.[42] Examining the white slavery controversy within this context helps uncover how white slavery operated as a symbolic field that sustained and reproduced the whiteness of nation.

As much as the white slavery controversy and (in many instances) its contemporary counterpart appear to be fixated on sex, especially regarding the protection women and children, these controversies are one of the ways in which people make sense of national space and belonging. They rely on creating a precarious and vulnerable symbol of the nation, a symbol deeply imbued with norms of gender, race, and class. Indeed, Clifford G. Roe and B. S. Steadwell insisted that white slavery was not simply an issue of protecting individual women, but unless killed, white slavery "will crush out decent government, for when our homes are destroyed our government is ruined, because the home is the foundation of all government."[43] As with white slavery, contemporary concerns over sex trafficking have mobilized activists around the world. Yet, when considering calls to protect women and children, it is important to consider what kind of government and nation is being protected and for whom.

Notes

Introduction

1. "The Slave Trade and the Voter," *National Prohibitionist*, May 12, 1911, quoted in Jean Turner-Zimmermann, *Chicago's Black Traffic in White Girls* (Chicago: Chicago Rescue Mission, 1911), 12.
2. Clifford E. Roe and B. S. Steadwell, The Great War on White Slavery or Fighting for the Protection of Our Girls (1911), 14.
3. Roe and Steadwell, *The Great War on White Slavery*, 371.
4. I use the term "white womanhood" to reference a symbolic construct that is distinct from the embodied experience of actual women. My use of "white womanhood" is similar to Raka Shome's use of "white femininity." Raka Shome, *Diana and Beyond* (Champaign: University of Illinois Press, 2014), 20.
5. Hooks explains, "This phrase is useful precisely because it does not prioritize one system over another but rather offers us a way to think about the interlocking systems that work together to uphold and maintain cultures of domination. bell hooks, *Writing Beyond Race: Living Theory and Practice* (New York: Routledge, 2013), 4.
6. See Jessica R. Pliley, *Policing Sexuality* (Cambridge, MA: Harvard University Press, 2014); Gretchen Soderlund, *Sex Trafficking, Scandal, and the Transformation of Journalism, 1885–1917* (Chicago: University of Chicago Press, 2013); Brian Donovan, *White Slave Crusades: Race, Gender, and Anti-Vice Activism, 1887–1917* (Urbana: University of Illinois Press, 2006).

7. David J. Langum, *Crossing Over the Line: Legislating Morality and the Mann Act* (Chicago: University of Chicago Press, 2007); Brian Donovan, *Respectability on Trial* (Albany, NY: SUNY Press, 2016), 107; Judith R. Walkowitz, *City of Dreadful Delight* (Chicago: University of Chicago Press, 2013), 121; Bonnie J. Shucha, "White Slavery in the Northwoods: Early U.S. Anti-Sex Trafficking and Its Continuing Relevance to Trafficking Reform," *William & Mary Journal of Women and the Law* 23, no. 1 (2015); Timothy J. Gilfoyle, *City of Eros: New York City, Prostitution, and the Commercialization of Sex, 1790–1920* (New York: W. W. Norton, 1992), 283–97; Frederick K. Grittner, *White Slavery: Myth, Ideology, and American Law* (New York: Garland, 1990), 64.

    It is not unusual to see scholarship apply the concept of moral panic without a definition of the term, and it is accurate to say that there was public outrage (panic) over an issue of moral import with the white slavery controversy. Young explains, "All commentators agree, the disproportional reaction to a particular deviance is a key attribute of any moral panic" (J. Young, "Moral Panic: Its Origins in Resistance, Ressentiment and the Translation of Fantasy into Reality," *British Journal of Criminology* 49, no. 1 [2009]: 13). I am not concerned with assessing the material reality of prostitution during this time, attempting to determine if the response was disproportional. Instead, I critically engage the controversy to uncover how the rhetoric of white womanhood shapes national space.

8. Ruth Rosen, *The Lost Sisterhood: Prostitution in America, 1900–1918* (Baltimore: Johns Hopkins University Press, 1983), 114.

9. Rosen, *The Lost Sisterhood*, 134–35. Rosen explains that the "sale of women into forced prostitution" was the most "extreme" form of sexual exploitation.

10. Most contemporary scholarship uses the term "sex work" instead of "prostitution." I have chosen to use "prostitution" throughout because that was the common language of the Progressive Era. However, I have attempted to be careful to situate prostitution as something that a person does, rather than an intrinsic identity. Additionally, people who are not women can practice prostitution. However, activists during the time period of this study were explicitly concerned with protecting white women, not everyone practicing prostitution.

11. Some studies of white slavery have explicitly considered discourse. See Jo Doezema, "Loose Women or Lost Women? The Re-emergence of the Myth of White Slavery in Contemporary Discourses of Trafficking in Women," *Gender Issues* 18, no. 1 (1999); Mara L. Keire, "The Vice Trust: A Reinterpretation of the White Slavery Scare in the United States, 1907–1917," *Journal of Social History* 35, no. 1 (2001). Likewise, Soderlund focuses on journalistic practices. Gretchen Soderlund, "Covering Urban Vice: The *New York Times*, 'White Slavery,' and the Construction of Journalistic Knowledge," *Critical Studies in Media Communication* 19, no. 4 (2002): 438–60; Gretchen Soderlund,

Sex Trafficking, Scandal, and the Transformation of Journalism, 1885–1917 (Chicago: University of Chicago Press, 2013).
12. Donovan, *White Slave Crusades*, 19; Keire, "The Vice Trust," 7.
13. Rajini Srikanth, "Ventriloquism in the Captivity Narrative: White Women Challenge European American Patriarchy," in *White Women in Racialized Spaces*, ed. Samina Najmi and Rajini Srikanth (Albany, NY: SUNY Press, 2012); Grittner, *White Slavery*, 20. Srikanth argues that these captivity narratives were used by white women to resist patriarchal gender expectations, but in doing so they reified the creation of a racial Other (87). Hasian also finds the rhetoric of white slavery in an antebellum legal case where the court considered a case where a European woman, assumed to be mixed race, was enslaved. Marouf Hasian, "Performative Law and the Maintenance of Interracial Social Boundaries: Assuaging Antebellum Fears of 'White Slavery' and the Case of Sally Miller/Salome Müller," *Text and Performance Quarterly* 23, no. 1 (2003): 55–86.
14. David Zarefsky, "Echoes of the Slavery Controversy in the Current Abortion Debate," *Conference Proceedings—National Communication Association/American Forensic Association (Alta Conference on Argumentation)* (Washington, DC: National Communication Association, 1991), 89.
15. Nell Irvin Painter, *The History of White People* (New York: W. W. Norton, 2010), 34.
16. Mishuana Goeman, *Mark My Words: Native Women Mapping Our Nation* (Minneapolis: University of Minnesota Press, 2013), 48.
17. There has been substantial research on whiteness and white womanhood. See Kathleen M. Blee, *Inside Organized Racism* (Berkeley: University of California Press, 2003); Lisa B. Y. Calvente, Bernadette Marie Calafell, and Karma R. Chávez, "Here Is Something You Can't Understand: The Suffocating Whiteness of Communication Studies," *Communication and Critical/Cultural Studies* 17, no. 2 (2020): 203; Eva Cherniavsky, *That Pale Mother Rising: Sentimental Discourses and the Imitation of Motherhood in Nineteenth-Century America* (Bloomington: Indiana University Press, 1995), 2; Bryan J. McCann, Ashley Noel Mack, and Rico Self, "Communication's Quest for Whiteness: The Racial Politics of Disciplinary Legitimacy," *Communication and Critical/Cultural Studies* 17, no. 2 (2020), 244; Phil Chidester, "May the Circle Stay Unbroken: Friends, the Presence of Absence, and the Rhetorical Reinforcement of Whiteness," *Critical Studies in Media Communication* 25, no. 2 (2008): 158; Leda M. Cooks and Jennifer S. Simpson, "Introduction," in *Whiteness, Pedagogy, Performance*, ed. Leda M. Cooks and Jennifer S. Simpson (Lanham, MD: Lexington Books, 2008), 17; Carrie Crenshaw, "Resisting Whiteness' Rhetorical Silence," *Western Journal of Communication* 61, no. 3 (1997); Katerina Deliovsky, *White Femininity* (Toronto, ON: Brunswick Books, 2010), 48; Mohan J. Dutta, "Whiteness, Internationalization, and Erasure: Decolonizing Futures from the Global South," *Communication and*

Critical/Cultural Studies 17, no. 2 (2020); Stephanie L. Hartzell, "Whiteness Feels Good Here: Interrogating White Nationalist Rhetoric on Stormfront," *Communication and Critical/Cultural Studies* 17, no. 2 (2020): 131; Elizabeth Gillespie McRae, *Mothers of Massive Resistance* (Oxford: Oxford University Press, 2018); Dreama G. Moon and Michelle A. Holling, "'White Supremacy in Heels': (White) Feminism, White Supremacy, and Discursive Violence," *Communication and Critical/Cultural Studies* 17, no. 2 (2020): 254; Dreama G. Moon, "White Enculturation and Bourgeois Ideology: The Discursive Production of 'Good (White) Girls,'" in *Whiteness: A Communication of Social Identity*, ed. Thomas K. Nakayama and Judith N. Martin (Thousand Oaks, CA: Sage Publications, 1999), 178; Dreama G. Moon, "'Be/coming' White and the Myth of White Ignorance: Identity Projects in White Communities," *Western Journal of Communication* 80, no. 3 (2016); Thomas K. Nakayama and Robert L. Krizek, "Whiteness: A Strategic Rhetoric," *Quarterly Journal of Speech* 81, no. 3 (1995); Raka Shome, "Whiteness and the Politics of Location," in *Whiteness: The Communication of Social Identity*, ed. Thomas K. Nakayama and Judith N. Martin (Thousand Oaks, CA: Sage Publications, 1999), 108; Vron Ware, "Perfidious Albion: Whiteness and the International Imagination," in *The Making and Unmaking of Whiteness*, ed. Birgit Brander Rasmussen, Eric Klinenberg, Irene J. Nexica, and Matt Wray (Durham, NC: Duke University Press, 2001), 185; John T. Warren, *Performing Purity* (New York: Peter Lang, 2003), 29.

18. William Stead, "The Maiden Tribute of Modern Babylon—I: The Report of Our Secret Commission," *Pall Mall Gazette*, July 6, 1885.
19. For example, Woman's Christian Temperance Union, "Department for the Promotion of Social Purity, Co-Operating with the 'White Cross Army,' Plan of Work for 1886," 1, Frances E. Willard Scrapbooks, Frances Willard Library and Archives, Evanston, IL, scrapbook number 26, microfilm roll 35; Roe and Steadwell, *The Great War on White Slavery*, 13.
20. Shucha, "White Slavery in the Northwoods," 76.
21. Donovan, *White Slave Crusades*, 20.
22. Peggy Levitt, "Constructing Gender Across Borders: A Transnational Approach," in *Analyzing Gender, Intersectionality, and Multiple Inequalities*, ed. Esther Ngan-Ling Chow, Marcia Texler Segal, and Tan Lin (Bingley, UK: Emerald Group Publishing, 2011), 164–65. Shome, *Diana and Beyond*, 5.
23. Eleonore Kofman, "Feminist Political Geographies," in *A Companion to Feminist Geography*, ed. Lise Nelson and Joni Seager (Malden, MA: Blackwell, 2005), 528. Also see Eric Sheppard and Robert B. McMaster, "Introduction: Scale and Geographic Inquiry," in *Scale and Geographic Inquiry: Nature, Society, and Method* (Malden, MA: Blackwell Publishing, 2008), 15.
24. Benedict Richard O'Gorman Anderson, *Imagined Communities* (London: Verso, 1991), 25.
25. Edward A. Ross, *The Old World in the New: The Significance of Past and Present Immigration to the American People* (New York: Century Co., 1914), 21, 285;

Daniel E. Bender, *American Abyss: Savagery and Civilization in the Age of Industry* (Ithaca, NY: Cornell University Press, 2010), 1–3. According to Leonard, Ross popularized the term "social control" to refer to the capacity to mold societies to ensure their survival. Thomas C. Leonard, "Mistaking Eugenics for Social Darwinism: Why Eugenics Is Missing from the History of American Economics," *History of Political Economy* 37, supplement (2005): 200–233.

26. H. W. Brands, *The Reckless Decade: America in the 1890s* (Chicago: University of Chicago Press, 1995), 90–95.
27. Stewart E. Tolnay, "The African American 'Great Migration' and Beyond," *Annual Review of Sociology* 29 (2003): 209–32.
28. Leslie A. Hahner, *To Become an American: Immigrants and Americanization Campaigns of the Early Twentieth Century* (East Lansing: Michigan State University Press, 2017), 1; Grace Abbott, *The Immigrant and the Community* (New York: Century Co., 1917), vii.
29. Leroy G. Dorsey, *We Are All Americans, Pure and Simple: Theodore Roosevelt and the Myth of Americanism* (Tuscaloosa: University of Alabama Press, 2007), 49; Brands, *The Reckless Decade*, 100.
30. Sidney R. Bland, "Shaping the Life of the New Woman: The Crusading Years of the *Delineator*," *American Periodicals* 19, no.2 (2009): 168.
31. Sara M. Evans, *Born for Liberty* (New York: Simon & Schuster, 1997), 147.
32. Jacqueline Jones Royster, *Traces of a Stream: Literacy and Social Change among African American Women* (Pittsburgh: University of Pittsburgh Press, 2000), 160; Shirley Wilson Logan, *Liberating Language: Sites of Rhetorical Education in Nineteenth-Century Black America* (Carbondale: Southern Illinois University Press, 2008), 4.
33. Gail Bederman, *Manliness and Civilization: A Cultural History of Gender and Race in the United States, 1880–1917* (Chicago: University of Chicago Press, 1995), 25.
34. Ross, *The Old World in the New*, 21, 285.
35. Immigration Commission of the United States, *Dictionary of Races or Peoples* (Washington, DC: Government Printing Office: 1911), 2.
36. I am following Thomas C. Leonard in representing Progressive Era evolutionary ideas as "eugenics." However, Leonard notes that there were significant areas of disagreement among progressives regarding issues that included if inheritance was dictated by nature or nurture, if the unit of selection was the individual or the group, and the meaning and sites of competition. Leonard prefers eugenics to the term "social Darwinism" because he argues that there was no school of thought called "social Darwinism" at the time. Instead, the term was used as an epithet, and it does not accurately describe Progressive Era thought; Leonard, "Mistaking Eugenics for Social Darwinism," 216.
37. Leonard, "Mistaking Eugenics for Social Darwinism," 201.
38. Leonard, "Mistaking Eugenics for Social Darwinism," 221.
39. Dorsey, *We Are All Americans*, 53; Leonard, "Mistaking Eugenics for Social Darwinism," 226.

40. For example, Elizabeth J. Clapp, *Mothers of All Children: Women Reformers and the Rise of Juvenile Courts in Progressive Era America* (University Park: Pennsylvania State University Press, 1998); Lori D. Ginzberg, *Women and the Work of Benevolence* (New Haven, CT: Yale University Press, 1990).
41. Anne McClintock, "Family Feuds: Gender, Nationalism and the Family," *Feminist Review* 44 (1993): 62. Also, Nira Yuval-Davis, *The Politics of Belonging: Intersectional Contestations* (Thousand Oaks, CA: Sage Publications, 2011), 94.
42. Barbara Welter, "The Cult of True Womanhood: 1820–1860," *American Quarterly* 18, no. 2 (1966): 151–74; Mary Louise Roberts, "True Womanhood Revisited," *Journal of Women's History* 14, no. 1 (2002).

    For literature on how women appropriated and resisted these norms, see Robert Asen, "Women, Work, Welfare: A Rhetorical History of Images of Poor Women in Welfare Policy Debates," *Rhetoric & Public Affairs* 6, no. 2 (2003): 290–92; A. Cheree Carlson, "Creative Casuistry and Feminist Consciousness: The Rhetoric of Moral Reform," *Quarterly Journal of Speech* 78, no. 1 (1992); Linda K. Kerber, *No Constitutional Right to Be Ladies* (New York: Macmillan, 1999), 8–9; Tiffany Lewis, "Municipal Housekeeping in the American West: Bertha Knight Landes's Entrance into Politics," *Rhetoric & Public Affairs* 14, no. 3 (2011); Catherine H. Palczewski, "The 1919 Prison Special: Constituting White Women's Citizenship," *Quarterly Journal of Speech* 102, no. 2 (2016); Jennifer Burek Pierce, "Science, Advocacy, and 'the Sacred and Intimate Things of Life': Representing Motherhood as a Progressive Era Cause in Women's Magazines," *American Periodicals* 18, no. 1 (2008); Kristan Poirot, "(Un)Making Sex, Making Race: Nineteenth-Century Liberalism, Difference, and the Rhetoric of Elizabeth Cady Stanton," *Quarterly Journal of Speech* 96, no. 2 (2010); Alisse Portnoy, *Their Right to Speak* (Cambridge, MA: Harvard University Press, 2009); Angela G. Ray and Cindy Koenig Richards, "Inventing Citizens, Imagining Gender Justice: The Suffrage Rhetoric of Virginia and Francis Minor," *Quarterly Journal of Speech* 93, no. 4 (2007); Angela G. Ray, "The Rhetorical Ritual of Citizenship: Women's Voting as Public Performance, 1868–1875," *Quarterly Journal of Speech* 93, no. 1 (2007); Amy R. Slagell, "The Rhetorical Structure of Frances E. Willard's Campaign for Woman Suffrage, 1876–1896," *Rhetoric & Public Affairs* 4, no. 1 (2001); Belinda A. Stillion Southard, "Militancy, Power, and Identity: The Silent Sentinels as Women Fighting for Political Voice," *Rhetoric & Public Affairs* 10, no. 3 (2007); Susan Zaeske, *Signatures of Citizenship: Petitioning, Antislavery, and Women's Political Identity* (Chapel Hill: University of North Carolina Press, 2003).
43. Katie L. Gibson, "Judicial Rhetoric and Women's 'Place': The United States Supreme Court's Darwinian Defense of Separate Spheres," *Western Journal of Communication* 71, no. 2 (2007); Nan Johnson, "Reigning in the Court of Silence: Women and Rhetorical Space in Postbellum America," *Philosophy & Rhetoric* 33, no. 3 (2000).

44. Leslie J. Harris, "Home-Making, Nation-Making," in *Reading the Presidency: Advances in Presidential Rhetoric*, ed. Stephen J. Heidt and Mary E. Stuckey (New York: Peter Lang, 2019), 287.
45. Lauren Gail Berlant, *The Queen of America Goes to Washington City* (Durham, NC: Duke University Press, 1997), 6, 36.
46. Henri Lefebvre, *The Production of Space*, trans. Donald Nicholson-Smith, (Cambridge, MA: Blackwell, 1991), 26. Lefebvre explains space as a "conceptual triad" consisting of spatial practice, representations of space, and representational spaces (33). Also see Joan Faber McAlister, "Figural Materialism: Renovating Marriage through the American Family Home," *Southern Communication Journal* 76, no. 4 (2011): 291.
47. Doreen B. Massey, *Space, Place, and Gender* (Minneapolis: University of Minnesota Press, 1999), 120.
48. Raka Shome, "Space Matters: The Power and Practice of Space," *Communication Theory* 13, no. 1 (February 1, 2003): 40. Also see Timothy Barney, "'Gulag'—Slavery, Inc.': The Power of Place and the Rhetorical Life of a Cold War Map," *Rhetoric & Public Affairs* 16, no. 2 (2013): 322–23; Eun Young Lee, "Looking Forward: Decentering and Reorienting Communication Studies in the Spatial Turn," *Women's Studies in Communication* 39, no. 2 (2016): 133.
49. Isaac West, "PISSAR's Critically Queer and Disabled Politics," *Communication and Critical/Cultural Studies* 7, no. 2 (2010): 160.
50. Jayne Rodgers, "Doreen Massey," *Information, Communication & Society* 7, no. 2 (2004): 282.
51. See Roxanne Mountford, "On Gender and Rhetorical Space," *Rhetoric Society Quarterly* 31, no. 1 (2001): 42; Allison M. Prasch, "Reagan at Pointe Du Hoc: Deictic Epideictic and the Persuasive Power of 'Bringing Before the Eyes,'" *Rhetoric & Public Affairs* 18, no. 2 (2015): 253; Danielle Endres and Samantha Senda-Cook, "Location Matters: The Rhetoric of Place in Protest," *Quarterly Journal of Speech* 97, no. 3 (2011): 265; Joshua P. Ewalt, "Mapping Injustice: The World Is Witness, Place-Framing, and the Politics of Viewing on Google Earth," *Communication, Culture & Critique* 4, no. 4 (2011): 336; Greg Dickinson, Carole Blair, and Brian L. Ott, "Introduction: Rhetoric/Memory/Place," in *Places of Public Memory* (Tuscaloosa: University of Alabama Press, 2010), 24; Lee, "Looking Forward," 133.
52. Tim Cresswell, *On the Move: Mobility in the Modern Western World* (New York: Routledge, 2006), 4.
53. Daniel C. Brouwer, "From San Francisco to Atlanta and Back Again: Ideologies of Mobility in the AIDS Quilts Search for a Homeland," *Rhetoric & Public Affairs* 10, no. 4 (2007): 701–21.
54. Alyssa A. Samek, "Mobility, Citizenship, and 'American Women on the Move' in the 1977 International Women's Year Torch Relay," *Quarterly Journal of Speech* 103, no. 3 (2017); Armond R. Towns, "Geographies of Pain: #SayHerName and the Fear of Black Women's Mobility," *Women's Studies in*

Communication 39, no. 2 (2016): 122–26; Robert Topinka, "Resisting the Fixity of Suburban Space: The Walker as Rhetorician," *Rhetoric Society Quarterly* 42, no. 1 (2012): 65–84.

The study of mobility has also begun to emerge as a significant area of focused concern in some other areas of scholarship, especially as the twenty-first century has brought increasing large-scale movement of people and ideas. In their development of the "new mobilities paradigm," Anthony Elliott and John Urry outline an area of empirical research considering five types of mobilities: corporeal mobility, mobility of objects, imaginative travel, virtual travel, and communicative travel. See R. Law, "Beyond 'Women and Transport': Towards New Geographies of Gender and Daily Mobility," *Progress in Human Geography* 23, no. 4 (1999): 574; Kevin Hannam, Mimi Sheller, and John Urry, "Editorial: Mobilities, Immobilities and Moorings," *Mobilities* 1, no. 1 (2006): 1; Stephen B. Crofts Wiley, Daniel M. Sutko, and Tabita Moreno Becerra, "Assembling Social Space," *Communication Review* 13, no. 4 (2010): 342; Catherine J. Nash and Andrew Gorman-Murray, "LGBT Neighbourhoods and 'New Mobilities': Towards Understanding Transformations in Sexual and Gendered Urban Landscapes," *International Journal of Urban and Regional Research* 38, no. 3 (2014): 763; Anthony Elliott and John Urry, *Mobile Lives* (New York: Routledge, 2010), 15–16.

55. Towns, "Geographies of Pain," 123.
56. Alessandra Beasley Von Burg, "Stochastic Citizenship: Toward a Rhetoric of Mobility," *Philosophy and Rhetoric* 45, no. 4 (2012): 355; Cresswell, *On the Move*, 159.
57. Cresswell, *On the Move*, 4.
58. Carly S. Woods, "(Im)mobile Metaphors: Toward an Intersectional Rhetorical History," in *Standing in the Intersection: Feminist Voices, Feminist Practices in Communication Studies*, ed. Karma R. Chávez and Cindy L. Griffin (Albany, NY: SUNY Press, 2012), 78–96.
59. Lisa A. Flores, "Stoppage and the Racialized Rhetorics of Mobility," *Western Journal of Communication* 84, no. 3 (2020): 248.
60. Flores, "Stoppage and the Racialized Rhetorics," 257.
61. Cresswell, *On the Move*, 159.
62. Cresswell, *On the Move*, 197; Sarah Hallenbeck, *Claiming the Bicycle: Women, Rhetoric, and Technology in Nineteenth-Century America* (Carbondale: Southern Illinois University Press, 2016), xvii; Nash and Gorman-Murray, "LGBT Neighbourhoods," 762; Mary E. Stuckey, "The Donner Party and the Rhetoric of Western Expansion," *Rhetoric & Public Affairs* 14, no. 2 (2011): 248–50.
63. Joanne Sharp, "Feminisms," in *A Companion to Cultural Geography*, ed. James S. Duncan, Nuala C. Johnson, and Richard H. Schein (Malden, MA: Blackwell, 2004), 71; Towns, "Geographies of Pain," 123.
64. Doreen Massey, "Imagining Globalisation: Power-Geometries of Time-Space,"

in *Power-Geometries and the Politics of Space-Time*, ed. Michael Hoyler (Heidelberg, Germany: University of Heidelberg, 1999), 22.
65. Massey, "Imagining Globalisation," 13–14.
66. Joan Faber McAlister, "Ten Propositions for Communication Scholars Studying Space and Place," *Women's Studies in Communication* 39, no. 2 (2016): 115.
67. E. Cram argues that "emotional landscapes" mediate relationships to space. E. Cram, "Feeling Cartography," *Women's Studies in Communication* 39, no. 2 (2016): 141.
68. Jan Nespor, "Discursive Geographies," *Journal of Language & Politics* 13, no. 3 (2014): 492–93.
69. See Ronald Walter Greene and Kevin Douglas Kusa, "From the Arab Spring to Athens, From Occupy Wall Street to Moscow," *Rhetoric Society Quarterly* 42, no. 3 (2012): 271–88; Hannam, Sheller, and Urry, "Editorial," 12; Wiley, Sutko, and Moreno Becerra, "Assembling Social Space," 342–44.
70. See Jeremy Packer and Kathleen F. Oswald, "From Windscreen to Widescreen: Screening Technologies and Mobile Communication," *Communication Review* 13, no. 4 (2010): 309–39; Mimi Sheller, "Air Mobilities on the U.S.-Caribbean Border: Open Skies and Closed Gates," *Communication Review* 13, no. 4 (2010): 269–88; John M. Sloop and Joshua Gunn, "Status Control: An Admonition Concerning the Publicized Privacy of Social Networking," *Communication Review* 13, no. 4 (2010): 289–308; Stephen B. Crofts Wiley and Jeremy Packer, "Rethinking Communication after the Mobilities Turn," *Communication Review* 13, no. 4 (2010): 263–68.
71. Hallenbeck, *Claiming the Bicycle*.
72. Karlyn Kohrs Campbell, "Agency: Promiscuous and Protean," *Communication and Critical/Cultural Studies* 2, no. 1 (2005): 2.
73. Darrel Enck-Wanzer, "Tropicalizing East Harlem: Rhetorical Agency, Cultural Citizenship, and Nuyorican Cultural Production," *Communication Theory* 21, no. 4 (2011): 346; Stacey Sowards, "Rhetorical Agency as Haciendo Caras and Differential Consciousness through Lens of Gender, Race, Ethnicity, and Class: An Examination of Dolores Huerta's Rhetoric," *Communication Theory* 20, no. 2 (2010): 227.
74. Christine J. Gardner, "'Created This Way': Liminality, Rhetorical Agency, and the Transformative Power of Constraint among Gay Christian College Students," *Communication and Critical/Cultural Studies* 14, no. 1 (2017): 35; Casey Ryan Kelly, "Women's Rhetorical Agency in the American West: The New Penelope," *Women's Studies in Communication* 32, no. 2 (2009): 210; Erin J. Rand, *Reclaiming Queer* (Tuscaloosa: University of Alabama Press, 2014), 14.
75. Josue David Cisneros, "Reclaiming the Rhetoric of Reies López Tijerina: Border Identity and Agency in 'The Land Grant Question,'" *Communication Quarterly* 60, no. 5 (2012): 564.
76. Katherine McKittrick, *Demonic Grounds: Black Women and the Cartographies of Struggle* (Minneapolis: University of Minnesota Press, 2006).

77. Jenny Sharpe, *Ghosts of Slavery: A Literary Archaeology of Black Women's Lives* (Minneapolis: University of Minnesota Press, 2003), xvii.
78. For an example of how a scene can be used to shape the meanings of women's bodies, see Mari Boor Tonn, Valerie A. Endress, and John N. Diamond, "Hunting and Heritage on Trial: A Dramatistic Debate over Tragedy, Tradition, and Territory," *Quarterly Journal of Speech* 79 (1993): 177.

Chapter 1. Slavery Up North: White Women's Displacement in the Wisconsin Northwoods, 1887–1889

1. Carl Krog, "Marinette: A Lumber Camp Becomes a City, 1880–1910," *Old Northwest* 6, no. 1 (1980): 20.
2. "Spirited Away: A Girl Imprisoned in a Den in Wisconsin Woods," *Boston Daily Globe*, October 28, 1887; "A Revolting Recital," *Galveston Daily News*, November 3, 1887.
3. Mishuana Goeman, *Mark My Words: Native Women Mapping Our Nation* (Minneapolis: University of Minnesota Press, 2013), 70.
4. Liz Bondi and Joyce Davidson, "Situating Gender," in *A Companion to Feminist Geography*, ed. Lise Nelson and Joni Seager (Malden, MA: Blackwell, 2005), 20.
5. Ronald Walter Greene and Kevin Douglas Kusa, "From the Arab Spring to Athens, from Occupy Wall Street to Moscow," *Rhetoric Society Quarterly* 42, no. 3 (2012): 273.
6. William Francis Raney, *Wisconsin: A Story of Progress* (New York: Prentice-Hall, 1940), 233.
7. Raney, *Wisconsin*, 88–89.
8. Raney, *Wisconsin*, 234.
9. Robert C. Nesbit, *The History of Wisconsin*, vol. 3 (Madison: State Historical Society of Wisconsin, 1985), 46.
10. Nesbit, *The History of Wisconsin*, 59.
11. Raney, *Wisconsin*, 203–5.
12. Isaac West, "PISSAR's Critically Queer and Disabled Politics," *Communication and Critical/Cultural Studies* 7, no. 2 (2010): 158.
13. James Z. Schwartz, "Taming the 'Savagery' of Michigan's Indians," *Michigan Historical Review* 34, no. 2 (2008): 54.
14. Raney, *Wisconsin*, 77. Raney also explains that in the 1850 some small reservations were created (78).
15. Frederick Jackson Turner, *The Significance of the Frontier in American History* (Chicago: American Historical Association, 1893), 201–2.
16. Tiziano Bonazzi, "Frederick Jackson Turner's Frontier Thesis and the Self-Consciousness of America," *Journal of American Studies* 27, no. 2 (1993): 149–71. One commentator called it "the single most influential essay ever

written by an American historian." William Cronon, "Landscape and Home: Environmental Traditions in Wisconsin," *Wisconsin Magazine of History* 74, no. 2 (1990–1991): 94.

17. H. W. Brands, *The Reckless Decade: American in the 1890s* (Chicago: University of Chicago Press, 1995), 23.
18. Jason E. Pierce, *Making the White Man's West: Whiteness and the Creation of the American West* (Boulder: University Press of Colorado, 2016), 11; Brigitte Georgi-Findlay, *The Frontiers of Women's Writing: Women's Narratives and the Rhetoric of Western Expansion* (Tucson: University of Arizona Press, 1996), 2.
19. Catherine H. Palczewski, "The Male Madonna and the Feminine Uncle Sam: Visual Argument, Icons, and Ideographs in 1909 Anti-Woman Suffrage Postcards," *Quarterly Journal of Speech* 91, no. 4 (2005): 374; Cheryl R. Jorgensen-Earp, "The Lady, the Whore, and the Spinster: The Rhetorical Use of Victorian Images of Women," *Western Journal of Speech Communication* 54, no. 1 (1990): 85.
20. Georgi-Findlay, *The Frontiers of Women's Writing*, 8.
21. For example, see Brian T. Thorn, "'Peace Is the Concern of Every Mother': Communist and Social Democratic Women's Antiwar Activism in British Columbia, 1948–1960," *Peace & Change* 35, no. 4 (2010): 626–57; Marilyn Fischer, "Addams's Internationalist Pacifism and the Rhetoric of Maternalism," *NWSA Journal* 18, no. 3 (2006): 1–19; Sara Hayden, "Family Metaphors and the Nation: Promoting a Politics of Care through the Million Mom March," *Quarterly Journal of Speech* 89, no. 3 (2003): 196–215; Angela McRobbie, "Feminism, the Family and the New 'Mediated' Maternalism," *New Formations*, no. 80/81 (2013): 119–37; Karen Foss and Kathy L. Domenici, "Haunting Argentina: Synecdoche in the Protests of the Mothers of Plaza de Mayo," *Quarterly Journal of Speech* 87 (2001); D. Lynn O'Brien Hallstein, "Introduction to Mothering Rhetorics," *Women's Studies in Communication* 40, no. 1 (2017): 1–10; Lisa D. Brush, "Love, Toil, and Trouble: Motherhood and Feminist Politics," *Signs* 21, no. 2 (1996): 429; Allison M. Prasch, "Maternal Bodies in Militant Protest: Leymah Gbowee and the Rhetorical Agency of African Motherhood," *Women's Studies in Communication* 38, no. 2 (2015): 187–205; Mari Boor Tonn, "Militant Motherhood: Labor's Mary Harris 'Mother' Jones," *Quarterly Journal of Speech* 82, no. 1 (1996): 1; Elizabeth J. Clapp, *Mothers of All Children: Women Reformers and the Rise of Juvenile Courts in Progressive Era America* (University Park: Pennsylvania State University Press, 1998); Jennifer A. Peeples and Kevin M. DeLuca, "The Truth of the Matter: Motherhood, Community and Environmental Justice," *Women's Studies in Communication* 29, no. 1 (2006): 59–87.
22. Ruth Bordin, *Frances Willard: A Biography* (Chapel Hill: University of North Carolina Press, 1986), 112.
23. The Department for the Suppression of Social Evil officially began in 1883, but the department never gained momentum and did not have consistent

leadership. The Stead exposé created momentum to revitalize the program under the name of Promotion of Social Purity. Frances E. Willard, "Social Purity: The Latest and Greatest Crusade," *Voice Extra*, June 1886, 12, Frances E. Willard Scrapbooks, Frances Willard Library and Archives, Evanston, IL (FWS hereafter), scrapbook number 26, microfilm roll 35.

24. Woman's Christian Temperance Union, "Department for the Promotion of Social Purity, Co-Operating with the 'White Cross Army,' Plan of Work for 1886," 1, FWS, scrapbook number 26, microfilm roll 35.
25. *New York Post Express*, January 30, 1886, FWS, scrapbook number 26, microfilm roll 35.
26. Frances E. Willard, "Social Purity: The Latest and Greatest Crusade," *Voice Extra*, June 1886, 11, FWS, scrapbook number 26, microfilm roll 35.
27. Frances E. Willard, "A White Life for Two, 1890," in *Man Cannot Speak for Her: Key Texts of the Early Feminists*, ed. Karlyn Kohrs Campbell, vol. 2 (Westport, CT: Praeger, 1989), 323.
28. Willard, "A White Life," 327.
29. Willard, "A White Life," 327.
30. Willard, "A White Life," 328.
31. Willard, "A White Life," 326.
32. Gretchen Soderlund, *Sex Trafficking, Scandal, and the Transformation of Journalism, 1885–1917* (Chicago: University of Chicago Press, 2013), 73; Bonnie J. Shucha, "White Slavery in the Northwoods: Early U.S. Anti-Sex Trafficking and Its Continuing Relevance to Trafficking Reform," *William & Mary Journal of Women and the Law* 23, no. 1 (2015): 80.
33. Soderlund, *Sex Trafficking*, 85.
34. Shucha, "White Slavery in the Northwoods," 81.
35. "Record of Crime: A Female Fiend in the Tolls for Enticing Girls to Dens of Infamy," *Burlington Hawk-Eye*, October 30, 1887. The disorderly conduct case against Maud Cassidy was dismissed, so there was no successful prosecution in the Howden case. However, Cassidy was served with an abduction charge for another young woman before she even left the courtroom.
36. "Dens of Horror," *Lemars Globe*, January 11, 1888.
37. "Spirited Away"; "Dens of Horror"; "Record of Crime"; "The Truth about the Northern Dives," *Eau Claire Daily Free Press*, February 13, 1888; "Wisconsin's Disgrace," *Columbus Daily Herald*, October 31, 1887; "Horrors of the Pinery Dens," *National Police Gazette*, January 26, 1889.
38. *The Great Wisconsin Pineries Scandal: Infamy, Horrors and Vices of Wisconsin's Vile Dens* (Chicago: G. S. Baldwin, 1889), 4.
39. "The Truth about the Northern Dives." This report was a reprint from the *Madison Journal* and provides an example of an exception.
40. *The Great Wisconsin Pineries Scandal*, 2.
41. Indiana WCTU, May 5, 1888, White Slavery Investigation, Wisconsin Governor Investigations, 1851–1959, Wisconsin State Historical Society,

Madison, WI (WGI hereafter), series 81, box 6, folder 1; Mrs. John Graham, "Petition from Ladies of Hurley," June 12, 1888, WGI, series 81, box 6, folder 1; A. K. Godshall, "Letter from Chairman of the Board of Suppression, Town of Florance," January 19, 1888, WGI, series 81, box 6, folder 1; Aaron Morris, "Philanthropic Committee of Indiana Yearly Meeting of Friends," 1888, WGI, series 81, box 6, folder 1; R. D. Whitehead, "Wisconsin Humane Society," July 2, 1888, WGI, series 81, box 6, folder 1; "Letter from Hillsboro Union WCTU," February 9, 1888, WGI, series 81, box 6, folder 2.

42. Gerard A. Hauser, "Vernacular Discourse and the Epistemic Dimension of Public Opinion," *Communication Theory* 17 (2007): 334.
43. Hauser, "Vernacular Discourse," 335.
44. Mary E. Stuckey, *Political Vocabularies: FDR, the Cleary Letters, and the Elements of Political Argument* (East Lansing: Michigan State University Press, 2018), xxxiv.
45. A. N., February 11, 1888, WGI, series 81, box 6, folder 1.
46. Julie R. Lemouse, October 31, 1887, WGI, series 81, box 6, folder 1; S. C. Corey, November 10, 1887, WGI, series 81, box 6, folder 1; a woman, WGI, series 81, box 6, folder 1; a mother, February 9, 1888, WGI, series 81, box 6, folder 2.
47. J. T. Woodhead, "Methodist Pastor," November 22, 1887, WGI, series 81, box 6, folder 1; J. J. Thompson, January 8, 1887, WGI, series 81, box 6, folder 1; John J. Jenkins, January 19, 1889, WGI, series 81, box 6, folder 1; L. J. Burch, June 26, 1888, WGI, series 81, box 6, folder 1; "Letter to Governor Rusk," 1888, WGI, series 81, box 6, folder 2; William Jaques, July 30, 1889, WGI, series 81, box 6, folder 2.
48. E. A. Morgan, April 7, 1889, WGI, series 81, box 6, folder 1; L. J. Burch, June 26, 1888, WGI, series 81, box 6, folder 1.
49. C. C. McCabe, February 2, 1889, series 81, box 6, folder 1. Similarly: "Miss. Bushnell is known to me and I must accept her account as substantially correct." Arthur Edwards, January 7, 1889, Wisconsin State Historical Society, Madison, WI (WSHS hereafter), William Dempster Hoard—Additions, box 3, folder 8.
50. C. C. McCabe, December 27, 1888, WGI, series 81, box 6, folder 1.
51. A. N., February 11, 1888, WGI, series 81, box 6, folder 1.
52. a woman, WGI, series 81, box 6, folder 1.
53. A. N., February 11, 1888, WGI, series 81, box 6, folder 1.
54. C. C. McCabe, December 27, 1888, WGI, series 81, box 6, folder 1; C. C. McCabe, December 19, 1888, WGI, series 81, box 6, folder 1; C. C. McCabe, April 17, 1889, WGI, series 81, box 6, folder 2; John J. Jenkins, January 19, 1889, WGI, series 81, box 6, folder 1; George Esterly, February 15, 1889, WGI, series 81, box 6, folder 2; Hannah Patchin, January 17, 1889, WGI, series 81, box 6, folder 2.
55. Kristin Kobes DuMez, *A New Gospel for Women: Katharine Bushnell and the Challenge of Christian Feminism* (Oxford: Oxford University Press, 2015), 12.
56. DuMez, *A New Gospel for Women*, 23–24.

57. DuMez, *A New Gospel for Women*, 45.
58. "A Good Work," *Inter Ocean*, February 13, 1886, Frances E. Willard Scrapbooks, Frances Willard Library and Archives, Evanston, IL (FWS hereafter), scrapbook number 26, microfilm roll 35.
59. Kate Bushnell, "As Bound with Them," *The Challenge*, September 2, 1886, FWS, scrapbook number 26: Establishment of Social Purity Department in W.C.T.U. (1886).
60. Bushnell, "As Bound with Them."
61. "Meeting of Women in New York: Addresses by Miss Greenwood, Dr. Kate Bushnell, and Bishop Fallows," *Chicago Daily Tribune*, October 22, 1888.
62. "Slavery Up North," *Inter Ocean*, January 6, 1889, WSHS, William Dempster Hoard—Additions, box 3, folder 8.
63. "Slavery Up North."
64. Eva A. Wolfe, November 13, 1887, WGI, series 81, box 6, folder 1.
65. A. N., February 11, 1888, WGI, series 81, box 6, folder 1; Aaron Morris, "Philanthropic Committee of Indiana Yearly Meeting of Friends," 1888, WGI, series 81, box 6, folder 1; C. C. McCabe, December 19, 1888, WGI, series 81, box 6, folder 1; W. H. Noyes, February 9, 1888, WGI, series 81, box 6, folder 2.
66. C. C. McCabe, December 27, 1888, WGI, series 81, box 6, folder 1; "Letter from Eau Claire, WI," WGI, series 81, box 6, folder 2; W. H. Noyes, February 9, 1888, WGI, series 81, box 6, folder 2.
67. Jo Doezema, "Loose Women or Lost Women? The Re-Emergence of the Myth of White Slavery in Contemporary Discourses of Trafficking in Women," *Gender Issues* 18, no. 1 (1999): 29.
68. M. J. Coggeshall, "Social Purity: Read Before the Polk County W.S.A.," *Woman's Standard*, June 3, 1889, 2.
69. *The Great Wisconsin Pineries Scandal*, 5.
70. Coggeshall, "Social Purity," 1.
71. "A Hell on Earth: A Woman's Awful Experience in One of Wisconsin's Dens of Infamy," *St. Paul Daily News*, January 26, 1889, FWS, scrapbook number 10.
72. "Another Marinette Victim," FWS, scrapbook number 10, microfilm roll 31.
73. J. M. Rusk, "Rusk Defends," *Milwaukee Daily Journal*, January 19, 1889.
74. Jeremiah M. Rusk, "Letter to Marinette District Attorney Fairchild," October 29, 1887, WSHS, Jeremiah M. Rusk Papers, box 7. Private Book September 19, 1887–December 13, 1888, 15–16.
75. "An Answer to Gov. Rusk," *Milwaukee Daily Journal*, November 1, 1887; Fairchild, "Letter to Governor Rusk," October 31, 1887, WGI, series 81, box 6, folder 1.
76. "Fielding in Court," *Milwaukee Daily Journal*, January 19, 1889.
77. James Fielding, "Report to Governor Rusk," December 20, 1887, WGI, series 81, box 6, folder 1.
78. Kate Bushnell, "Work in Northern Wisconsin," *W.C.T.U. State Work*, November 1888, 1.

79. "Mills' Hard Job," *Milwaukee Sentinel*, January 11, 1889; "Disappointed in Dr. Bushnell," *Milwaukee Daily Journal*, January 17, 1889.
80. "Fielding in Court," *Milwaukee Daily Journal*, January 19, 1889.
81. "The Case against James Fielding," *Wisconsin State Register*, May 11, 1889; "Mr. Fielding's Arrest," *Milwaukee Sentinel*, January 23, 1889; "She Must Come Back," *Wisconsin State Register*, February 16, 1889; "Bushnell's Fizzle," *Milwaukee Daily Journal*, May 3, 1889; "James Fielding Vindicated," *Daily Inter Ocean*, May 4, 1889; "Multiple News Items," *Milwaukee Journal*, January 19, 1889.
82. "Deposition of Patrick Clifford, Sheriff of Marinette County," WGI, series 81, box 6, folder 1.
83. E. R. Pethenck, WGI, series 81, box 6, folder 2.
84. "About the State," *Milwaukee Daily Sentinel*, February 13, 1889.
85. Bushnell, "Work in Northern Wisconsin," 1. Bushnell reports that Fielding admitted to authoring the report and admitted that the report published anonymously in the newspaper was inconsistent with his report to the governor.
86. Bushnell, "Work in Northern Wisconsin," 2.
87. "About the State," *Milwaukee Daily Sentinel*, February 13, 1889.
88. "Deposition of Patrick Clifford, Sheriff of Marinette County," WGI, series 81, box 6, folder 1.
89. "Slavery Up North."
90. Bushnell, "Work in Northern Wisconsin," 2.
91. J. J. Miles, WGI, series 81, box 6, folder 1.
92. J. K. Parish, January 24, 1889, WGI, series 81, box 6, folder 2.
93. E. R. Pethenck, WGI, series 81, box 6, folder 2.
94. Fairchild, November 2, 1887, WGI, series 81, box 6, folder 1.
95. James Fielding, "Report to Governor Rusk," December 20, 1887, WGI, series 81, box 6, folder 1.
96. Bushnell, "Work in Northern Wisconsin," 2.
97. Bushnell, "Work in Northern Wisconsin," 2; "Disappointed in Dr. Bushnell."
98. Shucha, "White Slavery in the Northwoods," 102.
99. "Mills' Hard Job," *Milwaukee Sentinel*, January 11, 1889.
100. "Mills' Hard Job."
101. Shucha, "White Slavery in the Northwoods," 103.
102. "A Woman's Scorn," *Milwaukee Sentinel*, January 19, 1889.
103. Of course, the newspapers did not report the specific language that was considered offensive. The closest indication of what was said came from the *Milwaukee Daily Journal* that reported, "He and Miss Bushnell had a quarrel the other day and he told her there was just as much truth in what people said about her as there was in stories circulated in reference to himself and his connection with the investigation of dives under the direction of Gov. Rusk" ("Disappointed in Dr. Bushnell."). This statement appears particularly biting because Bushnell was the primary person circulating

criticisms of Fielding. Also, "Bushnell's Fizzle," *Milwaukee Daily Journal*, May 3, 1889.
104. "She Must Come Back," *Wisconsin State Register*, February 16, 1889; "May Prosecute Dr. Bushnell," *Milwaukee Daily Journal*, February 13, 1889.
105. "A Woman's Scorn," *Milwaukee Sentinel*, January 19, 1889.
106. Shucha, "White Slavery in the Northwoods," 90.
107. Shucha, "White Slavery in the Northwoods," 91.
108. James Boyd White, *When Words Lose Their Meaning: Constitutions and Reconstitutions of Language, Character, and Community* (Chicago: University of Chicago Press, 1984), 266.
109. "Wisconsin," *Daily Inter Ocean*, January 28, 1887. Reports of white slavery in northern Wisconsin appear to have begun in the winter of 1886 ("A Revolting Recital," *Galveston Daily News*, November 3, 1887). Both Wisconsin and Michigan passed similar laws in 1887 (Shucha, "White Slavery in the Northwoods," 101).
110. Citing Bushnell's recollections, some historians have claimed that newspapers informally called the 1889 legislation the "Kate Bushnell Bill" even though Bushnell did not participate in crafting the legislation. While I have not found any primary source evidence to substantiate this claim, WCTU publications tended to be aggressive in spinning positive publicity. I have found no evidence of popular Wisconsin newspapers using that name for the bill, and one paper reported, "The woman [Bushnell] made herself so obnoxious to members of the legislature that her mere presence is liable to kill several bills the W.C.T.U. is making a special hobby of" ("May Prosecute Dr. Bushnell"). Regardless of the bill's informal title, it is likely the controversy created political pressure for legislative action.

Chapter 2. Mobility and the Danger of the City: Moral Reform in Chicago, 1907–1914

1. "Conference for the Suppression of the White Slave Traffic: Noted Reformers Discuss the Evil from Social, Legal and Medical Standpoints, and Point Out Remedies," *Union Signal*, February 18, 1909, 3. The comparison of white slavery to the enslavement of people of African descent was often explicit. Other examples include the Chicago Vice Commission that described white slavery as "more terrible than any black slavery that ever existed in this or any other country." Vice Commission of Chicago, *The Social Evil in Chicago: A Study of Existing Conditions with Recommendations* (Chicago: City of Chicago, 1911), 26–27.
2. "Convention Proceedings," *Union Signal*, November 11, 1909, 4.
3. Lloyd Wendt and Herman Kogan, *Lords of the Levee: The Story of Bathhouse John and Hinkydink* (Indianapolis: Bobbs-Merrill Co., 1943); Jack Lait and

Lee Mortimer, *Chicago Confidential* (New York: Crown Publishers, 1950), 21–31.
4. George Kibbe Turner, "The City of Chicago: A Study of the Great Immoralities," *McClure's Magazine*, April 1907, 575.
5. In the twenty-first century, this anxiety is currently evidenced in much of the opposition to immigration, including refugees.
6. Kevin Lynch, *The Image of the City* (Cambridge, MA: MIT Press, 1960), 4.
7. Lynch, *The Image of the City*, 3.
8. Jan Nespor, "Discursive Geographies," *Journal of Language & Politics* 13, no. 3 (2014): 493–94.
9. Jacob Dickerson, "Metonymy and Indexicality," *Rhetoric Review* 31, no.4 (2012): 405–21.
10. Turner, "The City of Chicago," 575.
11. Gretchen Soderlund, *Sex Trafficking, Scandal, and the Transformation of Journalism, 1885–1917* (Chicago: University of Chicago Press, 2013), 103.
12. Soderlund, *Sex Trafficking*, 110. Ernest Bell did not specifically name the Turner article, but in a pamphlet he labels 1907 as the year that a crusade began. "The Cross Confronting the Night," 1913, 4, Ernest A. Bell Collection, Chicago History Museum (EAB hereafter), 6–13.
13. Attendance estimates vary. One report indicates that 27,529,400 people were admitted to the fair. Robert W. Rydell, *All the World's a Fair: Visions of Empire at American International Expositions, 1876–1916* (Chicago: University of Chicago Press, 1987). However, the estimates of over 20 million may have been inflated because they do not account for repeat visitors, and other scholars estimate attendance to have been between twelve and sixteen million. Neil Harris, "Memory and the White City," in *Grand Illusions: Chicago's World's Fair of 1893*, ed. Wim De Wit, James Gilbert, and Robert W. Rydell (Chicago: Chicago Historical Society, 1993), 1–40.
14. William Thomas Stead, *If Christ Came to Chicago! A Plea for the Union of All Who Love in the Service of All Who Suffer* (Chicago: Laird & Lee, 1894).
15. Donald L. Miller, *City of the Century: The Epic of Chicago and the Making of America* (New York: Simon & Schuster, 1996), 17.
16. Turner, "The City of Chicago," 579.
17. "A Prophet with Honor," *Northwestern Christian Advocate*, January 8, 1913, EAB, 4–8; "Midnight Mission Letterhead," EAB, 4–7. It is unclear that Bell entirely bought into this reputation. At the bottom of a profile held in the Bell collection of the Chicago History Museum Archives, Bell wrote, "How shall I ever live up to this?"
18. Olive Bell Daniels, *From the Epic of Chicago: A Biography, Ernest A. Bell, 1865–1928* (Menasha, WI: George Banta Publishing Co., 1932), 3, 30.
19. The Midnight Mission would often call for volunteers specifying that they needed middle-aged or "mature" adults for missionary work. M.P. Boynton, "Letter to Dear Friend," December 19, 1908, EAB, 4–7; Rev. M. P. Boynton,

"Letter to: My Dear Brother," June 17, 1910, EAB, 4–7; "What the Judge and the Doctors Say" (Midnight Mission), EAB, 6–14; Mabel L. Conklin, "Our Work for Purity," *Union Signal*, November 15, 1900.
20. "The Mid-Night Mission: Minutes of Meeting of June 24th, 1907, at the University Club, 116 Dearborn Street," EAB, 4–9; "The Midnight Mission," 1912, 1, EAB, 4–8.
21. Ernest A. Bell, "Midnight Evangelism Among the Red Lights," 1906, 2, EAB, 4–7.
22. Rufus Simmons, "Letter to Mr. Victor F. Lawson," September 30, 1909, 3, EAB, 4–9.
23. Ernest A. Bell, "Midnight Evangelism among the Red Lights," 1906, 3, EAB, 4–7; Rufus Simmons, "Letter to Mr. Victor F. Lawson," September 30, 1909, 2, EAB, 4–9; Ernest A. Bell. "Letter to Hon. Carter H. Harrison, Mayor of Chicago," November 29, 1912, EAB, 4–8. There were also reports of police interference. M. P. Boynton, "Letter to Captain William Cudmore, 22nd Street Police Station, Chicago," November 2, 1909, EAB, 4–7.
24. Ernest A. Bell, "Letter to Board of Directors," January 28, 1910, 2, EAB, 4–7.
25. "The Midnight Mission," 1910, 18, EAB, 6–13; "The Cross Confronting the Night," 1913, 5, EAB, 6–13. Bell may have been an early advocate of the legislation, but the story of the actual legislation is more complicated than is represented by the Midnight Mission.
26. "Midnight Mission Letterhead," EAB, 4–7. The Midnight Mission also aided the Chicago Vice Commission. "The Midnight Mission: President's Report January 31st, 1911," 5, EAB, 5–1; Vice Commission of Chicago, *Social Evil in Chicago*, 9.
27. Aaron Powell, *The National Purity Congress: Its Papers, Addresses, and Portraits* (New York: American Purity Alliance, 1896).
28. David J. Pivar, *Purity and Hygiene: Women, Prostitution, and the "American Plan," 1900–1930* (Westport, CT: Greenwood, 2002), 44.
29. Pivar, *Purity and Hygiene*, 76.
30. Pivar, *Purity and Hygiene*, 76.
31. Pivar, *Purity and Hygiene*, 37, 43.
32. "White Slave Traffic," *Union Signal*, January 4, 1912.
33. Vice Commission of Chicago, *Social Evil in Chicago*, 45.
34. Vice Commission of Chicago, *Social Evil in Chicago*, 25.
35. It is interesting to note that Clifford Barnes claimed that the *Tribune* secretly financed white slavery investigations and prosecutions. The *Tribune* was in competition with the *Times*. Clifford W. Barnes, "'The Tribune' and White Slavery," *Chicago Tribune*, July 15, 1910, Clifford W. Barnes Papers, Chicago History Museum, Chicago, IL (CWB hereafter), 2–1.
36. Graham Taylor, "War against Vice Citywide Unending," May 23, 1914, CWB, 2–4; "Committee of Fifteen Fights 'White Slavers': Suppression of Traffic in Girls Is Object of Enlarged and Incorporated Body Headed by Clifford G. Roe," 1911, CWB, 2–1.

37. "The Midnight Mission: President's Report January 31st, 1911," 5, EAB, 5–1.
38. "Wanted! Reinforcements on the Firing Line against Commercialized Vice: Statement by the Committee of Fifteen" (Committee of Fifteen, 1913[?]), CWB, 2–3.
39. "Demand Officials Prosecute Owners of Vice Property," *Chicago Tribune*, June 13, 1913, CWB, 2–3; "Committee of 15 Plans Complete Vice Elimination," June 13, 1913, CWB, 2–3.
40. "Mayor as Sleuth: Closes 17 Saloons in Vice District," July 4, 1913, CWB, 2–3; "Mayor Revokes 17 Licenses of Levee Saloons," July 4, 1913, CWB, 2–3; "Mayor Cleans Levee: 17 Licenses Revoked," July 4, 1913, CWB, 2–3; "Harrison Views Vice in Levee: Closes Saloons," July 4, 1913, CWB, 2–3. One newspaper accused Harrison of having "deliberately encouraged the growth of the underworld." "Encouragement of Vice by Mayor Harrison," EAB, 6–2.
41. Karen Abbott, *Sin in the Second City: Madams, Ministers, Playboys, and the Battle for America's Soul* (New York: Random House, 2008), 232–33.
42. "The Cross Confronting the Night," 1913, 4, EAB, 6–13. Also, "the daily papers and the church papers, and then the magazines, gave publicity to the terrible facts. At least 50,000,000 pages owe their inspiration to the crusade then inaugurated." ("The Midnight Mission," 1910, 13, EAB, 6–13.)
43. Jean Turner-Zimmermann, *Chicago's Black Traffic in White Girls* (Chicago: Chicago Rescue Mission[?], 1911); Edward O. Janney, *The White Slavery Traffic in America* (New York City: National Vigilance Committee, 1911).
44. See Wendy Lucas Castro, "Stripped: Clothing and Identity in Colonial Captivity Narratives," *Early American Studies: An Interdisciplinary Journal* 6, no. 1 (March 24, 2008): 104–36; Greg Goodale and Jeremy Engels, "Black *and* White: Vestiges of Biracialism in American Discourse," *Communication and Critical/Cultural Studies* 7, no.1 (2010): 70–89; Susan M. Griffin, "Awful Disclosures: Women's Evidence in the Escaped Nun's Tale," *PMLA* 111, no. 1 (1996): 93–107; Lawrence A. Peskin, *Captives and Countrymen: Barbary Slavery and the American Public, 1785–1816* (Baltimore: Johns Hopkins University Press, 2009); Audra Simpson, "From White into Red: Captivity Narratives as Alchemies of Race and Citizenship," *American Quarterly* 60, no. 2 (2008): 251–57.
45. "Chicago Metropolitan Population," in *The Encyclopedia of Chicago*, ed. James R. Grossman, Ann Durkin Keating, and Janice L. Reiff (Chicago: University of Chicago Press, 2004), 1011.
46. Robert G. Spinney, *City of Big Shoulders: A History of Chicago* (DeKalb: Northern Illinios University Press, 2000), 123.
47. Walter Nugent, "Demography: Chicago as a Modern World City," in *The Encyclopedia of Chicago*, ed. James R. Grossman, Ann Durkin Keating, and Janice L. Reiff (Chicago: University of Chicago Press, 2004), 235; Leroy G. Dorsey, *We Are All Americans, Pure and Simple: Theodore Roosevelt and the Myth of Americanism* (Tuscaloosa: University of Alabama Press, 2007), 53; Thomas C.

Leonard, "Mistaking Eugenics for Social Darwinism: Why Eugenics Is Missing from the History of American Economics," *History of Political Economy* 37, supplement (2005): 226.
48. Doreen B. Massey, *Space, Place, and Gender* (Minneapolis: University of Minnesota Press, 1999), 5 and 147. Also see Armond R. Towns, "Geographies of Pain: #SayHerName and the Fear of Black Women's Mobility," *Women's Studies in Communication* 39, no. 2 (2016): 123.
49. Karma R. Chávez, "Border (In)Securities: Normative and Differential Belonging in LGBTQ and Immigrant Rights Discourse," *Communication and Critical/Cultural Studies* 7, no. 2 (2010): 138. Underhill explains that Progressive Era activists often constructed immigrant neighborhoods as emblematic of that perceived threat. Stephen M. Underhill, "Urban Jungle, Ferguson: Rhetorical Homology and Institutional Critique," *Quarterly Journal of Speech* 102, no. 4 (2016): 405.
50. Aaron Powell, "The President's Opening Address," in *The National Purity Congress: Its Papers, Addresses, Portraits*, ed. Aaron Powell (New York: American Purity Alliance, 1896), 2. Also see Janney, *The White Slavery Traffic in America*, 106.
51. There are many examples. See Rose Woodallen Chapman, "The Traffic in Women," *Union Signal*, May 5, 1910, 5; Ernest A. Bell, "Progress against the White Slave Trade," *Union Signal*, August 4, 1910, 3; Owen O. Wiard, "Will You Help Me out of Here?," *Union Signal*, May 2, 1912, 4; Margaret Dye Ellis, "Our Washington Letter," *Union Signal*, August 28, 1913, 5; Jack Lloyd, "Sidewalk Lizards," *The Light*, September–October 1919, 15, Frances Willard Library and Archives, Evanston, IL (FWLA hereafter); James Asa White, "Conservation of Moral Resources," *The Light*, July–August 1918, 24, FWLA.
52. Ernest A. Bell, *White Slavery Up to Date or White Slavery Today* (Chicago: Darrow, 1917), image 4; Edwin W. Sims, "Menace of the White Slave Trade," in *Fighting the Traffic in Young Girls: Or War on the White Slave Trade*, ed. Ernest A. Bell (Chicago, 1910), 72.
53. Jack Lloyd, "Behind the Scenes in a 'Coffee House,'" *The Light*, July–August 1919, 9, FWLA.
54. Turner-Zimmermann, *Chicago's Black Traffic in White Girls*, 8–9.
55. "The Hunters Hunted," *Union Signal*, July 2, 1908, 9.
56. Turner, "The City of Chicago," 581.
57. See "Civilization's Crowning Infamy: The Liquor Traffic's Foul Consort, the White Slave Trade, in Full Glare of Investigation," *National Prohibitionist*, December 16, 1909, 2, EAB, 4–7; Edwin W. Sims, "The White Slave Trade of Today," in *Fighting the Traffic in Young Girls: Or, War on the White Slave Trade*, ed. Ernest A Bell (Chicago, 1910), 47–60; Turner-Zimmermann, *Chicago's Black Traffic in White Girls*, 6.
58. Rev. M. P. Boynton, "Letter to: My Dear Brother," June 17, 1910, EAB, 4–7. The slippage between literal darkness and metaphorical darkness was common.

For example, "American, Bohemian, Italian, Lithuanian, Swede, Arab, Hindoo and Japanese have knelt with us in our house of prayer, in the black and dark night; and some of these, we know, have been redeemed from the blacker, darker night of their own sin." Ernest A. Bell, "The Midnight Mission: Superintendent's Report for 1910," 1, EAB, 5-1.
59. "The Cross Confronting the Night," 1913, 2, EAB, 6-13.
60. Lurenda B. Smith, "Superintendents, Department of Rescue Work," *Union Signal*, January 17, 1907. Other examples include M.P. Boynton, "What of the Night? Sunday Evening Comment at the Lexington Avenue Baptist Church by Dr. M. P. Boynton before His Regular Sermon," October 6, 1912, 3, EAB, 4-8; "The Purity Convention," *Union Signal*, October 17, 1901.
61. M. P. Boynton, "What of the Night? Sunday Evening Comment at the Lexington Avenue Baptist Church by Dr. M. P. Boynton before His Regular Sermon," October 6, 1912, 3, EAB, 4-8.
62. Turner-Zimmermann, *Chicago's Black Traffic in White Girls*, 54.
63. Vice Commission of Chicago, *Social Evil in Chicago*, 35.
64. "Address of Ernest A. Bell," *Friends' Intelligencer Supplement*, October 10, 1908, 73, EAB, 6-7; Sims, "The White Slave Trade of Today"; "The Vigil" (Illinois Vigilance Association, No 11), 2, EAB, 6-12; Ernest A. Bell, "The Twin Destroyers of Our Young People—Liquor and Vice," *Union Signal*, April 24, 1913, 4; James Asa White, "Conservation of Moral Resources," *The Light*, July-August 1918, 24, FWLA.
65. Helen Dare, "Girls Blame Nickel Dance Halls for Their Downfall: White Slave Cases Arouse Even Callous Police Court Habitues," *San Francisco Chronicle*, June 14, 1910, EAB, 4-7.
66. Some editions of the book had the images all in the beginning, creating what seemed to be a pictorial journey that ended in the brothel. Other editions had the images scattered throughout the book, but the journey language remained. Also see T. A. Faulkner, *From the Ballroom to Hell* (Chicago: R. F. Henry, 1892).
67. Turner-Zimmermann, *Chicago's Black Traffic in White Girls*, 27.
68. Lurenda B. Smith, "The War against the Social Evil," *Union Signal*, March 27, 1913, 11.
69. Bell, *White Slavery Up to Date or White Slavery Today*, 96.
70. Robin E. Jensen, *Dirty Words: The Rhetoric of Public Sex Education, 1870-1924* (Urbana: University of Illinois Press, 2010), 18; Nancy Tomes, *The Gospel of Germs: Men, Women, and the Microbe in American Life* (Cambridge, MA: Harvard University Press, 1999), 205.
71. Vice Commission of Chicago, *Social Evil in Chicago*, 25.
72. The association between character and illness has a long history. See Susan Sontag, *Illness as Metaphor and Aids and Its Metaphors* (New York: Anchor Books, 1990), 46.
73. Ernest A. Bell, "Midnight Evangelism among the Red Lights," 1906, 3,

EAB, 4–7; William Burgess, "Race Decadence: An Open Letter to Theodore Roosevelt," *The Vigil*, EAB, 5–2.
74. See "What the Judge and the Doctors Say" (Midnight Mission), EAB, 6–14; Mabel L. Conklin, "Our Work for Purity," *Union Signal*, November 15, 1900, 5.
75. "The Midnight Mission: President's Report January 31st, 1911," 5, EAB, 5–1; Ernest A. Bell, "Midnight Evangelism among the Red Lights," 1906, 4, EAB, 4–7; "Vice Situation in Chicago," *Union Signal*, February 3, 1910, 8.
76. Estrela Manley, "To the Board of Directors," September 1914, EAB, 5–5; Bell, *White Slavery Up to Date or White Slavery Today*, 28.
77. Jacobson v. Massachusetts, 197 U.S. 11 (1905).
78. David Zarefsky, *President Johnson's War On Poverty: Rhetoric and History* (Tuscaloosa: University Alabama Press, 2005), 29.
79. Zarefsky, *President Johnson's War*, 32.
80. "The Midnight Mission," 1910, 27, EAB, 6–13.
81. M. P. Boynton, "Annual Report of the Secretary of the Midnight Mission of Chicago for the Year 1910," 1910, 2, EAB, 5–1; "An Anti-Vice Crusade in Chicago," *Continent*, October 10, 1912, CWB, 2–2; Mabel L. Conklin, "Our Work for Purity," *Union Signal*, November 15, 1900, 5. The "Annual Report" also refers to "Christian soldiers" (1).
82. "Wanted! Reinforcements on the Firing Line Against Commercialized Vice" (Committee of Fifteen, 1913[?]), CWB, 2–3. Also, "Eleven Hundred Offer Services in Vice War," *Republican Herald*[?], May 20, 1914, CWB, 2–4; Vice Commission of Chicago, *Social Evil in Chicago*, 47.
83. Estrela Manley, "To the Board of Directors: Going to Church on Congress Street," September 4, 1914, EAB, 5–5; Graham Taylor, "Where We Are in the Segregation War," February 23, 1912, CWB, 2–2; Lurenda B. Smith, "Superintendents, Department of Rescue Work," *Union Signal*, January 17, 1907.
84. Tim Cresswell, *On the Move: Mobility in the Modern Western World* (New York: Routledge, 2006), 159.
85. Mimi Sheller and John Urry, "The New Mobilities Paradigm," *Environment and Planning A* 38, no. 2 (2006): 241.
86. On some occasions, railroads attempted to protect women by providing separate cars or guards. "Railroads Aid in Fight on Traffic in Women," *Union Signal*, May 9, 1912, 8. Also, "the carelessness and lack of common sense shown by multitudes of parents in the oversight of their girls is almost beyond belief. Young girls are often dressed in such a manner as to attract notice and comment, and are then allowed to frequent railroad stations and other public places unattended, or with silly companions." Janney, *The White Slavery Traffic in America*, 85.
87. For example, "When a young girl has once been induced to enter a house of prostitution or any of the feeders to such a place she is seldom allowed to leave until too broken in spirit to try to escape, or until she is thrown out, diseased and unfit for business. The end of these girls is most pitiful, and

many of them commit suicide." Agnes M. Rex, "The White Slave Traffic and Public Vice," *The Light*, 1918, 43.

88. Ernest A. Bell, *Fighting the Traffic in Young Girls: Or War on the White Slave Trade* (Chicago, 1910), 98.

89. Catherine H. Palczewski, "The 1919 Prison Special: Constituting White Women's Citizenship," *Quarterly Journal of Speech* 102, no. 2 (2016).

90. Turner-Zimmermann, *Chicago's Black Traffic in White Girls*, 13. Also see "Incident at the Midnight Mission: Sunday Evening, October—1911," October 1911, EAB, 5-2; "Incident at the Midnight Mission: Saturday Night, November 4th 1911," November 4, 1911, EAB, 5-2; Bell, *White Slavery Up to Date or White Slavery Today*, 38; Lurenda B. Smith, "Superintendents, Department of Rescue Work," *Union Signal*, January 17, 1907, 10.

91. Turner-Zimmermann, *Chicago's Black Traffic in White Girls*, 13.

92. Sims, "The White Slave Trade of Today." Also see Clifford G. Roe, "Exterminating the White Slave Traffic," *Union Signal*, August 13, 1908, 2, 12, 16; Lurenda B. Smith, "Superintendents, Department of Rescue Work," *Union Signal*, January 17, 1907, 10; Rose Woodallen Chapman, "The Traffic in Women. III. Two Vital Lessons," *Union Signal*, May 26, 1910.

93. "The 'White Slave' Traffic," *Union Signal*, July 11, 1907, 8-9; "Alcohol and the White Slave Traffic," *Union Signal*, March 28, 1912, 8.

94. William N. Gemmill, "The Terror That Walketh in Darkness," *Northwestern Christian Advocate*, January 25, 1911, EAB, 5-2.

95. Sims, "Menace of the White Slave Trade," 70-71.

96. Sims, "The White Slave Trade of Today," 48. Also see Sims, "The White Slave Trade of Today," *Woman's World*, September 1908, EAB, 6-2; "The Illinois Vigilance Association Pamphlet," EAB, 6-12. Sims tells parents to not trust their daughters. They have to check on their daughters who live in the city, and he explicitly tells them to get information from someone other than the daughter. Rose Woodallen Chapman, "The Traffic in Women. III. Two Vital Lessons," *Union Signal*, May 26, 1910, 5.

97. Bell, *White Slavery Up to Date or White Slavery Today*, 96. Bell also warns "girls": "Don't leave the country for the city without having first secured safe employment and a safe home. Your minister, your banker, or your postmaster could give you good advice—or your school teacher or the editor of your home paper or your family physician." Occasionally, some activist explicitly blamed parents. For example, "If some of the present-day mothers gave more time and attention to the rearing of children than to poodle dogs, cats and fine horses, card parties, and progressive games, the theater and the like, there might be some hope for relief." James Asa White, "Conservation of Moral Resources," *The Light*, July–August 1918, 26, FWLA.

98. Occasionally activists were referring to children. For example, "The white slave problem is also a children's problem. An [sic] this is the most serious of all its aspects. I have already said that the first thing the white slaver has to do

is to break down the barriers of virtue. Hundreds of thousands of these men are around in New York city, ruining little girls while they are almost babies." Margaret Luther, "The Problem of White Slavery," *The Light*, 1918, 38.

99. Turner-Zimmermann, *Chicago's Black Traffic in White Girls*, 7.
100. Ernest A. Bell, "To the Directors," October 8, 1912, EAB, 4–9.
101. "Minutes of Meeting of the Midnight Mission Directors of Chicago, At City Club, September 8th, 1914," September 8, 1914, EAB, 5–5.

Chapter 3. The Science of Social Mobility: John D. Rockefeller Jr. and the Science of Reform, 1910–1917

1. George Kibbe Turner, "The Daughters of the Poor: A Plain Story of the Development of New York City as a Leading Center of the White Slave Trade of the World, Under Tammany Hall," *McClure's Magazine*, November 1909, 45.
2. Turner, "The Daughters of the Poor," 58.
3. Turner, "The Daughters of the Poor," 62.
4. John Ensor Harr and Peter J. Johnson, *The Rockefeller Century: Three Generations of America's Greatest Family* (New York: Scribner, 1988), 109.
5. Raymond B. Fosdick, *John D. Rockefeller, Jr.: A Portrait* (New York: Harper & Brothers, 1956), 137.
6. Harr and Johnson, *The Rockefeller Century*, 110.
7. "John D. Rockefeller, Jr., Is Foreman of Grand Jury to Probe 'White Slave' Trade," January 3, 1910, Office of the Messrs. Rockefeller, Rockefeller Boards, Record Group III, series 20, Rockefeller Archives Center, Sleepy Hollow, NY (OMR hereafter), box 8, folder 56.
8. Harr and Johnson, *The Rockefeller Century*, 110.
9. Harr and Johnson, *The Rockefeller Century*, 114.
10. Fosdick, *John D. Rockefeller, Jr.: A Portrait*, 140.
11. Harr and Johnson, *The Rockefeller Century*, 23, 61.
12. John D. Rockefeller Jr., "Grand Jury Statement to Judge O'Sullivan," May 11, 1910, OMR, box 8, folder 56. There is some evidence that Rockefeller generally supported the cause, making relatively small donations to organizations like the Committee of Fourteen in New York. However, the grand jury investigation appears to have been the catalyst to the sustained and significant commitment that followed. Frederick Whitin, "Letter to John D. Rockefeller, Jr.," November 18, 1907, OMR, box 6, folder 40; John P. Peters, "Letter to John D. Rockefeller, Jr.," February 26, 1909, OMR, box 6, folder 40.
13. Examples include: John D. Rockefeller Jr., "Letter to Mr. Gustavus Myers, Sanford, Florida," February 10, 1910, OMR, box 8, folder 56; John D. Rockefeller Jr., "Letter to Editor, Evening Journal, New York," April 5, 1910, OMR, box 8, folder 56; John D. Rockefeller Jr., "Letter to Gaston Netter, New York," January 8, 1910, OMR, box 8, folder 56; John D. Rockefeller Jr., "Letter to Miss Frances A. Kellor, New York," March 19, 1910, OMR, box 8, folder 56.

14. A. Brisbane, "Letter to John D. Rockefeller," April 19, 1910, OMR, box 8, folder 56.
15. "Judge O'Sullivan Discharge Statement to Grand Jury," June 1910, 3-4, OMR, box 8, folder 57.
16. James Reynolds, "Letter to John D. Rockefeller, Jr.," July 14, 1910, OMR, box 8, folder 57.
17. Starr L. Murphy, "Letter to John D. Rockefeller, Jr.," January 25, 1910, OMR, box 8, folder 56; John D. Rockefeller Jr., "Letter to Mrs. William H. Baldwin, Jr.," February 1, 1910, OMR, box 8, folder 56; John D. Rockefeller Jr., "Letter to Mrs. W.H. Baldwin, Jr.," February 25, 1910, OMR, box 8, folder 56.
18. Clifford G. Roe, "Letter to Chas. O. Heydt, New York," August 10, 1912, OMR, box 6, folder 30; John D. Rockefeller Jr., "Letter to Clifford G. Roe," May 9, 1911, OMR, box 7, folder 42; "Press Release," August 8, 1912, OMR, box 7, folder 53; James Reynolds, "Letter to John D. Rockefeller, Jr., New York," June 23, 1910, OMR, box 8, folder 57.
19. John D. Rockefeller Jr., "Letter to John P. Peters, New York," December 23, 1910, OMR, box 8, folder 60; John D. Rockefeller Jr., "Letter to Raymond B. Fosdick, New York," December 30, 1910, OMR, box 8, folder 60.
20. John D. Rockefeller Jr., "Letter to Walter T. Sumner, Chiago," March 27, 1912, OMR, box 7, folder 42; John D. Rockefeller Jr., "Letter to Clifford Roe," January 26, 1911, OMR, box 7, folder 42.
21. Clifford G. Roe, "Report to Committee of Three, April 1, 1911–1912," OMR, box 7, folder 42.
22. Starr L. Murphy, "Letter to Clifford G. Roe, New York," January 5, 1912, OMR, box 7, folder 42.
23. For example, Abraham Flexnor, *Prostitution in Europe* (New York: Century Co., 1914); George J. Kneeland, *Commercialized Prostitution in New York City* (Montclair, NJ: Patterson Smith, 1969).
24. John D. Rockefeller Jr., "Letter to Abraham Flexner, Paris," March 13, 1912, OMR, box 7, folder 55; John D. Rockefeller Jr., "Letter to Abraham Flexner, New York City," July 18, 1913, OMR, box 7, folder 55; Abraham Flexner, "Letter to John D. Rockefeller Jr., Seal Harbor, Maine," July 22, 1913, OMR, box 7, folder 55; Starr L. Murphy, "Minutes of a Meeting of the Bureau of Social Hygiene," February 6, 1913, Bureau of Social Hygiene Records, Rockefeller Archives Center, Sleepy Hollow, NY (BSH hereafter), series 1, box 2, folder 25.

Fosdick ultimately became Rockefeller's authorized biographer. Rockefeller continued to employ Kneeland after the completion of his book, and in 1914, the police were calling Kneeland a "wizard." Rockefeller continued to quietly support Kneeland even as the investigator was being treating for the advanced stages of syphilis in 1918. Raymond B. Fosdick, "Letter to John D. Rockefeller, Jr., Seal Harbor, Maine," September 10, 1914, OMR, box 8, folder 62; John A. Fordyce, "Letter to John D. Rockefeller, Jr., New York," May 27, 1918, OMR, box 8, folder 62.

25. Rockefeller agreed to fund the lab for up to $200,000. John D. Rockefeller Jr., "To the Bureau of Social Hygiene," April 3, 1912, OMR, box 6, folder 35; Starr L. Murphy, "Minutes of a Meeting of the Bureau of Social Hygiene," April 3, 1912, BSH, series 1, box 2, folder 23.
26. Katharine B. Davis, "Letter to John D. Rockefeller Jr.," November 9, 1911, OMR, box 6, folder 31.
27. John D. Rockefeller Jr., "Letter to Paul Warburg, New York," November 24, 1911, OMR, box 6, folder 31.
28. Jerome D. Greene, "Letter to Herman Biggs, New York City," October 17, 1912, OMR, box 8, folder 63; "Bureau of Social Hygiene," OMR, box 8, folder 63. There was one report that the Bedford Hills research continued outside of the institution on women who had not consented. "Rockefeller Board Tricks Working Girls into 'Morality' Test," *New York Call*, March 26, 1916, Rockefeller Archives Center, Sleepy Hollow, NY (RAC hereafter), Rockefeller Foundation Records, Record Group 1.1 Projects, series 200, box 15, folder 157.
29. John D. Rockefeller Jr., "[Commission Recommendation]," 1910, 1, OMR, box 8, folder 57.
30. John D. Rockefeller Jr., "The Origin, Work and Plans of the Bureau of Social Hygiene," January 27, 1913, OMR, box 6, folder 31. Rockefeller sent copies of Reginald Wright Kauffman's *The House of Bondage* to large numbers of people as an example of white slavery literature that supposedly avoids sentimentalism. Interestingly, Emma Goldman came to a similar conclusion about Kauffman's book because he highlighted economic and structural issues that pushed women into prostitution. Emma Goldman, "The Traffic in Women," *Hastings Women's Law Journal* 13 (2002): 10.
31. David J. Pivar, *Purity and Hygiene: Women, Prostitution, and the "American Plan," 1900–1930* (Westport, CT: Greenwood, 2002), 128–29. Prior to the creation of the American Social Hygiene Association (ASHA), Rockefeller supported a merger of the National Vigilance Committee and the American Purity Alliance to form the American Vigilance Association (AVA) through funding and publicity. The AVA and American Federation for Sex Hygiene were the primary organizations in the merger that created the ASHA. Documents that illustrate Rockefeller's behind-the-scenes work include: John D. Rockefeller Jr., "Letter to James B. Reynolds, New York," July 11, 1913, OMR, box 6, folder 30; John D. Rockefeller Jr., "Letter to Clifford Roe," January 26, 1912, OMR, box 6, folder 30; John D. Rockefeller Jr., "Letter to John A. Sleicher, Leslie's Weekly," March 6, 1912, OMR, box 6, folder 30; John D. Rockefeller Jr., "Letter to Clifford Barnes, Chicago," April 23, 1912, OMR, box 6, folder 30; Clifford G. Roe, "Letter to John D. Rockefeller, Jr., New York," August 5, 1912, OMR, box 6, folder 30; John D. Rockefeller Jr., "Letter to Clifford Roe, Chicago," September 3, 1912, OMR, box 6, folder 30; John D. Rockefeller Jr., "Letter to James B. Reynolds," August 22, 1912, OMR, box 6, folder 30; John D. Rockefeller Jr., "Letter to Dr. Edward L. Keyes, Jr.," July 18, 1913, OMR, box 6,

folder 30; John D. Rockefeller Jr., "Letter to Clifford Barnes, New York City," December 19, 1912, OMR, box 6, folder 39; "Memo Re Conference at the House of Miss Grace H Dodge," July 18, 1911, OMR, box 7, folder 42.

32. J. Michael Hogan, "Introduction: Rhetoric and Reform in the Progressive Era," in *Rhetoric and Reform in the Progressive Era*, vol. 6, *A Rhetorical History of the United States: Significant Moments in American Public Discourse* (East Lansing: Michigan State University Press, 2003), xv.

33. Vicky M. MacLean and Joyce E. Williams, "'Ghosts of Sociologies Past': Settlement Sociology in the Progressive Era at the Chicago School of Civics and Philanthropy," *American Sociologist* 43, no. 3 (2012): 240; Joyce E. Williams and Vicky M. Maclean, "In Search of the Kingdom: The Social Gospel, Settlement Sociology, and the Science of Reform in America's Progressive Era," *Journal of the History of the Behavioral Sciences* 48, no. 4 (2012): 349.

34. John Louis Recchiuti, *Civic Engagement: Social Science and Progressive-Era Reform in New York City* (Philadelphia: University of Pennsylvania Press, 2007), 2–3.

35. Estelle B. Freedman, *Their Sisters' Keepers: Women's Prison Reform in America, 1830–1930* (Ann Arbor: University of Michigan Press, 1981), 110.

36. Freedman, *Their Sisters' Keepers*, 111.

37. John Angus Campbell and Keith R. Benson, "Review Essay: The Rhetorical Turn in Science Studies," *Quarterly Journal of Speech* 82 (1996): 75.

38. Leah Ceccarelli, "Rhetorical Criticism and the Rhetoric of Science," *Western Journal of Communication* 65, no. 3 (2001): 321.

39. John A. Lynch, "Articulating Scientific Practice: Understanding Dean Hamer's 'Gay Gene' Study as Overlapping Material, Social and Rhetorical Registers," *Quarterly Journal of Speech* 95, no. 4 (2009): 442.

40. Brett Jacob Bricker, "Feigning Environmentalism: Antienvironmental Organizations, Strategic Naming, and Definitional Argument," *Western Journal of Communication* 78, no. 5 (2014): 636–52; Jeffrey St. John, "Matters of Public Concern: Reconceptualizing Public Employee Free Speech through Definitional Argument," *Rhetoric & Public Affairs* 6, no. 2 (2003): 261–84; David Zarefsky, "Presidential Rhetoric and the Power of Definition," *Presidential Studies Quarterly* 34, no. 3 (2004): 607–19; David Zarefsky, "Strategic Maneuvering through Persuasive Definitions: Implications for Dialectic and Rhetoric," *Argumentation* 20, no. 4 (2006): 399–416.

41. Paul Sandfort, "Letter to James B. Reynolds," October 6, 1910, OMR, box 8, folder 57.

42. "Definition of White Slave," OMR, box 8, folder 56.

43. "Definition of White Slave," OMR, box 8, folder 56.

44. Marcus Braun, "Letter to John D. Rockefeller, Jr.," April 2, 1910, OMR, box 6, folder 38.

45. Kneeland, *Commercialized Prostitution*, 89.

46. Kneeland, *Commercialized Prostitution*, 89.

47. "Memo Re Conference at the House of Miss Grace H Dodge," July 18, 1911, OMR, box 7, folder 42.
48. Jane Addams, "A New Conscience and an Ancient Evil," *McClure's Magazine*, November 1911, 3.
49. Kneeland, *Commercialized Prostitution*, 103.
50. Kneeland, *Commercialized Prostitution*, 103–4.
51. Annie W. Allen, "How to Save the Girls Who Have Fallen," *The Survey* 24, no. 19 (1910): 690.
52. Kneeland, *Commercialized Prostitution*, 106.
53. Kneeland, *Commercialized Prostitution*, 15–16.
54. Addams, "A New Conscience and an Ancient Evil."
55. Kneeland, *Commercialized Prostitution*, 104.
56. Kneeland, *Commercialized Prostitution*, 88.
57. Addams, "A New Conscience and an Ancient Evil."
58. Allen, "How to Save the Girls Who Have Fallen," 686.
59. Alvin S. Johnson, "Letter to John D. Rockefeller Jr.," OMR, box 6, folder 39.
60. Kneeland, *Commercialized Prostitution*, 39.
61. Kneeland, *Commercialized Prostitution*, 79.
62. Brian Donovan and Tori Barnes-Brus, "Narratives of Sexual Consent and Coercion: Forced Prostitution Trials in Progressive-Era New York City," *Law & Social Inquiry* 36, no. 3 (2011): 606. The defense proved that the women were in their twenties, not fifteen, and had been previously involved in prostitution. While their testimony complicated the narrow view of agency common in white slavery narratives, it seems clear that they were not the virginal, innocent children described by the prosecution.
63. Donovan and Barnes-Brus, "Narratives of Sexual Consent and Coercion," 606.
64. Kneeland, *Commercialized Prostitution*, 298.
65. Marcy S. Sacks, *Before Harlem: The Black Experience in New York City Before World War I* (Philadelphia: University of Pennsylvania Press, 2006), 63.
66. William McAdoo, *Guarding a Great City* (New York: Harper, 1906), 95.
67. McAdoo, *Guarding a Great City*, 98.
68. Kneeland, *Commercialized Prostitution*, 108.
69. Kneeland, *Commercialized Prostitution*, 110.
70. Leslie A. Hahner, *To Become an American* (East Lansing: Michigan State University Press, 2017), 127.
71. Anne E Bowler, Chrysanthi S Leon, and Terry G Lilley, "'What Shall We Do With the Young Prostitute? Reform Her or Neglect Her?': Domestication as Reform at the New York State Reformatory for Women at Bedford, 1901–1913," *Journal of Social History* 47, no. 2 (2013): 462.
72. Kneeland, *Commercialized Prostitution*, ix.
73. Evelyn Ruggles-Brise, "An English View of the American Penal System," *Journal of the American Institute of Criminal Law and Criminology* (1911): 361–62; Katherine Bement Davis, "Probation and Parole (Report of the Committee

of the American Prison Association)," *Journal of the American Institute of Criminal Law and Criminology* 7, no. 2 (1916): 167.
74. Cheryl D. Hicks, "'Bright and Good Looking Colored Girl': Black Women's Sexuality and 'Harmful Intimacy' in Early-Twentieth-Century New York," *Journal of the History of Sexuality* 18, no. 3 (2009): 242.
75. Jerome D. Greene, "Memorandum on Proposed Facilities for Diagnosis and Treatment of Venereal Diseases at the Bedford Reformatory for Women," 1, OMR, box 8, folder 63.
76. Robin E. Jensen, *Dirty Words: The Rhetoric of Public Sex Education, 1870–1924* (Urbana: University of Illinois Press, 2010), 18.
77. Ida M. Tarbell, "What Shall We Do with the Young Prostitute? Reform Her or Neglect Her? Reprinted from American Magazine, December, 1912" (Charity Organization Society of the City of New York, March 28, 1913), 5, OMR, box 9, folder 76.
78. Allen, "How to Save the Girls Who Have Fallen," 694.
79. Kneeland, *Commercialized Prostitution*, 269.
80. Kneeland, *Commercialized Prostitution*, 170.
81. Tarbell, "What Shall We Do with the Young Prostitute?," 12.
82. Bowler, Leon, and Lilley, "What Shall We Do," 465.
83. Tarbell, "What Shall We Do with the Young Prostitute?," 22.
84. Bowler, Leon, and Lilley, "What Shall We Do," 460.
85. James Adams, "Taming Wild Girls: The Midnight Mission and the Campaign to Reform Philadelphia's Moral Fabric, 1915–1918," *Pennsylvania Magazine of History and Biography* 135, no. 2 (2011): 131.
86. "Annual Report of the Fiftieth Year of the Chicago Refuge for Girls," 1913, 9, Chicago History Museum Archives (CHM hereafter).
87. "Coulter House Home for Girls," CHM, Misc. Pamphlets, F38KG.C82.
88. Tarbell, "What Shall We Do with the Young Prostitute?," 5.
89. Tarbell, "What Shall We Do with the Young Prostitute?," 4.
90. Sander L. Gilman, "Black Bodies, White Bodies: Toward an Iconography of Female Sexuality in Late Nineteenth-Century Art, Medicine, and Literature," *Critical Inquiry* 12, no. 1 (1985): 206.
91. Catherine H. Palczewski, "The 1919 Prison Special: Constituting White Women's Citizenship," *Quarterly Journal of Speech* 102, no. 2 (2016): 121.
92. Evelynn M. Hammonds, "Toward a Genealogy of Black Female Sexuality: The Problematic Silence," in *Feminist Genealogies, Colonial Legacies, Democratic Futures*, ed. M. Jacqui Alexander and Chandra Talpade Mohanty (New York: Routledge, 1997), 173.
93. Sacks, *Before Harlem*, 39.
94. Sacks, *Before Harlem*, 60.
95. Timothy J. Gilfoyle, *City of Eros: New York City, Prostitution, and the Commercialization of Sex, 1790–1920* (New York: W. W. Norton & Company, 1992), 415n49.

96. Sacks, *Before Harlem*, 43.
97. Kneeland, *Commercialized Prostitution*, 165.
98. Tarbell, "What Shall We Do with the Young Prostitute?," 5–6.
99. Kneeland, *Commercialized Prostitution*, 164.
100. Freedman, *Their Sisters' Keepers*, 139.

Chapter 4. A National Solution: Protecting Whiteness Through the 1910 Mann Act

1. 45 Cong. Rec. 812 (January 19, 1910).
2. James Boyd White, *When Words Lose Their Meaning: Constitutions and Reconstitutions of Language, Character, and Community* (Chicago: University of Chicago Press, 1984), xi.
3. David J Langum, *Crossing over the Line: Legislating Morality and the Mann Act* (Chicago: University of Chicago Press, 1994), 10–11.
4. Langum, *Crossing over the Line*, 39.
5. Langum, *Crossing over the Line*, 40.
6. Langum, *Crossing over the Line*, 44.
7. Jack M. Balkin, "Commerce," *Michigan Law Review* 109, no. 1 (2010): 1–51; Randy E. Barnett, "The Original Meaning of the Commerce Clause," *University of Chicago Law Review* 68, no. 1 (2001): 101.
8. Robert Lowry Clinton, "Judicial Review, Nationalism, and the Commerce Clause: Contrasting Antebellum and Postbellum Supreme Court Decision Making," *Political Research Quarterly* 47, no. 4 (1994): 857; Vicki Lens, "The Supreme Court, Federalism, and Social Policy: The New Judicial Activism," *Social Service Review* 75, no. 2 (2001): 318–36.
9. Langum, *Crossing over the Line*, 42.
10. Ariela R. Dubler, "Immoral Purposes: Marriage and the Genus of Illicit Sex," *Yale Law Journal* 115, no. 4 (2006): 761–62.
11. Committee on Interstate and Foreign Commerce, White Slave Traffic, H.R. Rep. 61–47 at 11 (December 21, 1909). The Commission on Immigration also released a report with the same language.
12. 45 Cong. Rec. 821 (January 19, 1910).
13. 45 Cong. Rec. 821 (January 19, 1910).
14. Ted Carageorge, "An Evaluation of Hoke Smith and Thomas E. Watson as Georgia Reformers" (PhD diss., University of Georgia, 1963), 19; William W. Brewton, *The Life of Thomas E. Watson* (Atlanta: William W. Brewton, 1926). The author describes the Civil War as a "ruthless aggressor war," which provides insightful context for Brewton's praise of Watson (20).
15. "Watson of Georgia Dies in Washington," *New York Times*, September 27, 1922.

16. "Author and Publisher," *Hickory Hill*, http://www.hickory-hill.org. Hickory Hill is managed by the Watson-Brown Foundation, which was named after Thomas E. Watson and Walter J. Brown.
17. The biography on the Hickory Hill website praises Watson for his early anti-racist work but does not engage his white supremacist writings. Interestingly, their website includes an icon for "Georgia nonprofits stand against racism." Watson's biography is complicated, in part, because much of the biographical work on him is limited to hagiography. While it is possible that Watson became a white supremacist after 1900, as some secondary sources imply, it appears likely that his agrarian populism may have only incidentally benefited some Black Americans. For instance, Carageorge describes Watson's political stance as primarily in support of white farmers, and potential alliances with Black farmers were ineffective means of solidifying power. The best evidence (of which I am aware) of Watson's supposed anti-racism is an article in *The Arena* where he argued that the Black population of the South was not going anywhere, and Black and white farmers should unite under the People's Party. It is important to note that this appeal was an explicit attempt to carve space for a third party in a political context where Democratic and Republican votes were split along racial lines, and Watson was explicit that he was not advocating for social equality. (Thomas E. Watson, "The Negro Question in the South," *The Arena*, October 1892.) Cashin argued that Watson was primarily interested in power, explaining some contradictions in his positions over time. (Edward L. Cashin, "Thomas E. Watson and the Catholic Laymen's Association of Georgia" [PhD diss., Fordham University, 1962], 7.)
18. Thomas E. Watson, "The Hearst Paper, the Egyptian Sphinx, and the Negro," *Watson's Jeffersonian Magazine* 3, no. 2 (1909): 97.
19. Watson, "The Hearst Paper," 85.
20. 45 Cong. Rec. 811 (January 19, 1910).
21. 45 Cong. Rec. 821 (January 19, 1910). The Congressional representative was referring to the following article: Thomas E. Watson, "A Lady Missionary Defends Present System," *Watson's Jeffersonian Magazine* 3, no. 9 (1909): 667.
22. 45 Cong. Rec. 821 (January 19, 1910). Similarly, Representative Sims stated, "Mr. Speaker, I can not conceive, from my humble standpoint, one legitimate reason that can justify a civilized man in voting against this bill." 45 Cong. Rec. 812 (January 19, 1910).
23. 45 Cong. Rec. 812 (January 19, 1910).
24. 45 Cong. Rec. 550 (January 11, 1910).
25. Committee on Interstate and Foreign Commerce, White Slave Traffic Views of the Minority, H.R. Rep. 61–47 at 3 (January 5, 1910).
26. 45 Cong. Rec. 526 (January 11, 1910).
27. 45 Cong. Rec. 522 (January 11, 1910). This speech was in reference to a bill coming out of the Immigration Committee, but that bill was almost identical

to the Mann Act. Some legislators were explicit in the Congressional Record that their objections applied to both bills.
28. 45 Cong. Rec. 523 (January 11, 1910).
29. 45 Cong. Rec. 810 (January 19, 1910).
30. 45 Cong. Rec. 527 (January 11, 1910).
31. 45 Cong. Rec. 809 (January 19, 1910).
32. White Slave Traffic Act of June 25, 1910, S. 61–702 at 20 (1910).
33. 45 Cong. Rec. 820 (January 19, 1910).
34. Sanford J. Ungar, *FBI* (Boston: Little, Brown, 1976), 40. Max Lowenthal, *The Federal Bureau of Investigation* (Westport, CT: Greenwood Press, 1971), 5.
35. Langum, *Crossing over the Line*, 49.
36. Jessica R. Pliley, *Policing Sexuality: The Mann Act and the Making of the FBI* (Cambridge, MA: Harvard University Press, 2014), 86.
37. Langum, *Crossing over the Line*, 55–56.
38. Pliley, *Policing Sexuality*, 90.
39. Langum, *Crossing over the Line*; Pliley, *Policing Sexuality*, 100.
40. Pliley, *Policing Sexuality*, 92.
41. The Baltimore Police Department issued a rule in July 1913 that said that women could not easily leave the house they were in and not move from brothel to brothel—women practicing prostitution said that this made them vulnerable to madams and brothel owners because they could not leave. Pliley, *Policing Sexuality*, 93.
42. Armond R. Towns, "Geographies of Pain: #SayHerName and the Fear of Black Women's Mobility," *Women's Studies in Communication* 39, no. 2 (2016): 123.
43. Fon L. Gordon, "Early Motoring in Florida: Making Car Culture and Race in the New South, 1903–1943," *Florida Historical Quarterly* 95, no. 4 (2017): 523.
44. Derek H. Alderman, Joshua Inwood, and James A. Tyner, "Jack Johnson versus Jim Crow: Race, Reputation, and the Politics of Black Villainy; the Fight of the Century," *Southeastern Geographer* 58, no. 3 (2018): 236; E. M. Beck, "South Polls: Judge Lynch Denied; Combating Mob Violence in the American South, 1877–1950," *Southern Cultures* 21, no. 2 (2015): 118; Tia Sherèe Gaynor, Seong C. Kang, and Brian N. Williams, "Segregated Spaces and Separated Races: The Relationship between State-Sanctioned Violence, Place, and Black Identity," *RSF* 7, no. 1 (2021): 54.
45. Ersula J. Ore, *Lynching: Violence, Rhetoric, and American Identity* (Jackson: University Press of Mississippi, 2019), 26.
46. William D. Carrigan and Clive Webb, "The Lynching of Persons of Mexican Origin or Descent in the United States, 1848 to 1928," *Journal of Social History* 37, no. 2 (2003): 413; M. J. Pfeifer, "At the Hands of Parties Unknown? The State of the Field of Lynching Scholarship," *Journal of American History* 101, no. 3 (2014): 836–37.
47. Gail Bederman, *Manliness and Civilization: A Cultural History of Gender and*

Race in the United States, 1880–1917 (Chicago: University of Chicago Press, 1995), 49.

48. Estelle B. Freedman, "'Crimes Which Startle and Horrify': Gender, Age, and the Racialization of Sexual Violence in White American Newspapers, 1870–1900," *Journal of the History of Sexuality* 20, no. 3 (2011): 472; Christopher Waldrep, "War of Words: The Controversy over the Definition of Lynching, 1899–1940," *Journal of Southern History* 66, no. 1 (2000): 76. For an example of challenging lynching while accepting the myth that Black men raped white women, see the analysis of Willard's rhetoric in Maegan Parker, "Desiring Citizenship: A Rhetorical Analysis of the Wells/Willard Controversy," *Women's Studies in Communication* 31, no. 1 (2008). For an analysis of federal anti-lynching legislation, see Niall Palmer, "More Than a Passive Interest," *Journal of American Studies* 48, no. 2 (2014).
49. Alderman, Inwood, and Tyner, "Jack Johnson versus Jim Crow," 230.
50. "The White Man's Real Hope Is That the Better Man Is Not Cheated," *Chicago Daily Tribune*, July 4, 1910.
51. Phillip Hutchison, "Hyping White Hopes: Press Agentry and Its Media Affiliations during the Era of Jack Johnson, 1908–1915," *Journal of Public Relations Research* 23, no. 3 (2011): 336–37; Bederman, *Manliness and Civilization*, 3.
52. "Jack Johnson's Wife Self-Shot," *Chicago Daily Tribune*, September 12, 1912.
53. "Jack Johnson's Wife, Ill—Kills Self," *Chicago Defender*, September 14, 1912.
54. "Jack Johnson Fascinates Beautiful White Girl: Lucille Cameron of Minneapolis Goes Slumming in Chicago," *Los Angeles Times*, October 18, 1912.
55. "Jail Girl to Foil Pugilist Johnson," *Chicago Daily Tribune*, October 18, 1912.
56. "Jack Johnson Fascinates Beautiful White Girl: Lucille Cameron of Minneapolis Goes Slumming in Chicago," *Los Angeles Times*, October 18, 1912.
57. "Johnson Arrested: Weeps and Pleads when Handcuffed; Negro Pugilist Indicted on New Charge of Violating the Mann Act," *Chicago Daily Tribune*, November 8, 1912.
58. "Council Strikes at Jack Johnson: Aldermen Adopt Resolution Urging Mayor to Saloon License; Denounced as Depraved Cameron Girl Collapses during Confession before U. S., Grand Jury Inquiry," *Chicago Daily Tribune*, October 23, 1912.
59. "Condemns J. Johnson's Acts," *Chicago Daily Tribune*, October 21, 1912. Also "His wild and unlawful talk through the columns of the public press performed its part well in causing the vast majority of the unthinking and the unreasoning people to look upon Johnson as a hideous black demon who should be shot down on sight for attempting to steal or abduct a beautiful and lamb like innocent white girl." "John Arthur Johnson the Heavy Weight Champion Prize Fighter of the World Not Guilty of Abducting Miss Lucile Cameron," *Broad Ax*, November 23, 1912.
60. "Condemns J. Johnson's Acts," *Chicago Daily Tribune*, October 21, 1912.

61. "Indicts Johnson Four Times More," *Chicago Daily Tribune*, November 12, 1912.
62. "Johnson Arrested: Weeps and Pleads when Handcuffed; Negro Pugilist Indicted on New Charge of Violating the Mann Act," *Chicago Daily Tribune*, November 8, 1912.
63. "Jail Bends Spirit of Jack Johnson: Negro Pugilist, Held on White Woman's Charges, Meekly Seeks Freedom; U.S. Fight Opens Today—Attorney before Supreme Court Will Demand Writ and Attack Mann Act," *Chicago Daily Tribune*, November 11, 1912.
64. "Johnson Appeals for 'Just a Fine': Negro Pugilist Begs Wilkerson Not to Insist Upon a Penitentiary Term," *Chicago Daily Tribune*, November 17, 1912; "Indicts Johnson Four Times More," *Chicago Daily Tribune*, November 12, 1912.
65. "John Arthur Johnson vs. the United States of America, in the United States Circuit Court of Appeals for the Seventh Circuit. October Term, 1912," 12, Briefs and Appendices, 1891–1959 (Record Group 276), National Archives, Chicago, IL (NAC hereafter).
66. "John Arthur Johnson vs. the United States of America, in the United States Circuit Court of Appeals for the Seventh Circuit. October Term, 1912," 66, NAC.
67. "John Arthur Johnson vs. United States of America, United States Circuit Court of Appeals for the Seventh Circuit, Petition for the United States for Rehearing, October Term, 1913, No. 2017," 10, NAC.
68. "U.S. Jury Finds Johnson Guilty: May Go to Prison; Negro Bruiser Convicted of Violating Mann Act against Trafficking in Women," *Chicago Daily Tribune*, May 14, 1913.
69. "Joliet Sentence for Jack Johnson: Year and a Day and Fine of $1,000 for Violating Mann White Slave Law; Judge Denies New Trial," *Chicago Daily Tribune*, June 5, 1913.
70. Ida B. Wells-Barnett, "Big Mass Meeting for Jack Johnson," *Chicago Defender*, November 16, 1912.
71. "2,000 Citizens Condemn U.S. Judges," *Chicago Defender*, November 23, 1912; "L'Accuse!," *Chicago Defender*, October 26, 1912.
72. "Daily Newspapers Try to Incite Riot," *Chicago Defender*, October 26, 1912.
73. "Daily Newspapers Try to Incite Riot," *Chicago Defender*, October 26, 1912.
74. "George Thompson Did Not Betray Emma Hanson," *Chicago Defender*, July 19, 1913.
75. "Negroes Uphold Mann Act," *Chicago Defender*, November 16, 1912; "Slavery-Black and White," *Chicago Defender*, December 14, 1912.
76. Langum, *Crossing over the Line*, 60.
77. Cynthia M. Blair, *I've Got to Make My Livin* (Chicago: University of Chicago Press, 2018), 188.

78. Frank A. Young, "Colored Girl Outraged in Cook County Hospital," *Chicago Defender*, October 26, 1912.
79. "White Man ... Little 15 Year Old ...," *Chicago Defender*, November 23, 1912.
80. "Mother at Fifteen, November 30th," *Chicago Defender*, November 9, 1912; "John Arthur Johnson, Champion Heavy Weight Prize Fighter of the World," *Broad Ax*, October 26, 1912. Black newspapers continued to draw a comparison between McFerrin's case and other cases. For example, George Tompson was charged with a Mann Act violation after crossing state lines to marry a fifteen-year-old white girl. The *Chicago Defender* insisted that Tompson was being honorable by marrying the girl, whereas McFerrin was shamed and abandoned. "George Tompson Did Not Betray Emma Hanson," *Chicago Defender*, July 19, 1913.
81. "John Arthur Johnson, Champion Heavy Weight Prize Fighter of the World," *Broad Ax*, October 26, 1912.
82. "Mator M'Ferrin's Assailant Found Guilty and Sent to Jail," *Chicago Defender*, November 30, 1912.
83. "Little Mator M'ferrin Becomes Mother in the Cook County Hospital Wednesday," *Chicago Defender*, November 16, 1912. Also "The white man has gained all he can and is slowly but surely retrograding, going back to the beast which is shown in their lust for human blood." "White Gentleman Commits Rape," *Chicago Defender*, October 7, 1911.
84. "Dies for Resenting Insult," *Chicago Defender*, November 11, 1911.
85. P. K. S., "Welcoming Negroes into Canada, the Land of the Free," *Chicago Defender*, May 13, 1911; "Southern White Gentleman Rapes Colored Lady; Is Killed by Husband," *Chicago Defender*, November 4, 1911; "John Arthur Johnson the Heavy Weight Prize Fighting Champion of the World," *Broad Ax*, November 16, 1912; "White Gentlemen and Colored Girls," *Broad Ax*, November 16, 1912.
86. "Negroes Uphold Mann Act," *Chicago Defender*, November 16, 1912. Also "Plenty Work for the Mann Act," *Chicago Defender*, July 25, 1914.
87. Mildred Miller, "No Excuse for Immoral Living: Marry," *Chicago Defender*, April 13, 1912.
88. "The Laws on the 'White Slave' Traffic Should Protection the Women of All Races," *Broad Ax*, November 9, 1912.
89. "Mothers Taking Innocent Daughters to Houses of Ill Fame," *Chicago Defender*, March 26, 1910.
90. Tim Cresswell, *On the Move: Mobility in the Modern Western World* (New York: Routledge, 2006), 151.
91. Lisa A. Flores, "Stoppage and the Racialized Rhetorics of Mobility," *Western Journal of Communication* 84, no. 3 (2020): 248.
92. Flores, "Stoppage and the Racialized Rhetorics of Mobility," 253.

Chapter 5. White Slavery and Yellow Peril: Immigration and Transnational Threat

1. Frank Julian Warne, *The Immigrant Invasion* (New York: Dodd, Mead, 1913), 2.
2. Edward Alfred Steiner, *The Immigrant Tide* (New York: Fleming H. Revell, 1909), 363. Steiner argues that this number does not account for immigrant departures, and he estimates the net immigration during this time to be 5,240,200.
3. Warne, *The Immigrant Invasion*, 40; Jeremiah Whipple Jenks, William Jett Lauck, and Rufus D. Smith, *The Immigration Problem: A Study of American Immigration Conditions and Needs* (New York: Funk & Wagnalls Company, 1926), 26.
4. Mary Clark Barnes and Lemuel Call Barnes, *The New America: A Study in Immigration* (New York: Fleming H. Revell Company, 1913), 103.
5. Erika Lee, *The Making of Asian America* (New York: Simon and Schuster, 2015), 65.
6. Lee, *The Making of Asian America*, 90–91.
7. For example, H. A. Millis, *The Japanese Problem in the United States* (New York: MacMillan Company, 1915), 230.
8. Edward W. Said, *Orientalism* (New York: Vintage, 1979), 5.
9. Corey Johnson, Reece Jones, Anssi Paasi, Louise Amoore, Alison Mountz, Mark Salter, and Chris Rumford, "Interventions on Rethinking 'the Border' in Border Studies," *Political Geography* 30, no. 2 (2011): 62.
10. D. Robert Dechaine, "Bordering the Civic Imaginary: Alienization, Fence Logic, and the Minuteman Civil Defense Corps," *Quarterly Journal of Speech* 95, no. 1 (2009): 46.
11. Lisa A. Flores, "Constructing Rhetorical Borders: Peons, Illegal Aliens, and Competing Narratives of Immigration," *Critical Studies in Media Communication* 20, no. 4 (2003). Also Lisa A. Flores, "Stoppage and the Racialized Rhetorics of Mobility," *Western Journal of Communication* 84, no. 3 (2020): 248; Jeremy Packer, "Homeland Subjectivity: The Algorithmic Identity of Security," *Communication and Critical/Cultural Studies* 4, no. 2 (2007): 212.
12. Lucy E. Salyer, *Laws Harsh as Tigers* (Chapel Hill: University of North Carolina Press, 2000), 2.
13. A. Warner Parker, "Letter to Mr. Sargent," May 28, 1908, 2, Records of the Immigration and Naturalization Service (Record Group 85), National Archives, Washington, DC (NADC hereafter), box 211, Subject and Policy Files, folder, Kellor Report on Problems of Immigrants, 51777/164.
14. Leroy G. Dorsey, *We Are All Americans, Pure and Simple: Theodore Roosevelt and the Myth of Americanism* (Tuscaloosa: University Alabama Press, 2007), 126–27.

15. K. C. Councilor, "Feeding the Body Politic: Metaphors of Digestion in Progressive Era US Immigration Discourse," *Communication and Critical/Cultural Studies* 14, no. 2 (2017).
16. Karma R. Chávez, "Border (In)Securities: Normative and Differential Belonging in LGBTQ and Immigrant Rights Discourse," *Communication and Critical/Cultural Studies* 7, no. 2 (2010): 138.
17. Chávez, "Border (In)Securities," 138; Dechaine, "Bordering the Civic Imaginary."
18. J. David Cisneros, "Contaminated Communities: The Metaphor of 'Immigrant as Pollutant' in Media Representations of Immigration," *Rhetoric and Public Affairs* 11, no. 4 (2008): 569–601.
19. Dechaine, "Bordering the Civic Imaginary," 44.
20. Jenks, Lauck, and Smith, *The Immigration Problem*, 366.
21. Jenks, Lauck, and Smith, *The Immigration Problem*, 49a.
22. Prescott F. Hall, *Immigration and Its Effects upon the United Sates* (New York: Henry Holt, 1906), 101.
23. Jenks, Lauck, and Smith, *The Immigration Problem*, 374.
24. Jenks, Lauck, and Smith, *The Immigration Problem*, 375; Kerry Abrams, "Polygamy, Prostitution, and the Federalization of Immigration Law," *Columbia Law Review* 105 (2005): 643.
25. Abrams, "Polygamy, Prostitution, and the Federalization of Immigration Law," 695.
26. Abrams, "Polygamy, Prostitution, and the Federalization of Immigration Law," 698.
27. Lee, *The Making of Asian America*, 60, 67.
28. Abrams, "Polygamy, Prostitution, and the Federalization of Immigration Law," 711.
29. Lee, *The Making of Asian America*, 95.
30. Lee, *The Making of Asian America*, 112.
31. Jenks, Lauck, and Smith, *The Immigration Problem*, 375–76.
32. Jenks, Lauck, and Smith, *The Immigration Problem*, 377, 380.
33. "Confidential Circular," (March 19, 1909), NADC, box 595, Subject and Policy Files, folder, White Slave Traffic Ellis Island, 52484/3.
34. Kristofer Allerfeldt, "Marcus Braun and 'White Slavery,'" *Journal of Global Slavery* 4, no. 3 (2019): 347.
35. Allerfeldt, "Marcus Braun and 'White Slavery,'" 348–49.
36. "Marcus Braun Report," September 29, 1908, 1, NADC, box 594, Subject and Policy Files, folder, Braun Report of Sept. 29, 1908, 52484 1-A.
37. "Marcus Braun Report," September 29, 1908, 2, NADC, box 594, Subject and Policy Files, folder, Braun Report of Sept. 29, 1908, 52484 1-A.
38. "Marcus Braun Report," September 29, 1908, 2, NADC, box 594, Subject and Policy Files, folder, Braun Report of Sept. 29, 1908, 52484 1-A.

39. "Marcus Braun Report," September 29, 1908, 7, 23, 29, NADC, box 594, Subject and Policy Files, folder, Braun Report of Sept. 29, 1908, 52484 1-A.
40. John H. Clark, "To Walter E. Carr," April 11, 1911, NADC, box 1, Records of Field Offices District No. 15, Office Files of Order and Circulars, 1907–1911, entry A1 243, book 1.
41. John H. Clark, "10873," April 12, 1911, NADC, box 1, Records of Field Offices District No. 15, Office Files of Order and Circulars, 1907–1911, entry A1 243, book 1.
42. On another occasion, Clark advised officers to be on the lookout for a specific woman. Despite failing to have a description, he noted, "In general appearance she bespeaks her reputation." John H. Clark, "To All Boards of Special Inquiry," September 8, 1911, NADC, box 1, Records of Field Offices District No. 15, Office Files of Order and Circulars, 1907–1911, entry A1 243, Ray D. Gould Personal File 1910–1911.
43. Erika Lee and Judy Yung, *Angel Island: Immigrant Gateway to America* (Oxford: Oxford University Press, 2010), 20.
44. Lee and Yung, *Angel Island*, 31. Karma R. Chávez explains that there is a significant legacy of quarantine of migrant women who are deemed immoral because they were thought to present both a moral and public health threat to the nation. Karma R. Chávez, *The Borders of AIDS: Race, Quarantine, and Resistance* (Seattle: University of Washington Press, 2021), 39.
45. Lisa A. Flores, *Deportable and Disposable: Public Rhetoric and the Making of the "Illegal" Immigrant* (University Park: Pennsylvania State Press, 2021), 5.
46. "Sir," March 10, 1909, 52484/2 (File number), 51777/197-C, NADC, box 59, Subject and Policy Files, folder, White Slave Traffic, Ellis Island, 1909, 52484/3.
47. Marcus Braun, "To Commissioner General of Immigration," August 9, 1908, NADC, box 594, Subject and Policy Files, folder, Braun, US Details White Slave Traffic, 52484/1.
48. Daniel J. Leonard, "To Commissioner of Immigration," May 2, 1912, NADC, box 838, Subject and Policy Files, folder, White Slavery, 1912–1913, 52809/7-E.
49. Paraskowja Posuch 52742/40, Benj. S. Cable, "No. 52742/40," January 19, 1910, NADC, box 785, Subject and Policy Files, 1893–1957, folder, Paraskowja Posuch 52742/40.
50. "In the Matter of Posuch, Parakowja (alias Postach, Paulie) and child Posuch, Michael," January 12, 1910, 6, 8, 10, NADC, box 785, Subject and Policy Files, 1893–1957, folder, Paraskowja Posuch 52742/40; Samuel Markewich, "In the Matter of Pauline Posach and Child Michael," January 15, 1910, NADC, box 785 Subject and Policy Files, 1893–1957, folder, Paraskowja Posuch 52742/40.
51. William R. Wheeler, "To Supervising Inspector, Immigration Services, San Antonio, TX," March 11, 1909, NADC, Box 1, Records of Field Offices District No. 15, Office Files of Order and Circulars, 1907–1911, entry A1 243, book 2.
52. Leslie J. Harris, "Home-Making, Nation-Making," in *Reading the Presidency: Advances in Presidential Rhetoric*, ed. Stephen J. Heidt and Mary E. Stuckey (New York: Peter Lang, 2019).

53. Jenks, Lauck, and Smith, *The Immigration Problem*, 216.
54. Steiner, *The Immigrant Tide*, 194.
55. Lee, *The Making of Asian America*, 121.
56. Natalia Molina, *How Race Is Made in America* (Berkeley: University of California Press, 2014), 90.
57. Elmer Clarence Sandmeyer, *The Anti-Chinese Movement in California* (Urbana: University of Illinois Press, 1973), 27.
58. Matthew Guterl and Christine Skwiot, "Atlantic and Pacific Crossings: Race, Empire, and 'the Labor Problem' in the Late Nineteenth Century," *Radical History Review* 2005, no. 91 (2005): 43.
59. Guterl and Skwiot, "Atlantic and Pacific Crossings," 47.
60. Warne, *The Immigrant Invasion*, 180.
61. Yu-Fang Cho, "'Yellow Slavery,' Narratives of Rescue, and Sui Sin Far/Edith Maude Eaton's 'Lin John' (1899)," *Journal of Asian American Studies* 12, no. 1 (2009): 44.
62. Barnes and Barnes, *The New America*, 114.
63. "Grave but Uncorroborated Accusation Are Made against Chief Sullivan and Captain Wittman," *San Francisco Call*, February 10, 1901.
64. "Girls Sold at Auction," *New York Times*, January 21, 1901.
65. "Girl Slave Traffic News to Police," *San Francisco Examiner*, February 7, 1901.
66. "Slaves of Chinese Ring Will Be Coerced," *San Francisco Examiner*, April 29, 1901.
67. M. G. C. Edholm, "A Stain on the Flag," in *Unbound Voices: A Documentary History of Chinese Women in San Francisco*, ed. Judy Yung (Berkeley: University of California Press, 1999, 135.
68. In re Lee Kan, alias Lee Kam, February 28, 1913, Department of Commerce and Labor, Immigration Division, NADC, box 838 Subject and Policy Files, 1893–1957, folder, White Slavery, 1912–1913, 52809/7-E.
69. Lee and Yung, *Angel Island*, 49; Judy Yung, *Unbound Feet: A Social History of Chinese Women in San Francisco* (Berkeley: University of California Press, 1995), 63.
70. Lee and Yung, *Angel Island*, 88.
71. Louise A. Littleton, "Worse Than Slaves: Servitude of All Chinese Wives," in *Unbound Voices: A Documentary History of Chinese Women in San Francisco*, ed. Judy Yung (Berkeley: University of California Press, 1999, 167.
72. Yung, *Unbound Feet*, 69.
73. "Committee Lays Bare Official Rottenness," *Los Angeles Times*, February 22, 1901.
74. Yung, *Unbound Feet*, 37.
75. Edholm, "A Stain on the Flag," 139.
76. Leslie J. Harris, *State of the Marital Union: Rhetoric, Identity, and Nineteenth Century Marriage Controversies* (Waco, TX: Baylor University Press, 2014), 137.
77. Harris, *State of the Marital Union*, 136.

78. Ariela R. Dubler, "Immoral Purposes: Marriage and the Genus of Illicit Sex," *Yale Law Journal* 115, no. 4 (2006): 777.
79. "Marcus Braun Report," September 29, 1908, 8, NADC, box 594, Subject and Policy Files, folder, Braun Report of Sept. 29, 1908, 52484 1-A.
80. "Marcus Braun Report," September 29, 1908, 9, NADC, box 594, Subject and Policy Files, folder, Braun Report of Sept. 29, 1908, 52484 1-A. Braun continued to insist that an American who marries a prostitute should lose their citizenship because they have proven themselves unworthy (13).
81. Lee, *The Making of Asian America*, 112–13.
82. "Memo: For the Acting Commissioner-General," October 19, 1908, 4, NADC, box 594, Subject and Policy Files, folder, Braun 52484 1-A.
83. Yamato Ichihashi, *Japanese Immigration: Its Status in California* (San Francisco: Marshall Press, 1915), 13.
84. *California and the Oriental: Japanese, Chinese, and Hindus* (Sacramento: California State Printing Office, 1920), 139.
85. *California and the Oriental: Japanese, Chinese, and Hindus*, 182.
86. Chester H. Rowell, "Chinese and Japanese Immigrants—a Comparison," *Annals of the American Academy of Political and Social Science* 34, no. 2 (1909): 10.
87. Immigration Commission of the United States, *Dictionary of Races or Peoples* (Washington, DC: Government Printing Office, 1911), 3.
88. Sandmeyer, *The Anti-Chinese Movement in California*, 37.
89. "Moral and Legal Points Outlined," *San Francisco Call*, November 23, 1901.
90. Nayan Shah, *Contagious Divides: Epidemics and Race in San Francisco's Chinatown* (Berkeley: University of California Press, 2001), 18.
91. Rowell, "Chinese and Japanese Immigrants," 7–8.
92. Lady Henry Somerset, "The Darker Side," *North American Review* 154, no. 422 (1892): 64.
93. Theodore Bingham, "Foreign Criminals in New York," *North American Review* 188, no. 634 (1908): 391.
94. "Wonderful Woman Coming to Dayton," *Dayton Daily News*, October 24, 1913.
95. "One Woman against New York's Underworld," *Oregon Daily Journal*, February 2, 1913; "One Woman against New York's Underworld: She Is Rose Livingston Who Fights 10,000 Policemen and Thousands of White Slavers," *Salt Lake Herald-Republican*, February 2, 1913.
96. "Hundreds of Women Hear Suffrage Talks," *North Adams Transcript*, February 8, 1915.
97. "Rose Livingston," *Dayton Daily News*, October 25, 1913.
98. Ethel R. Vorce, "My Dear Mrs. Laidlaw," March 5, 1913, Harriet Wright Burton Laidlaw Papers, Schlesinger Library, Radcliffe Institute, Harvard University, Cambridge, MA (HWBL hereafter), White Slavery, Rose Livingston, Correspondence, January–March 1913, A-63, folder 93.

99. Geo. Hugh Birney, "To Whom It May Concern," HWBL, White Slavery, Rose Livingston, Correspondence, January–March 1913, A-63, folder 93.
100. Mary Ting Yi Lui, "Saving Young Girls from Chinatown: White Slavery and Woman Suffrage, 1910–1920," *Journal of the History of Sexuality* 18, no. 3 (2009): 398–99.
101. Lui, "Saving Young Girls from Chinatown," 399; Isabelle Thompson Smart, "To Mr. Nathan A. Smyth," May 27, 1912, HWBL, White Slavery, Rose Livingston, Correspondence, May–June 1912, A-63, folder 91; Frank Moss, "To Messrs. Gerard and Smyth," June 11, 1912, HWBL, White Slavery, Rose Livingston, Correspondence, May–June 1912, A-63, folder 91; Warren B. Chapin, January 6, 1913, HWBL, White Slavery, Rose Livingston, Correspondence, January–March 1913, A-63, folder 93.
102. "One Woman against New York's Underworld," *Oregon Daily Journal*, February 2, 1913.
103. "Enlists Aid in Saving Girls from White Slavery," *Dayton Herald*, October 27, 1913.
104. "One Woman against New York's Underworld," *Oregon Daily Journal*, February 2, 1913.
105. "Oust Vice Meeting from Schoolhouse," *Brooklyn Daily Eagle*, June 20, 1913.
106. "Hundreds of Women Hear Suffrage Talks," *The North Adams Transcript*, February 8, 1915.
107. "City Wider Open Than in Time of Devery, Says Girl Slum Worker," *Times Union* (Brooklyn, NY), July 31, 1913.
108. "City Wider Open Than in Time of Devery."
109. "One Woman against New York's Underworld," *Oregon Daily Journal*, February 2, 1913.
110. "'Can Any of You Men Live on $3 Per Week?' Asks Rose Livingston," *Brooklyn Daily Eagle*, July 23, 1913.
111. "Girls Are Sold in Chinatown," *Quad-City Times* (Davenport, IA), December 21, 1912.
112. Michael Grossberg, *Governing the Hearth: Law and the Family in Nineteenth-Century America* (Chapel Hill: University of North Carolina Press, 1985), 282. As Grossberg explained, principles of coverture were clearly weakening by the end of the nineteenth century, but women's rights remained inconsistent and often dependent on judicial discretion.
113. Eleanor Flexner, *Century of Struggle: The Woman's Rights Movement in the United States* (New York: Atheneum, 1973), 308–9.
114. Harriet B. Laidlaw, "To Whom It May Concern," February 9, 1926, HWBL, White Slavery, Rose Livingston, Correspondence, 1918–1933, A-63, folder 100.
115. "'Angel of Chinatown' Hailed for Her Work," *New York Times*, December 27, 1949.
116. "Medals Honor Five for Social Service," *New York Times*, May 1, 1929.
117. Chávez, *The Borders of AIDS*, 5.

Chapter 6. White Slavery and Transnational Flow: International Sex Trafficking Activism before World War I

1. "The White Slavery of Europe," *The Shield* 7, no. 265/56 (June 17, 1876), 202.
2. Stephanie Limoncelli, *The Politics of Trafficking: The First International Movement to Combat the Sexual Exploitation of Women* (Stanford, CA: Stanford University Press, 2011), 157; David Held, Anthony McGrew, David Goldblatt, and Jonathan Perraton, "Globalization," *Global Governance* 5, no. 4 (1999): 484.
3. Gregory Blue, "Introduction," in *Colonialism and the Modern World*, ed. Gregory Blue, Martin Bunton, and Ralph C. Croizier (London: Routledge, 2001), 8.
4. Raka Shome, "Whiteness and the Politics of Location," in *Whiteness: The Communication of Social Identity*, ed. Thomas K. Nakayama and Judith N. Martin (Thousand Oaks, CA: Sage Publications, 1999), 108. Also see Vron Ware, "Perfidious Albion: Whiteness and the International Imagination," in *The Making and Unmaking of Whiteness*, ed. Birgit Brander Rasmussen, Eric Klinenberg, Irene J. Nexica, and Matt Wray (Durham, NC: Duke University Press, 2001), 185; Mohan J. Dutta, "Whiteness, Internationalization, and Erasure: Decolonizing Futures from the Global South," *Communication and Critical/Cultural Studies* 17, no. 2 (2020).
5. Richard Phillips, *Sex, Politics, and Empire: A Postcolonial Geography* (Manchester, UK: Manchester University Press, 2006), 19.
6. For example, the Netherlands adopted French criminal code in 1811 while the country was under French rule, but specific systems of regulation varied among municipalities and over time. Petra De Vries, "Josephine Butler and the Making of Feminism: International Abolitionism in the Netherlands (1870–1914)," *Women's History Review* 17, no. 2 (2008): 259. For dates of international regulation, see Limoncelli, *The Politics of Trafficking*, 23.
7. Judith R. Walkowitz, *Prostitution and Victorian Society* (Cambridge: Cambridge University Press, 1982), 1.
8. Josephine E. Butler, *Truth before Everything* (n.p., 1897), 19.
9. Walkowitz, *Prostitution and Victorian Society*, 93.
10. Walkowitz, *Prostitution and Victorian Society*, 115.
11. Walkowitz, *Prostitution and Victorian Society*, 117.
12. Butler, *Truth before Everything*, 9.
13. Butler, *Truth before Everything*, 9.
14. "London," *The Shield* 7, no. 282/73 (December 16, 1876), 368.
15. "Reasons for Opposing Certain Immoral Legislation Now in Operation in This Country, and Other Information in Regard to It," January, 1878, Wisconsin State Historical Society, Madison, WI (WSHS hereafter), pamphlet 58-2439c.
16. National Association for Repeal, "What Are the Contagious Diseases Acts?," WSHS, pamphlet 58-2437c. Also see "Reasons for Opposing Certain Immoral Legislation Now in Operation in This Country, and Other Information in

Regard to it," January, 1878, WSHS, pamphlet 58-2439c; Josephine E. Butler, "State Regulation of Vice," September 29, 1876, WSHS, pamphlet 58-2436a.

17. "Reasons for Opposing Certain Immoral Legislation Now in Operation in This Country, and Other Information in Regard to it," January, 1878, WSHS, pamphlet 58-2439c. Also see Central Vigilance Committee for the Repression of Immorality, "Annual Report," 1884, 3, WSHS, pamphlet 58-2441d.
18. "Mrs. Butler in Switzerland," *The Shield* 6, no. 224/15 (March 1, 1875); "London," *The Shield* 7, no. 282/73 (December 16, 1876).
19. National Association for Repeal, "What Are the Contagious Diseases Acts?," WSHS, pamphlet 58-2437c. Also see "Reasons for Opposing Certain Immoral Legislation Now in Operation in This Country, and Other Information in Regard to it," January, 1878, WSHS, pamphlet 58-2439c.
20. James John Garth Wilkinson, *The Forcible Introspection of Women for the Army and Navy by the Oligarchy* (London: F. Pitman, 1870), 23.
21. Josephine E. Butler, "Dear Friends," 1874, 2, WSHS, pamphlet 58-2436a.
22. Alfred S. Dyer, *The European Slave Trade in English Girls. A Narrative of Facts*, (London: Dyer Brothers, 1880), 31–32.
23. Dyer, *The European Slave Trade in English Girls*, 31.
24. Limoncelli, *The Politics of Trafficking*, 46.
25. "Art. v. the International Congress on Public Morality," *Englishwoman's Review* 54 (October 15, 1877): 475.
26. "The International Conference on the White Slave Traffic," *The Shield* 2, no. 25 (July 1, 1899), 42.
27. European colonialism, sexual exploitation, and prostitution regulation is a complex issue that varies among different cultures. For an analysis of regulation in India, see Stephen Legg, "Stimulation, Segregation and Scandal: Geographies of Prostitution Regulation in British, India, Between Registration (1888) and Suppression (1923)," *Modern Asian Studies* 46, no. 6 (2012); Philippa Levine, "Venereal Disease, Prostitution, and the Politics of Empire: The Case of British India," *Journal of the History of Sexuality* 4 (1994).
28. John Pope Hennessey, "Governor and Commander-in-Chief of Hong Kong on the Contagious Diseases Ordinance in That Colony," July, 1882, 7, WSHS, pamphlet 58-2439d.
29. Limoncelli, *The Politics of Trafficking*, 103.
30. Levine, "Venereal Disease, Prostitution, and the Politics of Empire," 581.
31. Levine, "Venereal Disease, Prostitution, and the Politics of Empire," 586.
32. Henrik Örnebring, "The Maiden Tribute and the Naming of Monsters: Two Case Studies of Tabloid Journalism as Alternative Public Sphere," *Journalism Studies* 7, no. 6 (2006): 855.
33. Deborah Gorham, "The 'Maiden Tribute of Modern Babylon' Re-examined: Child Prostitution and the Idea of Childhood in Late-Victorian England," *Victorian Studies* 21, no. 3 (1978): 360.
34. "Notice to Our Readers: A Frank Warning," *Pall Mall Gazette*, July 4, 1885.

35. William Stead, "The Maiden Tribute of Modern Babylon—I: The Report of Our Secret Commission," *Pall Mall Gazette*, July 6, 1885, 2.
36. William Stead, "The Maiden Tribute of Modern Babylon—III: The Report of Our Secret Commission," *Pall Mall Gazette*, July 8, 1885, 5.
37. William Stead, "The Maiden Tribute of Modern Babylon—II: The Report of Our Secret Commission," *Pall Mall Gazette*, July 7, 1885, 3; Stead, "The Maiden Tribute of Modern Babylon—I," 3.
38. Stead, "The Maiden Tribute of Modern Babylon—I," 2.
39. Stead, "The Maiden Tribute of Modern Babylon—II," 2.
40. Stead, "The Maiden Tribute of Modern Babylon—I," 6.
41. William Stead, "The Maiden Tribute of Modern Babylon—IV: The Report of Our Secret Commission," *Pall Mall Gazette*, July 10, 1885, 5.
42. Stead, "The Maiden Tribute of Modern Babylon—I," 6.
43. Stead, "The Maiden Tribute of Modern Babylon—III," 2.
44. Stead, "The Maiden Tribute of Modern Babylon—III," 3.
45. Stead, "The Maiden Tribute of Modern Babylon—IV," 3.
46. Stead, "The Maiden Tribute of Modern Babylon—I," 6.
47. Judith R. Walkowitz, *City of Dreadful Delight: Narratives of Sexual Danger in Late-Victorian London* (Chicago: University of Chicago Press, 2013), 97.
48. Rachael Attwood, "Stopping the Traffic: The National Vigilance Association and the International Fight against the 'White Slave' Trade (1899–c. 1909)," *Women's History Review* 24, no. 3 (2015): 326.
49. Attwood, "Stopping the Traffic" 327.
50. Attwood, "Stopping the Traffic."
51. "The International Conference on the White Slave Traffic," *The Shield* 2, no. 25 (July 1, 1899), 44.
52. Butler, *Truth before Everything*, 7–8.
53. Limoncelli, *The Politics of Trafficking*, 145.
54. Marcus Braun, "Final Report," October 2, 1909, 1, NADC, box 595, Subject and Policy Files, folder, 52484/1-G.
55. Marcus Braun, "Commissioner General of Immigration, Washington DC," June 23, 1909, 3–4, NADC, box 594, Subject and Policy Files, folder, 52484/1-D.
56. Marcus Braun, "Commissioner General of Immigration, Washington DC," June 23, 1909, 4, NADC, box 594, Subject and Policy Files, folder, 52484/1-D.
57. He also represented France at the 1910 conference. Jean Allain, "White Slave Traffic in International Law," *Journal of Trafficking and Human Exploitation* 1 (2017): 20, 24.
58. The Secretary of Commerce and Labor, October 14, 1909, NADC, box 595, Subject and Policy Files, folder, Continue 1-F 52484/1-F; Marcus Braun, Letter to Commissioner General of Immigration, September 16, 1909, NADC, box 595, Subject and Policy Files, folder, Continue 1-F 52484/1-F.
59. Robert Asen, "Reflections on the Role of Rhetoric in Public Policy," *Rhetoric & Public Affairs* 13, no. 1 (2010): 137; Leah Ceccarelli, "Polysemy: Multiple

Meanings in Rhetorical Criticism," *Quarterly Journal of Speech* 84, no. 4 (1998).
60. "Suppression of the White-Slave Traffic," S. Doc. No. 214, pt. 2, 61st Congress, 2d Session, NADC, box 594, Subject and Policy Files, folder, Continue-1-A R, International Conference Folder 1, July–Dec 1910, 52483/1-A.
61. Allain, "White Slave Traffic in International Law," 27.
62. American Legation, Madrid, Accompanying Dispatch No. 282, 1, NADC, box 594, Subject and Policy Files, folder, Continue-1-A R, International Conference Folder 1, July–Dec 1910, 52483/1-A.
63. American Legation, Madrid, Accompanying Dispatch No. 282, 1, NADC, box 594, Subject and Policy Files, folder, Continue-1-A R, International Conference Folder 1, July–Dec 1910, 52483/1-A.
64. Siobhán McGrath, and Samantha Watson, "Anti-Slavery as Development: A Global Politics of Rescue," *Geoforum* 93 (2018): 24.
65. Liat Kozma, *Global Women, Colonial Ports: Prostitution in the Interwar Middle East* (Albany, NY: SUNY Press, 2017), 210.
66. Kozma, *Global Women, Colonial Ports*, 51.
67. Antoinette Burton, *Burdens of History* (Chapel Hill: University of North Carolina Press, 2000), 130.
68. Philippa Levine, *Prostitution, Race, and Politics: Policing Venereal Disease in the British Empire* (New York: Routledge, 2003), 103; Burton, *Burdens of History*, 135.
69. Levine, *Prostitution, Race, and Politics*, 104.
70. Levine, *Prostitution, Race, and Politics*, 105.
71. Levine, *Prostitution, Race, and Politics*, 106.
72. Elizabeth Wheeler Andrew and Katharine Caroline Bushnell, *The Queen's Daughters in India* (London: Morgan and Scott, 1899), 50–51.
73. Andrew and Bushnell, *The Queen's Daughters in India*, 62.
74. Andrew and Bushnell, *The Queen's Daughters in India*, 86.
75. Andrew and Bushnell, *The Queen's Daughters in India*, 101.
76. Andrew and Bushnell, *The Queen's Daughters in India*, 102.
77. Gayatri Chakravorty Spivak, "Can the Subaltern Speak?," in *Colonial Discourse and Post-Colonial Theory*, ed. Patrick Williams and Laura Chrisman (New York: Columbia University Press, 1994).

Conclusion

1. Natalia Molina, *How Race Is Made in America: Immigration, Citizenship, and the Historical Power of Racial Scripts* (Berkeley: University of California Press, 2014), 21.
2. For example, moral reform literature called on white Americans to save innocent girls who were trapped in white slavery, and some Congressional

representatives represented themselves as heroes of innocent white girls who were exploited by (primarily Black and immigrant) men.
3. Carrie N. Baker, "An Examination of Some Central Debates on Sex Trafficking in Research and Public Policy in the United States," *Journal of Human Trafficking* 1, no. 3 (2015): 195; Alison Brysk and Austin Choi-Fitzpatrick, "Introduction: Rethinking Trafficking," in *From Human Trafficking to Human Rights: Reframing Contemporary Slavery*, ed. Alison Brysk and Austin Choi-Fitzpatrick (Philadelphia: University of Pennsylvania Press, 2011), 2.
4. Baker, "An Examination of Some Central Debates," 195.
5. Louise Shelley, *Human Trafficking* (Cambridge: Cambridge University Press, 2010), 5.
6. Kamala Kempadoo, "The Modern-Day White (Wo)Man's Burden: Trends in Anti-Trafficking and Anti-Slavery Campaigns," *Journal of Human Trafficking* 1, no. 1 (2015): 10.
7. Maggy Lee, *Trafficking and Global Crime Control* (Thousand Oaks, CA: Sage Publications, 2011), 20.
8. Siobhán McGrath and Samantha Watson, "Anti-slavery as Development: A Global Politics of Rescue," *Geoforum* 93 (2018): 23.
9. Kempadoo, "The Modern-Day White (Wo)Man's Burden," 9.
10. Lee, *Trafficking and Global Crime Control*, 21.
11. David Zarefsky, "Echoes of the Slavery Controversy in the Current Abortion Debate," in *Conference Proceedings—National Communication Association/American Forensic Association (Alta Conference on Argumentation)* (Washington, DC: National Communication Association, 1991), 89.
12. Ashton Kutcher, "Opening Statement to the Senate Foreign Relations Committee on Ending Modern Slavery and Human Trafficking," February 15, 2017, https://www.americanrhetoric.com/speeches/ashtonkutchercongressthorn.htm.
13. Annie Hill, "Producing the Crisis: Human Trafficking and Humanitarian Interventions," *Women's Studies in Communication* 41, no. 4 (2018): 315.
14. Eli Andrade, René Leyva, Mei-Po Kwan, Carlos Magis, Hugo Stainez-Orozco, and Kimberly Brouwer, "Women in Sex Work and the Risk Environment: Agency, Risk Perception, and Management in the Sex Work Environments of Two Mexico–U.S. Border Cities," *Sexuality Research & Social Policy* 16, no. 3 (2019): 317–28.
15. Jessica Contrera, "Abused Teen Waits, Waits, Waits in Jail," *Milwaukee Journal Sentinel*, December 29, 2019, 14.
16. Annie Bunting and Joel Quirk, "Contemporary Slavery as More Than Rhetorical Strategy? The Politics and Ideology of a New Political Cause," in *Contemporary Slavery: The Rhetoric of Global Human Rights Campaigns*, ed. Annie Bunting and Joel Quirk (Ithaca, NY: Cornell University Press, 2017), 9.
17. Some scholarship has specifically named the dislocation caused by the collapse of the Soviet Union as the force that spurred globalized sex trafficking.

Girish J. "Jeff" Gulati, "Representing Trafficking: Media in the United States, Great Britain, and Canada," in *From Human Trafficking to Human Rights: Reframing Contemporary Slavery*, ed. Alison Brysk and Austin Choi-Fitzpatrick (Philadelphia: University of Pennsylvania Press, 2011), 46.

18. Casey Ryan Kelly, "Feminine Purity and Masculine Revenge-Seeking in *Taken* (2008)," *Feminist Media Studies* 14, no. 3 (2014): 411.
19. Lee, *Trafficking and Global Crime Control*, 24.
20. Jessica Contrera, "A QAnon Con: How the Viral Wayfair Sex Trafficking Lie Hurt Real Kids," *Washington Post*, December 16, 2021.
21. Jessica Contrera, "A QAnon Con: How the Viral Wayfair Sex Trafficking Lie Hurt Real Kids," *Washington Post*, December 16, 2021. Also see the University of Maryland, "QAnon Crime Map," National Consortium for the Study of Terrorism and Responses to Terrorism, https://www.start.umd.edu/qanon-crime-maps.
22. Lee, *Trafficking and Global Crime Control*, 26.
23. Soren Andersen, "'Rape for Profit': A Heartbreaking Look at Underage Sex-Trafficking in Seattle," *Seattle Times*, December 13, 2012.
24. Brysk and Choi-Fitzpatrick, "Introduction: Rethinking Trafficking," 3.
25. Lee, *Trafficking and Global Crime Control*, 29.
26. Laura Herbert, "The Sexual Politics of U.S. Inter/National Security," in *From Human Trafficking to Human Rights: Reframing Contemporary Slavery*, ed. Alison Brysk and Austin Choi-Fitzpatrick (Philadelphia: University of Pennsylvania Press, 2011), 99.
27. Mariam Jordan, "QAnon Joins Vigilantes at the Southern Border," *New York Times*, May 9, 2022.
28. Amy Gutmann, "Introduction," in *Human Rights as Political and Idolatry* (Princeton, NJ: Princeton University Press, 2001) ix.
29. Austin Choi-Fitzpatrick, "Rethinking Trafficking: Contemporary Slavery," in *From Human Trafficking to Human Rights: Reframing Contemporary Slavery*, ed. Alison Brysk and Austin Choi-Fitzpatrick (Philadelphia: University of Pennsylvania Press, 2011), 19.
30. Alison Brysk, "Rethinking Trafficking: Human Rights and Private Wrongs," in *From Human Trafficking to Human Rights: Reframing Contemporary Slavery*, ed. Alison Brysk and Austin Choi-Fitzpatrick (Philadelphia: University of Pennsylvania Press, 2011), 74.
31. Emma Goldman, "The Traffic in Women," *Hastings Women's Law Journal* 13 (2002): 9–20.
32. There is a long history of women's rights advocates, like Victoria Woodhull, challenging a double standard of morality evident in the condemnation of prostitution and the social conditions that sustained prostitution. For an example of Woodhull's rhetoric on prostitution see Victoria Woodhull, "'And the Truth Shall Make you Free.' A Speech on the Principles of Social Freedom Delivered in Steinway Hall," November 20, 1871, Voices of Democracy:

The U.S. Oratory Project, https://voicesofdemocracy.umd.edu/victoria-c-woodhull-and-the-truth-shall-make-you-free-speech-text/. Likewise, free love advocate Voltairine de Cleyre used the phrase "sex slavery" to reference exploitation within marriage (Leslie J. Harris, *State of the Marital Union: Rhetoric, Identity, and Nineteenth-Century Marriage Controversies* [Waco, TX: Baylor University Press, 2014], 104). These precursors to the movement to end white slavery are clearly significant. However, these advocates are outside of the scope of the current study because they were not active in challenging white slavery as a system of sex trafficking.

33. Michael Ignatieff, *Human Rights as Political and Idolatry* (Princeton, NJ: Princeton University Press, 2001), 10.
34. For example, *Gendered Resistance: Women, Slavery, and the Legacy of Margaret Garner*, ed. Mary E. Frederickson and Delores W. Walters (Urbana: University of Illinois Press, 2013).
35. Robin E. Jensen, *Dirty Words: The Rhetoric of Public Sex Education, 1870–1924* (Urbana: University of Illinois Press, 2010), xvii.
36. Glen Gendzel, "What the Progressives Had in Common," *Journal of the Gilded Age and Progressive Era* 10, no. 3 (2011): 332.
37. Daniel T. Rodger, "Capitalism and Politics in the Progressive Era and in Ours," *Journal of the Gilded Age and Progressive Era* 13, no. 3 (2014): 379.
38. Gendzel, "What the Progressives Had in Common," 332.
39. Gail Bederman, *Manliness & Civilization: A Cultural History of Gender and Race in the United States, 1880–1917* (Chicago: University of Chicago Press, 1995), 25.
40. Jane Addams, *A New Conscience and an Ancient Evil* (New York: MacMillan, 1912).
41. For example, Kristy Maddux, *Practicing Citizenship: Women's Rhetoric at the 1893 Chicago World's Fair* (University Park: Pennsylvania State University Press, 2019), 109–12; Sara C. VanderHaagen, "'A Grand Sisterhood': Black American Women Speakers at the 1893 World's Congress of Representative Women," *Quarterly Journal of Speech* 107, no. 1 (2021): 1–25.
42. bell hooks, *Writing Beyond Race: Living Theory and Practice* (New York: Routledge, 2013), 4.
43. Clifford E. Roe and B. S. Steadwell, *The Great War on White Slavery or Fighting for the Protection of Our Girls* (1911), 371.

Bibliography

Archives and Major Collections

Chicago History Museum Archives (CHM)
Chicago History Museum, Chicago, IL, Clifford W. Barnes Papers (CWB)
Chicago History Museum, Chicago, IL, Ernest A. Bell Collection (EAB)
Frances Willard Library and Archives, Evanston, IL (FWLA)
Frances Willard Library and Archives, Evanston, IL, Frances E. Willard Scrapbooks (FWS)
National Archives, Chicago, IL, Briefs and Appendices, 1891–1959 (Record Group 276) (NAC)
National Archives, Washington, DC, Records of the Immigration and Naturalization Service (Record Group 85) (NADC)
Rockefeller Archives Center, Sleepy Hollow, NY (RAC)
Rockefeller Archives Center, Sleepy Hollow, NY, Bureau of Social Hygiene Records (BSH)
Rockefeller Archives Center, Sleepy Hollow, NY, Office of the Messrs. Rockefeller, Rockefeller Boards, Record Group III, Series 20 (OMR)
Schlesinger Library, Radcliffe Institute, Harvard University, Cambridge, MA, Harriet Wright Burton Laidlaw Papers (HWBL)
Wisconsin State Historical Society, Madison, WI (WSHS)
Wisconsin State Historical Society, Madison, WI, Wisconsin Governor Investigations, 1851–1959, White Slavery Investigation (WGI)

References

Abbott, Grace. *The Immigrant and the Community*. New York: Century Co., 1917.

Abrams, Kerry. "Polygamy, Prostitution, and the Federalization of Immigration Law." *Columbia Law Review* 105 (2005): 641–716.

Adams, James. "Taming Wild Girls: The Midnight Mission and the Campaign to Reform Philadelphia's Moral Fabric, 1915–1918." *Pennsylvania Magazine of History and Biography* 135, no. 2 (2011): 125–49.

Addams, Jane. "A New Conscience and an Ancient Evil." *McClure's Magazine*, November 1911.

———. *A New Conscience and an Ancient Evil*. New York: MacMillan Company, 1912.

Alderman, Derek H., Joshua Inwood, and James A. Tyner. "Jack Johnson versus Jim Crow: Race, Reputation, and the Politics of Black Villainy; the Fight of the Century." *Southeastern Geographer* 58, no. 3 (2018): 227–49.

Allain, Jean. "White Slave Traffic in International Law." *Journal of Trafficking and Human Exploitation* 1 (2017): 1–40.

Allen, Annie W. "How to Save the Girls Who Have Fallen." *The Survey* 24, no. 19 (1910): 684–96.

Allerfeldt, Kristofer. "Marcus Braun and 'White Slavery.'" *Journal of Global Slavery* 4, no. 3 (2019): 343–71.

Anderson, Benedict Richard O'Gorman. *Imagined Communities*. London: Verso, 1991.

Andrade, Eli, René Leyva, Mei-Po Kwan, Carlos Magis, Hugo Stainez-Orozco, and Kimberly Brouwer. "Women in Sex Work and the Risk Environment: Agency, Risk Perception, and Management in the Sex Work Environments of Two Mexico-U.S. Border Cities." *Sexuality Research & Social Policy* 16, no. 3 (2019): 317–28.

Andrew, Elizabeth Wheeler, and Katharine Caroline Bushnell. *The Queen's Daughters in India*. London: Morgan and Scott, 1899.

"Art. v. the International Congress on Public Morality." *Englishwoman's Review* 54 (October 15, 1877): 474–80.

Asen, Robert. "Reflections on the Role of Rhetoric in Public Policy." *Rhetoric & Public Affairs* 13, no. 1 (2010): 121–43.

———. "Women, Work, Welfare: A Rhetorical History of Images of Poor Women in Welfare Policy Debates." *Rhetoric & Public Affairs* 6, no. 2 (2003): 285–312.

Attwood, Rachael. "Stopping the Traffic: The National Vigilance Association and the International Fight against the 'White Slave' Trade (1899–c. 1909)." *Women's History Review* 24, no. 3 (2015): 325–50.

Balkin, Jack M. "Commerce." *Michigan Law Review* 109, no. 1 (2010): 1–51.

Baker, Carrie N. "An Examination of Some Central Debates on Sex Trafficking in Research and Public Policy in the United States." *Journal of Human Trafficking* 1, no. 3 (2015): 191–208.

Barnett, Randy E. "The Original Meaning of the Commerce Clause." *University of Chicago Law Review* 68, no. 1 (2001): 101–47.
Barnes, Mary Clark, and Lemuel Call Barnes. *The New America: A Study in Immigration*. New York: Fleming H. Revell Company, 1913.
Barney, Timothy. "'Gulag'—Slavery, Inc.': The Power of Place and the Rhetorical Life of a Cold War Map." *Rhetoric & Public Affairs* 16, no. 2 (2013): 317–53.
Beck, E. M. "South Polls: Judge Lynch Denied; Combating Mob Violence in the American South, 1877–1950." *Southern Cultures* 21, no. 2 (2015): 117–39.
Bederman, Gail. *Manliness and Civilization: A Cultural History of Gender and Race in the United States, 1880–1917*. Chicago: University of Chicago Press, 1995.
Bell, Ernest A. *Fighting the Traffic in Young Girls: Or War on the White Slave Trade*. Chicago, 1910.
———. *White Slavery Up to Date or White Slavery Today*. Chicago: Darrow, 1917.
Bender, Daniel E. *American Abyss: Savagery and Civilization in the Age of Industry*. Ithaca, NY: Cornell University Press, 2010.
Berlant, Lauren Gail. *The Queen of America Goes to Washington City*. Durham, NC: Duke University Press, 1997.
Bingham, Theodore. "Foreign Criminals in New York." *North American Review* 188, no. 634 (1908): 383–94.
Blair, Cynthia M. *I've Got to Make My Livin: Black Women's Sex Work in Turn-of-the-Century Chicago*. Chicago: University of Chicago Press, 2018.
Bland, Sidney R. "Shaping the Life of the New Woman: The Crusading Years of the Delineator." *American Periodicals* 19, no. 2 (2009): 165–88.
Blee, Kathleen M. *Inside Organized Racism: Women in the Hate Movement*. Berkeley: University of California Press, 2003.
Blue, Gregory. "Introduction." In *Colonialism and the Modern World*, edited by Gregory Blue, Martin Bunton, and Ralph C. Croizier, 3–22. London: Routledge, 2001.
Bonazzi, Tiziano. "Frederick Jackson Turner's Frontier Thesis and the Self-Consciousness of America." *Journal of American Studies* 27, no. 2 (1993): 149–71.
Bondi, Liz, and Joyce Davidson. "Situating Gender." In *A Companion to Feminist Geography*, edited by Lise Nelson and Joni Seager. Malden, MA: Blackwell, 2005.
Bordin, Ruth. *Frances Willard: A Biography*. Chapel Hill: University of North Carolina Press, 1986.
Bowler, Anne E., Chrysanthi S. Leon, and Terry G. Lilley. "'What Shall We Do with the Young Prostitute? Reform Her or Neglect Her?': Domestication as Reform at the New York State Reformatory for Women at Bedford, 1901–1913." *Journal of Social History* 47, no. 2 (2013): 458–81.
Brands, H. W. *The Reckless Decade: America in the 1890s*. Chicago: University of Chicago Press, 1995.
Brewton, William W. *The Life of Thomas E. Watson*. Atlanta: William W. Brewton, 1926.

Bricker, Brett Jacob. "Feigning Environmentalism: Antienvironmental Organizations, Strategic Naming, and Definitional Argument." *Western Journal of Communication* 78, no. 5 (2014): 636–52.

Brouwer, Daniel C. "From San Francisco to Atlanta and Back Again: Ideologies of Mobility in the AIDS Quilts Search for a Homeland." *Rhetoric & Public Affairs* 10, no. 4 (2007): 701–21.

Brush, Lisa D. "Love, Toil, and Trouble: Motherhood and Feminist Politics." *Signs* 21, no. 2 (1996): 429–54.

Brysk, Alison. "Rethinking Trafficking: Human Rights and Private Wrongs." In *From Human Trafficking to Human Rights: Reframing Contemporary Slavery*, edited by Alison Brysk and Austin Choi-Fitzpatrick, 73–85. Philadelphia: University of Pennsylvania Press, 2011.

Brysk, Alison, and Austin Choi-Fitzpatrick. "Introduction: Rethinking Trafficking." In *From Human Trafficking to Human Rights: Reframing Contemporary Slavery*, edited by Alison Brysk and Austin Choi-Fitzpatrick, 1–11. Philadelphia: University of Pennsylvania Press, 2011.

Bunting, Annie, and Joel Quirk. "Contemporary Slavery as More Than Rhetorical Strategy? The Politics and Ideology of a New Political Cause." In *Contemporary Slavery: The Rhetoric of Global Human Rights Campaigns*, edited by Annie Bunting and Joel Quirk, 5–35. Ithaca, NY: Cornell University Press, 2017.

Burton, Antoinette. *Burdens of History: British Feminists, Indian Women, and Imperial Culture, 1865–1915*. Chapel Hill: University of North Carolina Press, 2000.

Bushnell, Kate. "Work in Northern Wisconsin." *W.C.T.U. State Work* (November 1888).

Butler, Josephine E. *Truth before Everything*, 1897.

California State Board of Control. *California and the Oriental: Japanese, Chinese, and Hindus*. Sacramento: California State Printing Office, 1920.

Calvente, Lisa B. Y., Bernadette Marie Calafell, and Karma R. Chávez. "Here Is Something You Can't Understand: The Suffocating Whiteness of Communication Studies." *Communication and Critical/Cultural Studies* 17, no. 2 (2020): 202–9.

Campbell, John Angus, and Keith R. Benson, "Review Essay: The Rhetorical Turn in Science Studies." *Quarterly Journal of Speech* 82 (1996): 74–109.

Campbell, Karlyn Kohrs. "Agency: Promiscuous and Protean." *Communication and Critical/Cultural Studies* 2, no. 1 (2005): 1–19.

Carageorge, Ted. "An Evaluation of Hoke Smith and Thomas E. Watson as Georgia Reformers." PhD diss., University of Georgia, 1963.

Carlson, A. Cheree. "Creative Casuistry and Feminist Consciousness: The Rhetoric of Moral Reform." *Quarterly Journal of Speech* 78, no. 1 (1992): 16–32.

Carrigan, William D., and Clive Webb. "The Lynching of Persons of Mexican

Origin or Descent in the United States, 1848 to 1928." *Journal of Social History* 37, no. 2 (2003): 411–38.

Cashin, Edward L. "Thomas E. Watson and the Catholic Laymen's Association of Georgia." PhD diss., Fordham University, 1962.

Castro, Wendy Lucas. "Stripped: Clothing and Identity in Colonial Captivity Narratives." *Early American Studies: An Interdisciplinary Journal* 6, no. 1 (2008): 104–36.

Ceccarelli, Leah. "Polysemy: Multiple Meanings in Rhetorical Criticism." *Quarterly Journal of Speech* 84, no. 4 (1998): 395–415.

———. "Rhetorical Criticism and the Rhetoric of Science." *Western Journal of Communication* 65, no. 3 (2001): 314–29.

Chávez, Karma R. "Border (In)Securities: Normative and Differential Belonging in LGBTQ and Immigrant Rights Discourse." *Communication and Critical/Cultural Studies* 7, no. 2 (2010): 136–55.

———. *The Borders of AIDS: Race, Quarantine, and Resistance*. Seattle: University of Washington Press, 2021.

Cherniavsky, Eva. *That Pale Mother Rising: Sentimental Discourses and the Imitation of Motherhood in Nineteenth-Century America*. Bloomington: Indiana University Press, 1995.

"Chicago Metropolitan Population." In *The Encyclopedia of Chicago*, edited by James R. Grossman, Ann Durkin Keating, and Janice L. Reiff. Chicago: University of Chicago Press, 2004.

Chidester, Phil. "May the Circle Stay Unbroken: Friends, the Presence of Absence, and the Rhetorical Reinforcement of Whiteness." *Critical Studies in Media Communication* 25, no. 2 (2008): 157–74.

Cho, Yu-Fang. "'Yellow Slavery,' Narratives of Rescue, and Sui Sin Far/Edith Maude Eaton's 'Lin John' (1899)." *Journal of Asian American Studies* 12, no. 1 (2009): 35–63.

Choi-Fitzpatrick, Austin. "Rethinking Trafficking: Contemporary Slavery." In *From Human Trafficking to Human Rights: Reframing Contemporary Slavery*, edited by Alison Brysk and Austin Choi-Fitzpatrick, 13–24. Philadelphia: University of Pennsylvania Press, 2011.

Cisneros, J. David. "Contaminated Communities: The Metaphor of 'Immigrant as Pollutant' in Media Representations of Immigration." *Rhetoric and Public Affairs* (2008): 569–601.

———. "Reclaiming the Rhetoric of Reies López Tijerina: Border Identity and Agency in 'The Land Grant Question.'" *Communication Quarterly* 60, no. 5 (2012): 561–87.

Clapp, Elizabeth J. *Mothers of All Children: Women Reformers and the Rise of Juvenile Courts in Progressive Era America*. University Park: Pennsylvania State University Press, 1998.

Clinton, Robert Lowry. "Judicial Review, Nationalism, and the Commerce Clause:

Contrasting Antebellum and Postbellum Supreme Court Decision Making." *Political Research Quarterly* 47, no. 4 (1994): 857–76.

Connelly, Mark Thomas. *The Response to Prostitution in the Progressive Era.* Chapel Hill: University of North Carolina Press, 1980.

Cooks, Leda M., and Jennifer S. Simpson. "Introduction." In *Whiteness, Pedagogy, Performance*, edited by Leda M. Cooks and Jennifer S. Simpson, 1–23. Lanham, MD: Lexington Books, 2008.

Councilor, K. C. "Feeding the Body Politic: Metaphors of Digestion in Progressive Era US Immigration Discourse." *Communication and Critical/Cultural Studies* 14, no. 2 (2017): 139–57.

Cram, E. "Feeling Cartography." *Women's Studies in Communication* 39, no. 2 (2016): 141–46.

Crenshaw, Carrie. "Resisting Whiteness' Rhetorical Silence." *Western Journal of Communication* 61, no. 3 (1997): 253–78.

Cresswell, Tim. *On the Move: Mobility in the Modern Western World.* New York: Routledge, 2006.

Cronon, William. "Landscape and Home: Environmental Traditions in Wisconsin." *Wisconsin Magazine of History* 74, no. 2 (1990–1991): 83–105.

Daniels, Olive Bell. *From the Epic of Chicago: A Biography, Ernest A. Bell, 1865–1928.* Menasha, WI: George Banta Publishing Co., 1932.

Davis, Katherine Bement. "Probation and Parole (Report of the Committee of the American Prison Association)." *Journal of the American Institute of Criminal Law and Criminology* 7, no. 2 (1916): 165–72.

De Vries, Petra. "Josephine Butler and the Making of Feminism: International Abolitionism in the Netherlands (1870–1914)." *Women's History Review* 17, no. 2 (2008): 257–77.

Dechaine, D. Robert. "Bordering the Civic Imaginary: Alienization, Fence Logic, and the Minuteman Civil Defense Corps." *Quarterly Journal of Speech* 95, no. 1 (2009): 43–65.

Deliovsky, Katerina. *White Femininity: Race, Gender & Power.* Toronto, ON: Brunswick Books, 2010.

Dickerson, Jacob. "Metonymy and Indexicality." *Rhetoric Review* 31, no.4 (2012): 405–21.

Dickinson, Greg, Carole Blair, and Brian L. Ott, "Introduction: Rhetoric/Memory/Place." In *Places of Public Memory*, 1–54. Tuscaloosa: University of Alabama Press, 2010.

Doezema, Jo. "Loose Women or Lost Women? The Re-Emergence of the Myth of White Slavery in Contemporary Discourses of Trafficking in Women." *Gender Issues* 18, no. 1 (1999): 23–50.

Donovan, Brian. *Respectability on Trial: Sex Crimes in New York City, 1900–1918.* Albany, NY: SUNY Press, 2016.

———. *White Slave Crusades: Race, Gender, and Anti-Vice Activism, 1887–1917.* Urbana: University of Illinois Press, 2006.

Donovan, Brian, and Tori Barnes-Brus. "Narratives of Sexual Consent and Coercion: Forced Prostitution Trials in Progressive-Era New York City." *Law & Social Inquiry* 36, no. 3 (2011): 597–619.

Dorsey, Leroy G. *We Are All Americans, Pure and Simple: Theodore Roosevelt and the Myth of Americanism*. Tuscaloosa: University Alabama Press, 2007.

Dubler, Ariela R. "Immoral Purposes: Marriage and the Genus of Illicit Sex." *Yale Law Journal* 115, no. 4 (2006): 756–812.

DuMez, Kristin Kobes. *A New Gospel for Women: Katharine Bushnell and the Challenge of Christian Feminism*. Oxford: Oxford University Press, 2015.

Dutta, Mohan J. "Whiteness, Internationalization, and Erasure: Decolonizing Futures from the Global South." *Communication and Critical/Cultural Studies* 17, no. 2 (2020): 228–35.

Dyer, Alfred S. *The European Slave Trade in English Girls: A Narrative of Facts*. London: Dyer Brothers, 1880.

Edholm, M. G .C. "A Stain on the Flag." In *Unbound Voices: A Documentary History of Chinese Women in San Francisco*, edited by Judy Yung, 124–41. Berkeley: University of California Press, 1999.

Elliott, Anthony, and John Urry. *Mobile Lives*. New York: Routledge, 2010.

Enck-Wanzer, Darrel. "Tropicalizing East Harlem: Rhetorical Agency, Cultural Citizenship, and Nuyorican Cultural Production." *Communication Theory* 21, no. 4 (2011): 344–67.

Endres, Danielle, and Samantha Senda-Cook. "Location Matters: The Rhetoric of Place in Protest." *Quarterly Journal of Speech* 97, no. 3 (2011): 257–83.

Evans, Sara M. *Born for Liberty*. New York: Simon & Schuster, 1997.

Ewalt, Joshua P. "Mapping Injustice: The World Is Witness, Place-Framing, and the Politics of Viewing on Google Earth." *Communication, Culture & Critique* 4, no. 4 (2011): 333–54.

Faulkner, T. A. *From the Ballroom to Hell*. Chicago: R. F. Henry, 1892.

Fischer, Marilyn. "Addams's Internationalist Pacifism and the Rhetoric of Maternalism." *NWSA Journal* 18, no. 3 (2006): 1–19.

Flexner, Eleanor. *Century of Struggle: The Woman's Rights Movement in the United States*. New York: Atheneum, 1973.

Flexnor, Abraham. *Prostitution in Europe*. New York: Century Co., 1914.

Flores, Lisa A. "Constructing Rhetorical Borders: Peons, Illegal Aliens, and Competing Narratives of Immigration." *Critical Studies in Media Communication* 20, no. 4 (2003): 362–87.

———. *Deportable and Disposable: Public Rhetoric and the Making of the "Illegal" Immigrant*. University Park: Pennsylvania State Press, 2021.

———. "Stoppage and the Racialized Rhetorics of Mobility." *Western Journal of Communication* 84, no. 3 (2020): 247–63.

Fosdick, Raymond B. *John D. Rockefeller, Jr.: A Portrait*. New York: Harper & Brothers, 1956.

Foss, Karen, and Kathy L. Domenici. "Haunting Argentina: Synecdoche in the

Protests of the Mothers of Plaza de Mayo." *Quarterly Journal of Speech* 87 (2001).

Frederickson, Mary E., and Delores W. Walters, eds. *Gendered Resistance: Women, Slavery, and the Legacy of Margaret Garner.* Urbana: University of Illinois Press, 2013.

Freedman, Estelle B. "'Crimes Which Startle and Horrify': Gender, Age, and the Racialization of Sexual Violence in White American Newspapers, 1870–1900." *Journal of the History of Sexuality* 20, no. 3 (2011): 465–97.

———. *Their Sisters' Keepers: Women's Prison Reform in America, 1830–1930.* Ann Arbor: University of Michigan Press, 1981.

Gardner, Christine J. "'Created This Way': Liminality, Rhetorical Agency, and the Transformative Power of Constraint among Gay Christian College Students." *Communication and Critical/Cultural Studies* 14, no. 1 (2017): 31–47.

Gaynor, Tia Sherèe, Seong C. Kang, and Brian N. Williams. "Segregated Spaces and Separated Races: The Relationship between State-Sanctioned Violence, Place, and Black Identity." *RSF* 7, no. 1 (2021): 50–66.

Georgi-Findlay, Brigitte. *The Frontiers of Women's Writing: Women's Narratives and the Rhetoric of Western Expansion.* Tucson: University of Arizona Press, 1996.

Gendzel, Glen. "What the Progressives Had in Common." *Journal of the Gilded Age and Progressive Era* 10, no. 3 (2011): 331–39.

Gibson, Katie L. "Judicial Rhetoric and Women's 'Place': The United States Supreme Court's Darwinian Defense of Separate Spheres." *Western Journal of Communication* 71, no. 2 (2007): 159–75.

Gilfoyle, Timothy J. *City of Eros: New York City, Prostitution, and the Commercialization of Sex, 1790–1920.* New York: W. W. Norton & Company, 1992.

Gilman, Sander L. "Black Bodies, White Bodies: Toward an Iconography of Female Sexuality in Late Nineteenth-Century Art, Medicine, and Literature." *Critical Inquiry* 12, no. 1 (1985): 204–42.

Ginzberg, Lori D. *Women and the Work of Benevolence.* New Haven, CT: Yale University Press, 1990.

Goeman, Mishuana. *Mark My Words: Native Women Mapping Our Nation.* Minneapolis: University of Minnesota Press, 2013.

Goldman, Emma. "The Traffic in Women." *Hastings Women's Law Journal* 13 (2002): 9–20.

Goodale, Greg, and Jeremy Engels. "Black *and* White: Vestiges of Biracialism in American Discourse." *Communication and Critical/Cultural Studies* 7, no.1 (2010): 70–89.

Gordon, Fon L. "Early Motoring in Florida: Making Car Culture and Race in the New South, 1903–1943." *Florida Historical Quarterly* 95, no. 4 (2017): 517–37.

Gorham, Deborah. "The 'Maiden Tribute of Modern Babylon' Re-Examined: Child Prostitution and the Idea of Childhood in Late-Victorian England." *Victorian Studies* 21, no. 3 (1978): 353–79.

The Great Wisconsin Pineries Scandal: Infamy, Horrors and Vices of Wisconsin's Vile Dens. Chicago: G. S. Baldwin, 1889.

Greene, Ronald Walter, and Kevin Douglas Kusa. "From the Arab Spring to Athens, From Occupy Wall Street to Moscow." *Rhetoric Society Quarterly* 42, no. 3 (2012): 271–88.

Griffin, Susan M. "Awful Disclosures: Women's Evidence in the Escaped Nun's Tale." *PMLA* 111, no. 1 (1996): 93–107.

Grittner, Frederick K. *White Slavery: Myth, Ideology, and American Law.* New York: Garland Publishing, Inc., 1990.

Grossberg, Michael. *Governing the Hearth: Law and the Family in Nineteenth-Century America.* Chapel Hill: University of North Carolina Press, 1985.

Gulati, Girish J. [Jeff]. "Representing Trafficking: Media in the United States, Great Britain, and Canada." In *From Human Trafficking to Human Rights: Reframing Contemporary Slavery,* edited by Alison Brysk and Austin Choi-Fitzpatrick, 44–71. Philadelphia: University of Pennsylvania Press, 2011.

Guterl, Matthew, and Christine Skwiot. "Atlantic and Pacific Crossings: Race, Empire, and 'the Labor Problem' in the Late Nineteenth Century." *Radical History Review* 2005, no. 91 (2005): 40–61.

Gutmann, Amy. "Introduction," In *Human Rights as Political and Idolatry.* Princeton, NJ: Princeton University Press, 2001.

Hahner, Leslie A. *To Become an American: Immigrants and Americanization Campaigns of the Early Twentieth Century.* East Lansing: Michigan State University Press, 2017.

Hall, Prescott F. *Immigration and Its Effects upon the United Sates.* New York: Henry Holt, 1906.

Hallenbeck, Sarah. *Claiming the Bicycle: Women, Rhetoric, and Technology in Nineteenth-Century America.* Carbondale: Southern Illinois University Press, 2016.

Hallstein, D. Lynn O'Brien. "Introduction to Mothering Rhetorics." *Women's Studies in Communication* 40, no. 1 (2017): 1–10.

Hammonds, Evelynn M. "Toward a Genealogy of Black Female Sexuality: The Problematic Silence." In *Feminist Genealogies, Colonial Legacies, Democratic Futures,* edited by M. Jacqui Alexander and Chandra Talpade Mohanty. New York: Routledge, 1997.

Hannam, Kevin, Mimi Sheller, and John Urry. "Editorial: Mobilities, Immobilities and Moorings." *Mobilities* 1, no. 1 (2006): 1–22.

Harr, John Ensor, and Peter J. Johnson. *The Rockefeller Century: Three Generations of America's Greatest Family.* New York: Scribner, 1988.

Harris, Leslie J. "Home-Making, Nation-Making." In *Reading the Presidency: Advances in Presidential Rhetoric,* edited by Stephen J. Heidt and Mary E. Stuckey, 281–99. New York: Peter Lang, 2019.

———. *State of the Marital Union: Rhetoric, Identity, and Nineteenth Century Marriage Controversies.* Waco, TX: Baylor University Press, 2014.

Harris, Neil. "Memory and the White City." In *Grand Illusions: Chicago's World's Fair of 1893*, edited by Wim De Wit, James Gilbert, Robert W. Rydell, and Neil Harris, 1–40. Chicago: Chicago Historical Society, 1993.

Hartzell, Stephanie L. "Whiteness Feels Good Here: Interrogating White Nationalist Rhetoric on Stormfront." *Communication and Critical/Cultural Studies* 17, no. 2 (2020): 129–48.

Hasian, Marouf. "Performative Law and the Maintenance of Interracial Social Boundaries: Assuaging Antebellum Fears of 'White Slavery' and the Case of Sally Miller/Salome Müller." *Text and Performance Quarterly* 23, no. 1 (2003): 55–86.

Hauser, Gerard A. "Vernacular Discourse and the Epistemic Dimension of Public Opinion." *Communication Theory* 17 (2007): 333–39.

Hayden, Sara. "Family Metaphors and the Nation: Promoting a Politics of Care through the Million Mom March." *Quarterly Journal of Speech* 89, no. 3 (2003): 196–215.

Held, David, Anthony McGrew, David Goldblatt, and Jonathan Perraton. "Globalization." *Global Governance* 5, no. 4 (1999): 483–96.

Herbert, Laura. "The Sexual Politics of U.S. Inter/National Security." In *From Human Trafficking to Human Rights: Reframing Contemporary Slavery*, edited by Alison Brysk and Austin Choi-Fitzpatrick, 86–106. Philadelphia: University of Pennsylvania Press, 2011.

Hicks, Cheryl D. "'Bright and Good Looking Colored Girl': Black Women's Sexuality and 'Harmful Intimacy' in Early-Twentieth-Century New York." *Journal of the History of Sexuality* 18, no. 3 (2009): 418–56.

Hill, Annie. "Producing the Crisis: Human Trafficking and Humanitarian Interventions." *Women's Studies in Communication* 41, no. 4 (2018): 315–19.

Hogan, J. Michael. "Introduction: Rhetoric and Reform in the Progressive Era." In *Rhetoric and Reform in the Progressive Era*, ix–xxiv. East Lansing: Michigan State University Press, 2003.

hooks, bell. *Writing beyond Race: Living Theory and Practice*. New York: Routledge, 2013.

Hutchison, Phillip. "Hyping White Hopes: Press Agentry and Its Media Affiliations during the Era of Jack Johnson, 1908–1915." *Journal of Public Relations Research* 23, no. 3 (2011): 325–48.

Ichihashi, Yamato. *Japanese Immigration: Its Status in California*. San Francisco: Marshall Press, 1915.

Immigration Commission of the United States. *Dictionary of Races or Peoples*. Washington, DC: Government Printing Office, 1911.

Ignatieff, Michael. *Human Rights as Political and Idolatry*. Princeton, NJ: Princeton University Press, 2001.

Jenks, Jeremiah Whipple, William Jett Lauck, and Rufus D. Smith. *The Immigration Problem: A Study of American Immigration Conditions and Needs*. New York: Funk & Wagnalls Company, 1926.

Jensen, Robin E. *Dirty Words: The Rhetoric of Public Sex Education, 1870–1924*. Urbana: University of Illinois Press, 2010.

Johnson, Corey, Reece Jones, Anssi Paasi, Louise Amoore, Alison Mountz, Mark Salter, and Chris Rumford. "Interventions on Rethinking 'the Border' in Border Studies." *Political Geography* 30, no. 2 (2011): 61–69.

Johnson, Nan. "Reigning in the Court of Silence: Women and Rhetorical Space in Postbellum America." *Philosophy & Rhetoric* 33, no. 3 (2000): 221–42.

Jorgensen-Earp, Cheryl R. "The Lady, the Whore, and the Spinster: The Rhetorical Use of Victorian Images of Women." *Western Journal of Speech Communication* 54, no. 1 (1990): 82–98.

Keire, Mara L. "The Vice Trust: A Reinterpretation of the White Slavery Scare in the United States, 1907–1917." *Journal of Social History* 35, no. 1 (2001): 5–41.

Kelly, Casey Ryan. "Feminine Purity and Masculine Revenge-Seeking in *Taken* (2008)." *Feminist Media Studies* 14, no.3 (2014): 403–18.

———. "Women's Rhetorical Agency in the American West: The New Penelope." *Women's Studies in Communication* 32, no. 2 (2009): 203–31.

Kempadoo, Kamala. "The Modern-Day White (Wo)Man's Burden: Trends in Anti-Trafficking and Anti-Slavery Campaigns." *Journal of Human Trafficking* 1, no. 1 (2015): 8–20.

Kerber, Linda K. *No Constitutional Right to Be Ladies*. New York: Macmillan, 1999.

Kneeland, George. *Commercialized Prostitution in New York City*. Montclair, NJ: Patterson Smith, 1969.

Kofman, Eleonore. "Feminist Political Geographies." In *A Companion to Feminist Geography*, edited by Lise Nelson and Joni Seager, 519–33. Malden, MA: Blackwell, 2005.

Kozma, Liat. *Global Women, Colonial Ports: Prostitution in the Interwar Middle East*. Albany, NY: SUNY Press, 2017.

Krog, Carl. "Marinette: A Lumber Camp Becomes a City, 1880–1910." *Old Northwest* 6, no. 1 (1980): 19–41.

Lefebvre, Henri. *The Production of Space*. Translated by Donald Nicholson-Smith. Cambridge, MA: Blackwell, 1991.

Lait, Jack, and Lee Mortimer, *Chicago Confidential*. New York: Crown Publishers, 1950.

Langum, David J. *Crossing over the Line: Legislating Morality and the Mann Act*. Chicago: University of Chicago Press, 1994.

Law, R. "Beyond 'Women and Transport': Towards New Geographies of Gender and Daily Mobility." *Progress in Human Geography* 23, no. 4 (1999): 567–88.

Lee, Erika. *The Making of Asian America*. New York: Simon and Schuster, 2015.

Lee, Erika, and Judy Yung. *Angel Island: Immigrant Gateway to America*. Oxford: Oxford University Press, 2010.

Lee, Eun Young. "Looking Forward: Decentering and Reorienting Communication Studies in the Spatial Turn." *Women's Studies in Communication* 39, no. 2 (2016): 132–36.

Lee, Maggy. *Trafficking and Global Crime Control.* Thousand Oaks, CA: Sage Publications, 2011.

Legg, Stephen. "Stimulation, Segregation and Scandal: Geographies of Prostitution Regulation in British, India, between Registration (1888) and Suppression (1923)." *Modern Asian Studies* 46, no. 6 (2012): 1459–1505.

Lens, Vicki. "The Supreme Court, Federalism, and Social Policy: The New Judicial Activism." *Social Service Review* 75, no. 2 (2001): 318–36.

Leonard, Thomas C. "Mistaking Eugenics for Social Darwinism: Why Eugenics Is Missing from the History of American Economics." *History of Political Economy* 37, supplement (2005): 200–233.

Levine, Philippa. *Prostitution, Race, and Politics: Policing Venereal Disease in the British Empire.* New York: Routledge, 2003.

———. "Venereal Disease, Prostitution, and the Politics of Empire: The Case of British India." *Journal of the History of Sexuality* 4 (1994): 579–602.

Levitt, Peggy. "Constructing Gender Across Borders: A Transnational Approach." In *Analyzing Gender, Intersectionality, and Multiple Inequalities,* edited by Esther Ngan-Ling Chow, Marcia Texler Segal, and Tan Lin, 164–65. Bingley, UK: Emerald Group Publishing, 2011.

Lewis, Tiffany. "Municipal Housekeeping in the American West: Bertha Knight Landes's Entrance into Politics." *Rhetoric & Public Affairs* 14, no. 3 (2011): 465–91.

Limoncelli, Stephanie. *The Politics of Trafficking: The First International Movement to Combat the Sexual Exploitation of Women.* Stanford, CA: Stanford University Press, 2011.

Littleton, Louise A. "Worse Than Slaves: Servitude of All Chinese Wives." In *Unbound Voices: A Documentary History of Chinese Women in San Francisco,* edited by Judy Yung, 164–70. Berkeley: University of California Press, 1999.

Logan, Shirley Wilson. *Liberating Language: Sites of Rhetorical Education in Nineteenth-Century Black America.* Carbondale: Southern Illinois University Press, 2008.

Lowenthal, Max. *The Federal Bureau of Investigation.* Westport, CT: Greenwood Press, 1971.

Lui, Mary Ting Yi. "Saving Young Girls from Chinatown: White Slavery and Woman Suffrage, 1910–1920." *Journal of the History of Sexuality* 18, no. 3 (2009): 393–417.

Lynch, John A. "Articulating Scientific Practice: Understanding Dean Hamer's 'Gay Gene' Study as Overlapping Material, Social and Rhetorical Registers." *Quarterly Journal of Speech* 95, no. 4 (2009): 435–56.

Lynch, Kevin. *The Image of the City.* Cambridge, MA: MIT Press, 1960.

MacLean, Vicky M., and Joyce E. Williams. "'Ghosts of Sociologies Past': Settlement Sociology in the Progressive Era at the Chicago School of Civics and Philanthropy." *American Sociologist* 43, no. 3 (2012): 235–63.

Maddux, Kristy. *Practicing Citizenship: Women's Rhetoric at the 1893 Chicago World's Fair.* University Park: Pennsylvania State University Press, 2019.
Massey, Doreen. "Imagining Globalisation: Power-Geometries of Time-Space." In *Power-Geometries and the Politics of Space-Time,* edited Michael Hoyler, 9–23. Heidelberg, Germany: University of Heidelberg, 1999.
———. *Space, Place, and Gender.* Minneapolis: University of Minnesota Press, 1999.
McAdoo, William. *Guarding a Great City.* New York: Harper, 1906.
McAlister, Joan Faber. "Figural Materialism: Renovating Marriage through the American Family Home." *Southern Communication Journal* 76, no. 4 (2011): 279–304.
———. "Ten Propositions for Communication Scholars Studying Space and Place." *Women's Studies in Communication* 39, no. 2 (2016): 113–21.
McCann, Bryan J., Ashley Noel Mack, and Rico Self. "Communication's Quest for Whiteness: The Racial Politics of Disciplinary Legitimacy." *Communication and Critical/Cultural Studies* 17, no. 2 (2020): 243–52.
McClintock, Anne. "Family Feuds: Gender, Nationalism and the Family." *Feminist Review* 44 (1993): 61–80.
McGrath, Siobhán, and Samantha Watson. "Anti-Slavery as Development: A Global Politics of Rescue." *Geoforum* 93 (2018): 22–31.
McKittrick, Katherine. *Demonic Grounds: Black Women and the Cartographies of Struggle.* Minneapolis: University of Minnesota Press, 2006.
McRae, Elizabeth Gillespie. *Mothers of Massive Resistance.* Oxford: Oxford University Press, 2018.
McRobbie, Angela. "Feminism, the Family and the New 'Mediated' Maternalism." *New Formations,* no. 80/81 (2013): 119–37.
Miller, Donald L. *City of the Century: The Epic of Chicago and the Making of America.* New York: Simon & Schuster, 1996.
Millis, H. A. *The Japanese Problem in the United States.* New York: MacMillan Company, 1915.
Molina, Natalia. *How Race Is Made in America: Immigration, Citizenship, and the Historical Power of Racial Scripts.* Berkeley: University of California Press, 2014.
Moon, Dreama G. "'Be/coming' White and the Myth of White Ignorance: Identity Projects in White Communities." *Western Journal of Communication* 80, no. 3 (2016): 282–303.
———. "White Enculturation and Bourgeois Ideology: The Discursive Production of 'Good (White) Girls.'" In *Whiteness: A Communication of Social Identity,* edited by Thomas K. Nakayama and Judith N. Martin, 177–97. Thousand Oaks, CA: Sage Publications, 1999.
Moon, Dreama G., and Michelle A. Holling. "'White Supremacy in Heels': (White) Feminism, White Supremacy, and Discursive Violence." *Communication and Critical/Cultural Studies* 17, no. 2 (2020): 253–60.

Mountford, Roxanne. "On Gender and Rhetorical Space." *Rhetoric Society Quarterly* 31, no. 1 (2001): 41–71.
Nakayama, Thomas K., and Robert L. Krizek. "Whiteness: A Strategic Rhetoric." *Quarterly Journal of Speech* 81, no. 3 (1995): 291–309.
Nash, Catherine J., and Andrew Gorman-Murray. "LGBT Neighbourhoods and 'New Mobilities': Towards Understanding Transformations in Sexual and Gendered Urban Landscapes." *International Journal of Urban and Regional Research* 38, no. 3 (2014): 756–72.
Nesbit, Robert C. *The History of Wisconsin*, vol. 3. Madison: State Historical Society of Wisconsin, 1985.
Nespor, Jan. "Discursive Geographies." *Journal of Language & Politics* 13, no. 3 (2014), 493–94.
Nugent, Walter. "Demography: Chicago as a Modern World City." In *The Encyclopedia of Chicago*, edited James R. Grossman, Ann Durkin Keating, and Janice L. Reiff, 233–37. Chicago: University of Chicago Press, 2004.
Ore Ersula J. *Lynching: Violence, Rhetoric, and American Identity*. Jackson: University Press of Mississippi, 2019.
Örnebring, Henrik. "The Maiden Tribute and the Naming of Monsters: Two Case Studies of Tabloid Journalism as Alternative Public Sphere." *Journalism Studies* 7, no. 6 (2006): 851–68.
Packer, Jeremy. "Homeland Subjectivity: The Algorithmic Identity of Security." *Communication and Critical/Cultural Studies* 4, no. 2 (2007): 211–15.
Packer, Jeremy, and Kathleen F. Oswald. "From Windscreen to Widescreen: Screening Technologies and Mobile Communication." *Communication Review* 13, no. 4 (2010): 309–39.
Painter, Nell Irvin. *The History of White People*. New York: W. W. Norton, 2010.
Palczewski, Catherine H. "The Male Madonna and the Feminine Uncle Sam: Visual Argument, Icons, and Ideographs in 1909 Anti-Woman Suffrage Postcards." *Quarterly Journal of Speech* 91, no. 4 (2005): 365–94.
———. "The 1919 Prison Special: Constituting White Women's Citizenship." *Quarterly Journal of Speech* 102, no. 2 (2016): 107–32.
Palmer, Niall. "More Than a Passive Interest." *Journal of American Studies* 48, no. 2 (2014): 417–43.
Parker, Maegan. "Desiring Citizenship: A Rhetorical Analysis of the Wells/Willard Controversy." *Women's Studies in Communication* 31, no. 1 (2008): 56–78.
Peeples, Jennifer A., and Kevin M. DeLuca. "The Truth of the Matter: Motherhood, Community and Environmental Justice." *Women's Studies in Communication* 29, no. 1 (2006): 59–87.
Peskin, Lawrence A. *Captives and Countrymen: Barbary Slavery and the American Public, 1785–1816*. Baltimore: Johns Hopkins University Press, 2009.
Pfeifer, M. J. "At the Hands of Parties Unknown? The State of the Field of Lynching Scholarship." *Journal of American History* 101, no. 3 (2014): 832–46.

Phillips, Richard. *Sex, Politics and Empire: A Postcolonial Geography*. Manchester, UK: Manchester University Press, 2006.
Pierce, Jason E. *Making the White Man's West: Whiteness and the Creation of the American West*. Boulder: University Press of Colorado, 2016.
Pierce, Jennifer Burek. "Science, Advocacy, and 'the Sacred and Intimate Things of Life': Representing Motherhood as a Progressive Era Cause in Women's Magazines." *American Periodicals* 18, no. 1 (2008): 69–95.
Pivar, David J. *Purity and Hygiene: Women, Prostitution, and the "American Plan," 1900–1930*. Westport, CT: Greenwood Press, 2002.
Pliley, Jessica R. *Policing Sexuality: The Mann Act and the Making of the FBI*. Cambridge, MA: Harvard University Press, 2014.
Poirot, Kristan. "(Un)Making Sex, Making Race: Nineteenth-Century Liberalism, Difference, and the Rhetoric of Elizabeth Cady Stanton." *Quarterly Journal of Speech* 96, no. 2 (2010): 185–208.
Portnoy, Alisse. *Their Right to Speak: Women's Activism in the Indian and Slave Debates*. Cambridge, MA: Harvard University Press, 2009.
Powell, Aaron. *The National Purity Congress: Its Papers, Addresses, and Portraits*. New York: American Purity Alliance, 1896.
Prasch, Allison M. "Maternal Bodies in Militant Protest: Leymah Gbowee and the Rhetorical Agency of African Motherhood." *Women's Studies in Communication* 38, no. 2 (2015): 187–205.
———. "Reagan at Pointe Du Hoc: Deictic Epideictic and the Persuasive Power of 'Bringing Before the Eyes,'" *Rhetoric & Public Affairs* 18, no. 2 (2015): 247–75.
Rand, Erin J. *Reclaiming Queer: Activist and Academic Rhetorics of Resistance*. Tuscaloosa: University of Alabama Press, 2014.
Raney, William Francis. *Wisconsin: A Story of Progress*. New York: Prentice-Hall, 1940.
Ray, Angela G. "The Rhetorical Ritual of Citizenship: Women's Voting as Public Performance, 1868–1875." *Quarterly Journal of Speech* 93, no. 1 (2007): 1–26.
Ray, Angela G., and Cindy Koenig Richards. "Inventing Citizens, Imagining Gender Justice: The Suffrage Rhetoric of Virginia and Francis Minor." *Quarterly Journal of Speech* 93, no. 4 (2007): 375–402.
Recchiuti, John Louis. *Civic Engagement: Social Science and Progressive-Era Reform in New York City*. Philadelphia: University of Pennsylvania Press, 2007.
Roberts, Mary Louise. "True Womanhood Revisited." *Journal of Women's History* 14, no. 1 (2002): 150–55.
Rodger, Daniel T. "Capitalism and Politics in the Progressive Erin and in Ours." *Journal of the Gilded Age and Progressive Era* 13, no. 3 (2014): 379–86.
Rodgers, Jayne. "Doreen Massey." *Information, Communication & Society* 7, no. 2 (2004): 273–91.
Roe, Clifford E., and B. S. Steadwell. *The Great War on White Slavery or Fighting for the Protection of Our Girls*. 1911.

Rosen, Ruth. *The Lost Sisterhood: Prostitution in America, 1900–1918*. Baltimore: Johns Hopkins University Press, 1983.
Ross, Edward A. *The Old World in the New: The Significance of Past and Present Immigration to the American People*. New York: Century Co, 1914.
Rowell, Chester H. "Chinese and Japanese Immigrants—a Comparison." *Annals of the American Academy of Political and Social Science* 34, no. 2 (1909): 3–10.
Royster, Jacqueline Jones. *Traces of a Stream: Literacy and Social Change among African American Women*. Pittsburgh: University of Pittsburgh Press, 2000.
Ruggles-Brise, Evelyn. "An English View of the American Penal System." *Journal of the American Institute of Criminal Law and Criminology* (1911): 361–62.
Rydell, Robert W. *All the World's a Fair: Visions of Empire at American International Expositions, 1876–1916*. Chicago: University of Chicago Press, 1987.
Sacks, Marcy S. *Before Harlem: The Black Experience in New York City before World War I*. Philadelphia: University of Pennsylvania Press, 2006.
Said, Edward W. *Orientalism*. New York: Vintage, 1979.
Salyer, Lucy E. *Laws Harsh as Tigers: Chinese Immigrants and the Shaping of Modern Immigration Law*. Chapel Hill: University of North Carolina Press, 2000.
Samek, Alyssa A. "Mobility, Citizenship, and 'American Women on the Move' in the 1977 International Women's Year Torch Relay." *Quarterly Journal of Speech* 103, no. 3 (2017): 207–29.
Sandmeyer, Elmer Clarence. *The Anti-Chinese Movement in California*. Urbana: University of Illinois Press, 1973.
Schwartz, James Z. "Taming the 'Savagery' of Michigan's Indians." *Michigan Historical Review* 34, no. 2 (2008): 39–55.
Shah, Nayan. *Contagious Divides: Epidemics and Race in San Francisco's Chinatown*. Berkeley: University of California Press, 2001.
Sharp, Joanne. "Feminisms." In *A Companion to Cultural Geography*, edited by James S. Duncan, Nuala C. Johnson, and Richard H. Schein, 66–78. Malden, MA: Blackwell, 2004.
Sharpe, Jenny. *Ghosts of Slavery: A Literary Archaeology of Black Women's Lives*. Minneapolis: University of Minnesota Press, 2003.
Sheller, Mimi. "Air Mobilities on the U.S.-Caribbean Border: Open Skies and Closed Gates." *Communication Review* 13, no. 4 (2010): 269–88.
Sheller, Mimi, and John Urry. "The New Mobilities Paradigm." *Environment and Planning A* 38, no. 2 (2006): 207–26.
Shelley, Louise. *Human Trafficking*. Cambridge: Cambridge University Press, 2010.
Sheppard, Eric, and Robert B. McMaster. "Introduction: Scale and Geographic Inquiry." In *Scale and Geographic Inquiry: Nature, Society, and Method*, 1–22. Malden, MA: Blackwell Publishing, 2008.
Shome, Raka. *Diana and Beyond: White Femininity, National Identity, and Contemporary Media Culture*. Urbana: University of Illinois Press, 2014.
———. "Space Matters: The Power and Practice of Space." *Communication Theory* 13, no. 1 (2003): 39–56.

———. "Whiteness and the Politics of Location." In *Whiteness: The Communication of Social Identity*, edited by Thomas K. Nakayama and Judith N. Martin, 107–28. Thousand Oaks, CA: Sage Publications, 1999.

Shucha, Bonnie J. "White Slavery in the Northwoods: Early U.S. Anti-Sex Trafficking and Its Continuing Relevance to Trafficking Reform." *William & Mary Journal of Women and the Law* 23, no. 1 (2015): 75–115.

Simpson, Audra. "From White into Red: Captivity Narratives as Alchemies of Race and Citizenship." *American Quarterly* 60, no. 2 (2008): 251–57.

Sims, Edwin W. "Menace of the White Slave Trade," In *Fighting the Traffic in Young Girls: Or War on the White Slave Trade*, edited by Ernest A. Bell. Chicago, 1910.

———. "The White Slave Trade of Today." In *Fighting the Traffic in Young Girls: Or, War on the White Slave Trade*, edited by Ernest A Bell, 47–60. Chicago, 1910.

Slagell, Amy R. "The Rhetorical Structure of Frances E. Willard's Campaign for Woman Suffrage, 1876–1896." *Rhetoric & Public Affairs* 4, no. 1 (2001): 1–23.

Sloop, John M., and Joshua Gunn. "Status Control: An Admonition Concerning the Publicized Privacy of Social Networking." *Communication Review* 13, no. 4 (2010): 289–308.

Soderlund, Gretchen. "Covering Urban Vice: The *New York Times*, 'White Slavery,' and the Construction of Journalistic Knowledge." *Critical Studies in Media Communication* 19, no. 4 (2002): 438–60.

———. *Sex Trafficking, Scandal, and the Transformation of Journalism, 1885–1917*. Chicago: University of Chicago Press, 2013.

Somerset, Lady Henry. "The Darker Side." *North American Review* 154, no. 422 (1892): 64–68.

Sontag, Susan. *Illness as Metaphor and AIDS and Its Metaphors*. New York: Anchor Books, 1990.

Sowards, Stacey. "Rhetorical Agency as Haciendo Caras and Differential Consciousness through Lens of Gender, Race, Ethnicity, and Class: An Examination of Dolores Huerta's Rhetoric." *Communication Theory* 20, no. 2 (2010): 223–47.

Spinney, Robert G. *City of Big Shoulders: A History of Chicago*. DeKalb: Northern Illinios University Press, 2000.

Spivak, Gayatri Chakravorty. "Can the Subaltern Speak?" In *Colonial Discourse and Post-Colonial Theory*, edited by Patrick Williams and Laura Chrisman, 66–111. New York: Columbia University Press, 1994.

Srikanth, Rajini. "Ventriloquism in the Captivity Narrative: White Women Challenge European American Patriarchy." In *White Women in Racialized Spaces*, edited by Samina Najmi and Rajini Srikanth, 85–103. Albany, NY: SUNY Press, 2012.

Stead, William Thomas. *If Christ Came to Chicago! A Plea for the Union of All Who Love in the Service of All Who Suffer*. Chicago: Laird & Lee, 1894.

Steiner, Edward Alfred. *The Immigrant Tide*. New York: F. H. Revell, 1909.

Stillion Southard, Belinda A. "Militancy, Power, and Identity: The Silent Sentinels as Women Fighting for Political Voice." *Rhetoric & Public Affairs* 10, no. 3 (2007): 399–417.

St. John, Jeffrey. "Matters of Public Concern: Reconceptualizing Public Employee Free Speech through Definitional Argument." *Rhetoric & Public Affairs* 6, no. 2 (2003): 261–84.

Stuckey, Mary E. "The Donner Party and the Rhetoric of Western Expansion." *Rhetoric & Public Affairs* 14, no. 2 (2011): 229–60.

———. *Political Vocabularies: FDR, the Cleary Letters, and the Elements of Political Argument*. East Lansing: Michigan State University Press, 2018.

Thorn, Brian T. "'Peace Is the Concern of Every Mother': Communist and Social Democratic Women's Antiwar Activism in British Columbia, 1948–1960." *Peace & Change* 35, no. 4 (2010): 626–57.

Tolnay, Stewart E. "The African American 'Great Migration' and Beyond." *Annual Review of Sociology* 29 (2003): 209–32.

Tomes, Nancy. *The Gospel of Germs: Men, Women, and the Microbe in American Life*. Cambridge, MA: Harvard University Press, 1999.

Tonn, Mari Boor. "Militant Motherhood: Labor's Mary Harris 'Mother' Jones." *Quarterly Journal of Speech* 82, no. 1 (1996): 1–21.

Tonn, Mari Boor, Valerie A. Endress, and John N. Diamond. "Hunting and Heritage on Trial: A Dramatistic Debate over Tragedy, Tradition, and Territory." *Quarterly Journal of Speech* 79 (1993): 165–81.

Topinka, Robert. "Resisting the Fixity of Suburban Space: The Walker as Rhetorician." *Rhetoric Society Quarterly* 42, no. 1 (2012): 65–84.

Towns, Armond R. "Geographies of Pain: #SayHerName and the Fear of Black Women's Mobility." *Women's Studies in Communication* 39, no. 2 (2016): 122–26.

Turner, Frederick Jackson. *The Significance of the Frontier in American History*. Chicago: American Historical Association, 1893.

Turner-Zimmermann, Jean. *Chicago's Black Traffic in White Girls*. Chicago: Chicago Rescue Mission, 1911.

Turner, George Kibbe. "The City of Chicago: A Study of the Great Immoralities." *McClure's Magazine*, 1907.

———. "The Daughters of the Poor: A Plain Story of the Development of New York City as a Leading Center of the White Slave Trade of the World, Under Tammany Hall." *McClure's Magazine* 34, no. 1 (1909).

Underhill, Stephen M. "Urban Jungle, Ferguson: Rhetorical Homology and Institutional Critique." *Quarterly Journal of Speech* 102, no. 4 (2016): 396–417.

Ungar, Sanford J. *FBI*. Boston: Little, Brown, 1976.

VanderHaagen, Sara C. "'A Grand Sisterhood': Black American Women Speakers at the 1893 World's Congress of Representative Women." *Quarterly Journal of Speech* 107, no. 1 (2021): 1–25.

Vice Commission of Chicago. *The Social Evil in Chicago: A Study of Existing Conditions with Recommendations*. Chicago: City of Chicago, 1911.

Von Burg, Alessandra Beasley. "Stochastic Citizenship: Toward a Rhetoric of Mobility." *Philosophy and Rhetoric* 45, no. 4 (2012): 351–75.

Waldrep, Christopher. "War of Words: The Controversy over the Definition of Lynching, 1899–1940." *Journal of Southern History* 66, no. 1 (2000): 75–100.

Walkowitz, Judith R. *City of Dreadful Delight: Narratives of Sexual Danger in Late-Victorian London.* Chicago: University of Chicago Press, 2013.

———. *Prostitution and Victorian Society: Women, Class, and the State.* Cambridge: Cambridge University Press, 1982.

Ware, Vron. "Perfidious Albion: Whiteness and the International Imagination." In *The Making and Unmaking of Whiteness*, edited by Birgit Brander Rasmussen, Eric Klinenberg, Irene J. Nexica, and Matt Wray, 184–213. Durham, NC: Duke University Press, 2001.

Warne, Frank Julian. *The Immigrant Invasion.* New York: Dodd, Mead, 1913.

Warren, John T. *Performing Purity: Whiteness, Pedagogy, and the Reconstitution of Power.* New York: Peter Lang, 2003.

Watson, Thomas E. "The Hearst Paper, the Egyptian Sphinx, and the Negro." *Watson's Jeffersonian Magazine* 3, no. 2 (1909): 81–108.

———. "A Lady Missionary Defends Present System." *Watson's Jeffersonian Magazine* 3, no. 9 (1909): 659–75.

Welter, Barbara. "The Cult of True Womanhood: 1820–1860." *American Quarterly* 18, no. 2 (1966): 151–74.

Wendt, Lloyd, and Herman Kogan. *Lords of the Levee: The Story of Bathhouse John and Hinkydink.* Indianapolis: Bobbs-Merrill Co., 1943.

West, Isaac. "PISSAR's Critically Queer and Disabled Politics." *Communication and Critical/Cultural Studies* 7, no. 2 (2010): 156–75.

White, James Boyd. *When Words Lose Their Meaning: Constitutions and Reconstitutions of Language, Character, and Community.* Chicago: University of Chicago Press, 1984.

Wiley, Stephen B. Crofts, and Jeremy Packer. "Rethinking Communication after the Mobilities Turn." *Communication Review* 13, no. 4 (2010): 263–68.

Wiley, Stephen B. Crofts, Daniel M. Sutko, and Tabita Moreno Becerra. "Assembling Social Space." *Communication Review* 13, no. 4 (2010): 340–72.

Wilkinson, James John Garth. *The Forcible Introspection of Women for the Army and Navy by the Oligarchy.* London: F. Pitman, 1870.

Willard, Frances E. "A White Life for Two, 1890." In *Man Cannot Speak for Her: Key Texts of the Early Feminists*, edited by Karlyn Kohrs Campbell, vol. 2, 317–38. Westport, CT: Praeger, 1989.

Williams, Joyce E., and Vicky M. Maclean. "In Search of the Kingdom: The Social Gospel, Settlement Sociology, and the Science of Reform in America's Progressive Era." *Journal of the History of the Behavioral Sciences* 48, no. 4 (2012): 339–62.

Woods, Carly S. "(Im)Mobile Metaphors: Toward an Intersectional Rhetorical History." In *Standing in the Intersection: Feminist Voices, Feminist Practices in Communication Studies*, edited by Karma R. Chávez and Cindy L. Griffin, 78–96. Albany, NY: SUNY Press, 2012.

Young, J. "Moral Panic: Its Origins in Resistance, Ressentiment and the Translation of Fantasy into Reality." *British Journal of Criminology* 49, no. 1 (2009): 4–16.

Yung, Judy. *Unbound Feet: A Social History of Chinese Women in San Francisco*. Berkeley: University of California Press, 1995.

Yuval-Davis, Nira. *The Politics of Belonging: Intersectional Contestations*. Thousand Oaks, CA: Sage Publications, 2011.

Zaeske, Susan. *Signatures of Citizenship: Petitioning, Antislavery, and Women's Political Identity*. Chapel Hill: University of North Carolina Press, 2003.

Zarefsky, David. "Echoes of the Slavery Controversy in the Current Abortion Debate." In *Conference Proceedings—National Communication Association/ American Forensic Association (Alta Conference on Argumentation)*. Washington, DC: National Communication Association, 1991.

———. "Presidential Rhetoric and the Power of Definition." *Presidential Studies Quarterly* 34, no. 3 (2004): 607–19.

———. *President Johnson's War on Poverty: Rhetoric and History*. Tuscaloosa: University Alabama Press, 2005.

———. "Strategic Maneuvering through Persuasive Definitions: Implications for Dialectic and Rhetoric." *Argumentation* 20, no. 4 (2006): 399–416.

Index

A

Addams, Jane, 32, 58, 159–60
Advisory Committee on Traffic in Women and Children, 144
agency, xii, 79–80, 152; and identity, 3; mobility, xxiii, 158; and prostitution, 17, 23, 59–60; racism, 154; rhetorical, xxiii; sex work, 154; of women, 45
Agreement for the Suppression of the White Slave Traffic, 141
alienizing logic, 123
American Federation for Sex Hygiene, 186–87n31
American imaginary, xv; frontier thesis, 5; Indigenous populations, 15; linear progress of civilization in, xvi; white womanhood, xvii
Americanization, xvi, 5, 100
American Purity Alliance (APA), 30, 186–87n31
American Purity Federation, 30
American Social Hygiene Association (ASHA), 54, 122, 186–87n31
American Vigilance Association (AVA), 40, 186–87n31
Andrew, Elizabeth Wheeler, 144–48
Angel Island Immigration Station, 105, 110
Anti-Slavery International, 153
Armstrong, Eliza, 135, 137–38
Asia, xvi, xxvi, 34, 97, 108, 114; Asian immigration, 98–99, 112–13, 123; Asian women, 98–99, 105, 113, 123; Asian women as threat, 124; assimilation of, 100; racialization of immigrants from, 107

B

Bales, Kevin, 153
Barnes, Clifford, 31–32, 178n35

Barnes, Lemuel Call, 97, 108
Barnes, Mary Clark, 97, 108
Bartlett, Charles Lafayette, 80–81
Bedford Hills Laboratory of Social Hygiene, 53, 64–69, 186n28
Belgium, 104, 131, 134
Bell, Ernest A., 38–39, 43, 155, 177n12, 177n17, 183n97; Midnight Mission, 28–30, 35, 40–41, 47, 156, 177–78n19, 180–81n58
belonging, x, 105, 123, 152, 160; civic, 84–85; identity, 158; and mobility, xxi; national, xxvi; national identity, x, 150; and place, xx, xxiv; as racialized, xxvi, 101; and space, xxi; spatiotemporal, xviii; white woman's place, 8
Bitty, John, 74
Black Americans, xiii, xv, 15, 26, 85; mobility, and police traffic stops, xix–xx; mobility of, xxv; mobility of, as dangerous, 151; public space, 84; regulating mobility of, 84
Black women, xvi, 44, 57, 91, 151; as abject, 68–70; accusations of trafficking white women, 62–63; containment, xxiii–xxiv; displacement, xxiii–xxiv; immorality linked to, 68; as incapable of reform, 69–70; as promiscuous, 91–92; and prostitution, 68–69; public space, 68; trafficking of, 94; white men, treatment by, 92–93
borders, xiii, xxvi, 2, 133, 138, 147, 156; as between places of good and evil, 41; of city, 27, 39–40; invisible, 27; leakiness of, 101; national, 99, 122, 126–27, 152–53; porous, 99–101; porous, ideology, 100; and racialized logics of belonging, 101; rhetorical, 113; secure, 99–101, 123; topography, 113–14; vice districts, 40–41

Braun, Marcus, 103–4, 106, 112, 139–41, 200n80
British Committee for the Abolition of the State Regulation of Vice in India and throughout the British Dominions, 144
British, Continental and General Federation for the Abolition of the Government Regulation of Vice, 132, 144. *See also* International Abolitionist Federation
Broad Ax (newspaper), 92–94
Bureau of Immigration and Naturalization, 105–6
Bureau of Investigation, 82–83, 84. *See also* Federal Bureau of Investigation (FBI)
Bureau of Social Hygiene, 52, 55–58
Bushnell, Katherine, 11–12, 16–21, 144–48, 157–58, 175n85, 175–76n103, 176n110; "Slavery Up North" speech, 13–15
Busse, Fred, 25, 31
Butler, Josephine, 125, 128–31, 139, 144, 157–58

C

California, 81, 98, 102, 107, 109, 111, 113
Cameron, Lucille, 87–88
Canada, 45, 105, 135
Canton (China), 109, 116
Cantonments Act, 144
captivity narratives, xii, 32, 163n13
chaklas, xi, 144–45, 151
Challenge, The (newspaper), 12
Chaplin, Frank, 92–93
Chicago (IL), 1, 34, 72, 92, 152; Bubbly Creek, 28; Bushnell speech in, 13; Custom House district, 26; as dangerous, xxv, 27, 33; debate over vice districts in, 26; disparity in, 27–28; growth of, 28; immigrants

in, 32–33; Jack Johnson in, 85, 87–88; Levee district, 26, 28–30, 37, 42, 47; prostitution reform, 35–54, 56; rebuilding of, 27; reform institutions, 66–67; vice, 28, 30–31; Whisky Row, 28; white slavery in, 25–28, 31–32, 47, 52
Chicago Defender (newspaper), 92–93
Chicago Refuge for Girls, 66
Chicago Rescue Mission and Woman's Shelter, 33
Chicago Times (newspaper), 31, 178n35
Chicago Tribune (newspaper), 178n35
Chicago Vice Commission, 30–31, 36, 40, 42, 45, 176n1
Chicago Woman's Club, 25
Chicago World's Fair, 26, 27, 28, 177n13
China, 12, 97–98, 102, 115–16, 121, 124; arranged marriages, 109; Chinese slavery, 99, 109, 111; Chinese wives as enslaved, 109–10; Chinese women as prostitution and trafficking of, 109; invasion of white national space, 114; "yellow slaves," 108, 123
Chinatown, xxvi, 99, 111, 114, 117–18, 120; as dangerous, 116, 121; as place apart, 121; prostitution, 119; racial geography of, 122; racialization of Chinese space, 116; as separate, 115–16; as transnational threat, 121; white slaves, 116
Chinese Exclusion Act, 98, 102, 104, 107, 114
Chinese labor, 107, 108
Christian morality, 128–29
cities: city spaces, 39; as dangerous, xxv, 33, 39, 46; entrapment, 43; immigration and leakiness, 26; as leaky, 26, 47; as mobile, 48; mobile imagination, 47–48; mobility as locus of, 47; popular imaginary of, 32; as rhetorical construct, 27; scientific rhetoric, 48; as site of danger for white women, 37; as site of spatiotemporal dislocation, 35, 37; as urban jungles, 35, 37; white slavery, 27
citizenship, xx, xxi, xxv, 10, 42, 108; as good, 76, 99; masculinity, 108; material mobility as marker of, 94; as racialized, 99; women's, to whiteness, 76
Civil Rights Act (1875), 81
Civil War, 14–15, 77, 80, 107, 147, 190n14
Clark, John H., 104, 198n42
colonialism, xxvi, 125, 143, 147; British, 145–46, 148; justification for, 146
Committee of Fifteen (Chicago), 31–32, 42
Committee of Fourteen (New York), 184n12
Committee on Interstate and Foreign Commerce, 80
Committee on State Affairs, 21
Conference for the Suppression of the White Slave Traffic, 25
Contagious Disease (CD) Acts, 127–28, 131–33
Coote, William Alexander, 138
Coulter House, 66–67
coverture, 121–22, 201n112
Criminal Law Amendment (CLA) Act, 134–35, 138
criminology, 54

D

dance halls, 37–38
Darwinism, xvi, xvii, 101
Davis, Katharine B., 53, 64–66, 69
de Cleyre, Voltairine, 207–8n32
Department for the Suppression of Social Evil, 171–72n23
Dictionary of Races or Peoples (Dillingham Commission), xvii

disease, 16, 39, 77, 127–29, 134, 147–48; connection between morality and, 65; mobile imagination, 41; moral and physiological danger of, 41; prostitution, 40; rhetoric of, 41; spread of, 40; as vice, 41, 94
dislocation, 13–14, 37, 44, 46, 137; as national threat, 33; as spatio-temporal, 33; white slavery, 16
displacement, 24; of Black women, xxiii–xxiv; redemption, 2, 17; white slavery, 2; of white women, xxiv, 2, 16–17
domesticity, xviii, 5, 63, 123, 150; middle class, 69–70; privilege of, 59; prostitution, 63, 65–66; purity, 66; reformers maintaining, 70; reform institutions, 64; social mobility, 70; as solution to white slavery, 70; veil of, 47; whiteness, 56
domestic servants, 66
Dyer, Alfred, 131–32, 134

E

Edholm, Mary Grace Charlton, 111
England, xiii, 38–39, 125, 144–45, 147; development of white slavery controversy in, 6, 8; prostitution in, 128, 131–33; prostitution investigations in, 134–37; reform organizations in, 138–39; white slavery controversy in, 126–27
entrapment, 14–16, 19, 23, 43, 56–58, 60–61, 133, 135
epidemics, 41
eugenics, xvii, 39–40, 164–65n36
Europe, 25, 127, 131–33, 138–41, 143; immigration from, xvi, 34; investigating prostitution in, 52, 55
Everleigh Club, 26, 32, 89

F

Fairchild, Hiram O., 17, 20
"Fallen is Babylon" (Bell), 47
Federal Bureau of Investigation (FBI), x–xi, 72, 83–84. See also Bureau of Investigation
Federation of Churches, 30
Fielding, James, 17, 22, 175n85, 175–76n103; arrest of, 21
Fighting the Traffic in Young Girls (Bell), 38, 43–44
Finch, Stanley W., 83
Flexnor, Abraham, 52
Florence Crittenden League, 122
Fosdick, Raymond, 52
Fourth International Congress for the Repression of the White Slave Traffic, 142
France, 45, 104, 128–29, 139–41
Frank, Jason, 156–57
Free the Slaves, 152–53

G

Geary Act, 102
gender, xii, xv, 2, 22, 24, 105, 121; equality, 128; norms, 82, 113, 160; patriarchal, 163n13
globalization, xxvi, 125–26
Goldman, Emma, 157, 186n30
Great Migration, xv
Great Wisconsin Pineries Scandal, 9

H

Harrison, Carter Henry, 31–32
Hennessey, John Pope, 133
Hoard, William, 9
home: godly ideal of, 6; infantilizing of women, 46–47; national identity, xviii; as safe place, 46; spatial dislocation, 16; stasis, xxi; as

traditional sphere of women, 47; two-fold headship, 6-7; white womanhood tied to, xvii, 5-6; womanhood, protection of, 9
Homestead Act, 3
Home Missionary society, 118
Hong Kong (China), 133
House Committee on Interstate and Foreign Commerce, 72
Howden, Julia, 1-2, 8-9, 17-18, 24, 172n35
human trafficking, xxvi, 152-55, 156-57. *See also* sex trafficking

I

identity, xx, 11, 57, 162n10; agency, xxiii-xxiv, 3; American, 34, 70, 100; authority, 10; belonging, 150, 158; civic, 71; colonialism, 143; cultural, xxii; embodied, xxi; home and national, xviii; immigration and national, 99-101, 123; national, x-xxviii, 72, 126, 147, 156; Progressive Era and national, 159-60; public, xxvi; racial, 62; white womanhood, 149-51; women's, 122
If Christ Came to Chicago (Stead), 27
Illinois Vigilance Association, 30, 40
imagined community, xv, xviii
imagined mobility, national space, xviii
immigration, 15, 123, 157, 177n5; Americanization, xvi, 100; from Asia, 97-99, 108, 112-13; assimilation, 100, 113; from China, 97-98; city savagery, 34; and danger, 33-34; deportation, 105-6; federal control over, 102; hyphenating allegiance, 100; marriage, 111-12; material mobility, 99; mobility of, 34; "old" versus "new," xvi; and Others, 37; physiognomy, xvii; picture brides, 112-13; porous borders, 100; prostitution, 103-6; protection from immorality, 101; racial inferiority, 101; as racialized, 102; rates, xv, 32-33, 196n2; spatial landscape, 33; spatial location, 34; "sub-common," xvii; white slavery, 33, 98, 104-5
Immigration Act, 74-75
Immigration Bureau, 103-4
Immigration Commission, 100, 114
Immigration Commission Report, 79-80. *See also* Dillingham Commission
Immigration Law (1907), 103
immigration laws, 102, 103, 123-24
India, xi, 144-47, 148
Indian Contagious Diseases Act, 144
Indigenous populations, 3, 5, 15
industrialization, xv-xvi
International Abolitionist Federation, 132, 134. *See also* British, Continental and General Federation for the Abolition of the Government Regulation of Vice
International Convention for the Suppression of the White Slave Traffic, 141-42
International Labor Organization (ILO), 153

J

Janney, O. Edward, 30-31
Japan, 102, 104, 107, 112-13
Jeffries, James J., 85-86
Johnson, Etta, 86-87
Johnson, Jack, xxv-xxvi, 92, 193n59; larger-than-life persona, 85; open sexual relationships with white women, 86; prosecution of, 85;

Johnson, Jack (*continued*), trial of, 88–91; victory of, and white rioters, 85; violating Mann Act, 88, 91; violation of color line, 87–88, 90, 95

K

Kan, Lee, 109–10
Keefe, Daniel J., 113
Kellor, Frances A., 100
Kneeland, George, 52, 57, 59–64, 185n24

L

Ladies' National Association for the Repeal of the Contagious Diseases Acts (LNA), 128
Laidlaw, Harriet Burton, 117, 122
Laidlaw, James Lee, 117–18, 122
Leonard, Daniel, 106, 165n25
"Light the Night" (Bell), 35
Livingston, Rose, 116–21
London (England), 126, 135–37
lynching, 81, 84–85, 87–88

M

Mann Act, 71, 75–76, 151, 195n80; Black women, 91–92; development of, 30, 103; enforcement of, 85, 93; as enforcement mechanism, xxv–xxvi; immigration, 105–6; interstate commerce, 82–83; Jack Johnson, 88–90; as means of stoppage against men of color, 95; opposition to, 80–81, 95–96, 191–92n27; racialization of, 94–96; restricting Black people's mobility, 72; stoppage, 95–96; white men's innocence, 81–83, 95–96. *See also* White Slave Traffic Act

Mann, James R., 71–73, 75–76, 95
Marinette (WI), 1, 9, 16–19
marriage, 111, 112
marriage fraud, 99, 109, 113
material mobility, 94, 99
McAdoo, William, 63
McClure's (magazine), 26, 27, 32, 49
McFerrin, Mator, 92–93, 195n80
Mexico, 106, 156–57
migration, xix, 113–14, 153, 156; indenture, 107; voluntary, 102
mobile imagination, xviii, xix, xxiii; belonging, 150; of Black women, 57; of the body, 56; and cities, 47–48; citizenship, xxv; components of, xxi; and disease, 41; maintaining white American social imaginary, 70; and mobility, 151; modern-day slavery, 154; movement, 150; national identity, 150; of place, 2; of place and bodies, 24; potential for movement, 152; progress, 160; and race, xxv; representation and cultural entanglements, xx, xxii; social mobility, 70; white slavery, 38, 50, 158; of white womanhood, xxvi
mobility, 84, 96, 167–68n54; agency, xxiii, 158; belonging, xxi; bicycles, xxiii; of Black men, xxv; buses as markers of class and race, xxiii; citizenship, xxi, 42, 94; confluence of time and space, xix, xxi–xxii; containment, 26, 47–48; corporal, xix; crossing color line, xxv–xxvi; danger, xxv, 37; difference between movement and, 42; discursive, xx; embodied identity and spatiotemporally, xxi–xxii; fears associated with, 44; figurative, xx; immigration, 34; indicator of freedom, 94; interracial sex, xxv; material, xx; metaphor

of progress, 159; of people of color, xxv–xxvi; and prostitution, 84; race, xix; rhetoricity, xxi; stasis, xxi; stoppage as removal of, 94–95; white slavery, 47; white slavery controversy, xviii; white women, 37; of women, xxiv–xxv; women and negotiating of public space, xv

Moore, Belle, 62

moral panic, xi, 162n7

Morrow, Prince Albert, 30–31

N

National American Woman Suffrage Association (NAWSA), 117

National Association for the Repeal of the Contagious Diseases Acts, 128–30, 132–33

National Council of Jewish Women, 30

National Federation of Women's Clubs, 30

national identity, xv; boundaries, 99; and borders, 100; home, xviii; spatial network, xi; white womanhood, x

National Institute of Social Sciences, 122

National Purity Conference, 30

National Purity Congress, 33

National Vigilance Association (NVA), 138–39, 141

National Vigilance Committee, 30, 186–87n31

"new woman," xvi

New York City, xv, 15, 32, 61–62, 67, 106, 118, 183–84n98; Chinatown, 116–17, 122; reform in, xxv, 48, 54; Tammany Hall, 49–50; Tenderloin, 37; white slavery investigation, 49–53, 55–57; Woman's Night Court, 68

New York Training School, 65

nickel theaters, 37–38

nostalgia, xxii

O

O'Sullivan, Thomas C., 49–51

Others, 155, 163n13; as dangerous, 34; as foreign, 62; as immigrants, 37; as racialized, 3, 15, 34–35, 95

P

Page Act, 74, 102

Pall Mall Gazette (newspaper), xiii, 6, 134–35

Pares, Juana, 106

Parkin, Harry, 89–90

people of color, xix–xx, xxv–xxvi, 84

People's Party, 77, 191n17

Pethenck, E. R., 19–20

picture brides, 112

place, 2–3, 24, 41

Plessy v. Ferguson, xv, 84

polygamy, 98

polysemy, 140–41

Posouch, Paraskowja, 106

prison system, 54

progress, 159, 160

Progressive Era, xvi–xviii, 107, 149, 158–60; courts, 73; embrace of scientific methodologies, 54–55, 69; focus on criminology, 54; lynching, 85; preoccupation with medicine and science, 39; racial hierarchy, xvi–xvii; reformers, 67–68, 70, 121, 180n49; rhetoric of science, 54–55; social mobility, 70

Promotion of Social Purity, 171–72n23

prostitution, 18–20, 49, 162n7, 186n30; agency, xii, 17, 23, 59–60; arranged marriages, 109–10; Asian, xxvi, 109–11; Asian, and slavery, 109;

prostitution (*continued*), association with white slavery, xiii–xiv, 57–58, 61, 63, 69; '*awalim*, 143–44; Black women, 69–70; causes of, 31, 59–60; in Chinatowns, 116–17, 119–20; Christian morality, 128–29; consensual, and white slavery, xii; customers, 63; and disease, 40; domesticity, 63, 65–66; double standard, 207–8n32; entrapment, 60; "fallen" girls and women, 61; forced, as rare, xi; human trafficking, 156; immigration, 103–6; in India, 146–47; investigation of, 51–55, 139; and justice, 129–30; juvenile, 135–37, 188n62; law, 73–75; mobility, 84, 192n41; *mui tsai* system and, 111; pimps, and blame, 61–62; redeemable women, 58; redemption, 61; and reformers, 12–13, 17, 61, 69; regulation of, 129–30, 131–34, 143–44, 157–58; servant girls, 111; as sex slavery, xiv; sexual exploitation, xi, xiii–xiv, xxvi; social mobility as solution to, 61, 69; suspicion toward migrant women, 104; as term, 162n10; trafficking, 109; as victims, 59–61, 137, 182–83n87; victims and whores dichotomy, 60; of white women, 47, 70. *See also* sex work

public imaginary, xvi, xvii–xviii, 5, 14, 35, 108

public space, xv, 84, 152

purity, xiii, xviii, 7, 12; domesticity, 66; in home, 150–51; human progress and, 6–7; innocence, ix–x, 14–15, 132; moral, 64; movement, 30; organizations and white slavery, 30; reformers, 127, 133–34; significance of, 7; social, 26, 138–39; social, reformers, 40; social, with temperance, 5–6; suppression of vice, 138; as a marker of white American womanhood, 77; as a marker of whiteness, 14; of white womanhood, 149–51, 155; of womanhood, 76–77; of women, 5, 93; women's virtue, 76

Q

QAnon, 155–57
Queen's Daughters in India, The (Andrew and Bushnell), 144–46

R

race, 50, 57, 93, 157; class, 119; crime, 63–64, 68; erasure of, 146; mobile imagination, xxiii, 26, 95, 143; morality, 106; neutrality, 102; progress, xvi, 159–60; racial hierarchy, xv, xvi–xvii, 90; racial segregation, xv; suicide, xvii; whiteness, xii, 146

racism, 91, 117, 154, 191n17

Rape for Profit (documentary), 156

Reconstruction, 77, 80

redemption, 2, 29, 56, 61, 64, 91–92, 136; displacement, 17; grounded in language of racial absence, 67; mobile imagination, 2

reform, 55–56, 58, 65, 67; faith in, 54; race and, 68; rhetoric of, 70

reformers, 29–31, 35, 47–48, 55–56, 58, 63, 65, 143; faith in, 54; maintaining domesticity, 64, 70; race and, 68; reform institutions, 64, 66, 151; rhetoric of, 70; scientific approach of, 67–68

Reynolds, James, 51–52

rhetoric of science, 48, 55–56

rhetorical studies of space and place, xix

Richardson, William, 80–82
Rockefeller, John D., Jr., 64, 69, 186n30, 186–87n31; funding, 53–54, 185n24, 186n25; grand jury service, 49–52, 55–57, 155, 184n12
Rockefeller, John D., Sr., 50–51
Roe, Clifford G., ix–x, 52, 160
Roosevelt, Theodore, xvii, 83, 100, 103
Ross, Edward A., xv, xvii, 164–65n25
Rowell, Chester H., 114–16
Rusk, Jeremiah, 1, 8–12, 17–20, 22, 175–76n103; as Civil War hero, 14–15
Russell, Gordon J., 76–77, 79

S

Salvation Army, 134
Sandfort, Paul, 52, 56–57
San Francisco (CA), xix, 109–10, 114
Schreiber, Belle, 88–91
segregation, 84
Senate Foreign Relations Committee on Ending Modern Slavery and Human Trafficking, 153
sex slavery, 98, 122, 131–32
sex tourism, 153
sex trafficking, 144, 160, 207–8n32; of children, 155–56; investigation of, 13; law, 74; fear of mobility, 150; as transnational problem, 126–27, 139, 142, 206–7n17; white slavery, xiii, 132–33; as problem of women's rights, 157. *See also* human trafficking; white slavery
sex work, 154, 156, 162n10. *See also* prostitution
Sicka, Foma, 106
Sims, Edwin, 45–46, 72–73, 78–79, 155, 183n96
Sims, Thetus, 71
slavery, 13, 19, 147, 157; language of, 14; metaphor of, xii–xiii; modern day, 149, 153–54, 158–59; and North, 14; rhetoric of, 155; and rhetorical power of whiteness, xiii; as "up North," 15; and whiteness, 14; commonalities between, and white slavery, 158; of white women, 25. *See also* white slavery; yellow slavery
social Darwinism, 165n36
social hygiene movement, 30–31, 39, 40
social mobility, 70; prostitution as solution to, 61, 69; and redemption, 57; white domesticity, 66; white slavery as solution to, 50
social purity, 5–6
Society for the Sanitary and Moral Prophylaxis, 30
space, xxi, 3; movement through, xxii–xxiii; and power relations, xix; and whiteness, 15
spatial dislocation, 16
spatial location, 34
spatiotemporal rhetoric, 26, 33
stasis, xxii, 7, 44; of home, xxi, 46, 150; mobility, xxi; womanhood, xxi
State Board of Charities, 17–18
Stead, William T., 27–28, 136, 152, 156, 171–72n23; "The Maiden Tribute of Modern Babylon," xiii–xiv, 134–35, 137–38; tabloid journalism and, 134–35; white slavery expose of, 6
Steadwell, B. S., ix–x, 30, 160
Steiner, Edward A., 107, 196n2
Sterling, Violet, 74
stoppage, xxi, 94, 95–96, 151
Superintendent of Immigration, 103
syphilis, 40, 65, 185n24

T

Taft, William Howard, 73, 83
Taken (film), 155

Tarbell, Ida, 66, 68–69
temperance, xiii, 5–6, 144
topography, xxii, 113–14
trafficking, 45, 62, 155, 157–59
trafficking, forced labor, and modern slavery (TFLS), 153
transnational space, 121–22, 127, 131, 147
Turner, Frederick Jackson, 5
Turner, George Kibbe, 26–28, 34, 35, 49
Turner-Zimmerman, Jean, 33–36, 38, 44

U

United Nations (UN), 152, 155
United States, 116, 146, 151, 153, 156–58; as boundary between heathen and civilized worlds, 123; as civilized, 34–35; composition of, as changing, xv–xvi; frontier thesis, 5; imagined community of, xv, xviii; immigration to, xv–xvi, 97–99, 102–6, 108–10, 112–13; influence of Darwinism, 101; law, 42, 72, 74; law enforcement, 83–84, 90–91, 93; mobility, 94; national home and familial home, 107; open border of, 99–100; porous versus secure borders, 99–100; progress, xiv; prostitution in, 139; secure border ideology, 101; threat of Asian women, 124; transnational space, 121–22; urbanization, 28; white slave trade, xi–xiv, 105; white slavery treaties, 138–39, 141
United States v. Bitty, 74–75, 111–12
United States v. Gould, 81
urbanization, xv–xvi, 28
urban spaces, permeability of, 26

V

venereal disease, 53–54, 65, 143
vice, 28, 34–35, 45, 47; causes of, 31; commercialized, 42, 58; harms of, 40–41; hidden permeability of spaces, 38; organizations against, 30, 138; as permeable, 37; professional, 6; and race, 63, 94, 116
vice districts, 26, 28–29, 35; as permeable, 45; spread of disease, 40–41; white slavery, 37

W

Washington, Booker T., 87–88
Watson, Thomas E., 77–79, 190n14, 191n17
Wells-Barnett, Ida B., 91
White Life for Two, A (Willard), 6
whiteness, x, xxvi, 79, 96; American identity, 100; association between womanly virtue and civilization, 78; on bodies, 15; as cultural marker of innocence and purity, 14–15; and freedom, xiii, 15; good women's citizenship, 76; as integral to national identity, xxv, 72, 150; and North, 15; ownership of property, xiii; preserving of, 76; protecting women's purity, 150–51; protection of, 77; and race, 146; rhetorical power of slavery, xiii; slavery as antithetical to, 14; onto space, 15; trafficking, 63; uncivilized foreign men as threat to, 15; white slavery controversy, 160; and womanhood, 158–59
white slavery, 26–29, 51, 80–81; ambiguity of, 141–43; Asian immigration, 99, 108; association with people of African descent, xii; captivity narratives, xii, 32; and children, 183–84n98; class conflict, xii; commonalities with modern-day slavery, 158; comparison to Black slavery, 129, 176n1; definitions of,

xiv, 56–58, 76, 141–42; dislocation fears and, 16; displacement, 2; domesticity, as solution to, 70; in England, 6, 126–27; entrapment, 56, 133; expansion of federal powers, 83; as evocative phrase, xii–xiii; as female person, 57; as foreign, 42; on global scale, 126; immigration, 98, 104–5; and innocence, 188n62; language of, xii, 129; language of crusade, 42; language of sex trafficking, 132–33; language of traffic, 44; letter writing, 10–11; link to liquor traffic, 45; literature of, 37–38, 48, 186n30, 205–6n2; metaphor of war, 41–42; mobile imagination, 151, 158; mobility, xviii, 139; as moral failing, 58; moral panic, xi; moral reform literature, xxv; of national concern, 76; as national crisis, 72; national outcry against, 24; national outrage, 2; newspaper reporting, role in, 8–9, 11, 17, 21; opposition to vice districts, 26, 37; progress, 160; prohibition of, 139; prostitution and, xiii–xiv, 57–58, 61, 63, 69; public opinion, 10; purity organizations, 30; and race, 57; redemption, 56; as rhetorical construct, 127; rhetoric of, x–xi, 147, 149–52; risk to white womanhood, ix; Russian Jews, 33; scientific approach to, 54–55, 70; and shaping of national identity, xii, xviii, xix; shaping of transnational space, 127; slavery analogy, 58; as social evil, 58; social-hygiene movement, 39–40; social mobility, 50; spatiotemporal discourse of, 37; as startling disjuncture, 15; as term, xii, xiii, 163n13, 207–8n32; as threat, 47; threat to nation, ix; trafficking of, 25, 95; as transnational, xiv, 122, 131, 133, 147; treaties of, 138–43; and whiteness, 160; white woman's place, 2; in Wisconsin, 2, 8–18, 20–22, 24, 126, 144, 146; woman suffrage movement, 117–18, 121–22. *See also* slavery; yellow slavery

White Slavery Convention, 141

white slavery reformers, 33, 42, 55, 69

White Slave Traffic Act, xxv, 71–76. *See also* Mann Act

white supremacy, x–xi, 77–78, 159–60, 191n17

white womanhood, ix, 140, 161n4; agency, 43; Asian immigrants as threat to, xxvi, 124, 151; belonging, x, 8; Black Americans as threat to, 80, 151; containment of, 95, 144, 151; danger of mobility and, 26; danger to, 38–39, 46, 147; and debate over innocence, 82; displacement, 2, 24; entrapment, 43; goodness of, 76; mobile imagination, xxvi; mobility of, 43, 46, 95, 135, 142–43, 147, 151; national identity as central to, 70, 123, 147; national progress as critical to, xvii; national space, xiv–xv; as national virtue, 121; objects of movement, 79; and place, 2, 24; progress as central to, xvii; protection of, x–xi, 11, 42, 126, 141–43; public space threatening, 152; purity of, 149–50; racialized belonging, xxvi; as redeemable, xxv; redemption, 17; regulation of mobility for, 79; rhetoric of, 162n7; and sanctity of home, 123; sex trafficking rhetoric, xiii; shaping of national identity, x–xii, 126, 150; slavery of, 25; as symbolic construct, x;

white womanhood (*continued*), symbolizing of national identity, 149; tied to home, xvii, 5–6; as universalizing frame, 148; virtue and purity of, 77; as vulnerable, x; white national belonging reinforcing, xxvi; white woman's place, 5. *See also* womanhood

Wilkerson, James H., 90

Wilkinson, James John, 130–31

Willard, Frances E., 5–6, 7–8, 12, 157–58

Wilson, Woodrow, 117, 122

Wisconsin, xiv, 5, 19, 145, 154; abduction of unmarried women, 22–23; expansion in, 3; isolation of, 16; lumber and mining industries, 3; as masculine space, 16; Northwoods of, xxiv–xxv, 1–3, 9, 15–17, 24, 150; sex trafficking, 13; slavery in, of white women, 14; white slavery in, 2, 8–11, 14–18, 20–22, 24, 126, 144, 146

womanhood: double bind, 21; as good, xvii–xviii; and marriage, 111–12; national space, 123; protection of, 10; as racialized, 123; stasis, xxi; and whiteness, 158–59. *See also* white womanhood

Woman's Christian Temperance Union (WCTU), xxiv, 9–10, 13, 16, 18–20, 45, 176n110; Colorado branch, 145; Department for the Promotion of Social Purity, 5–6, 12; equal standard of morality for men and women, 5–6; *Unions Signal* (journal), 35, 38; White Cross Army, 7–8, 30

woman suffrage, 116–17, 119, 121–22

women: containment of, xxv; fallen women, 5, 12–13, 20–21; infantilization of, 46; introduction of speculum, 130–31; as objects of transportation, 82; structural violence against, xviii

women of color, xxv, xviii, 117

Wong, Soo Hoo Lam, 109–10

Woodhull, Victoria, 207–8n32

World Purity Federation, 30

World's Columbian Exposition, 26, 27, 28, 177n13

World War I, 122, 125

World Woman's Christian Temperance Union, 144

X

xenophobia, 100

Y

yellow peril, xxvi, 114

yellow slavery, xxvi, 98–99, 108, 123. *See also* slavery; white slavery